AQA Religious Studies: Ethics

AS

Exclusively endorsed by AQA

Robert Bowie
with
John Frye

Nelson Thornes

Published in 2008 by:
Nelson Thornes Ltd
Delta Place
27 Bath Road
CHELTENHAM
GL53 7TH
United Kingdom

12 / 10 9 8 7 6 5 4 3

A catalogue record for this book is available from the British Library

ISBN 978 0 7487 9819 3

Cover photograph: Alamy/Design Pics Inc.
Illustrations by Clinton Banbury; additional illustrations by Hart McLeod
Page make-up by Hart McLeod

Printed in China

The authors and publisher are grateful to the following for permission to reproduce photographs and other copyright material in this book:
p7 bulleted list from *Getting Saved from the Sixties: Moral Meaning in Conversion and Cultural Change*, Steven Tipton, University of California Press, 1984; p12 image © Bettmann/Corbis; p22 quote from *Utilitarianism*: *For and Against* pp98–9 © J.J.C. Smart and B. Williams 1973, reproduced by permission of Cambridge University Press; p44 exert from *Honest to God* pp110–15 © John A. T. Robinson 1963, reproduced by permission of SCM Press; p96 exert from Judith Jarvis Thompson, The Violinist Example, from 'A defence of abortion', quoted in Cahn and Markie, 1998, p738 'A defence of abortion', 1971, *Philosophy and Public Affairs*, Vol 1; 1963, reproduced by permission of Wiley-Blackwell Publishing; p120 photo © Design Pics Inc./Alamy; p137–8 letter to Lord Mackay from the Archbishop of Canterbury and the Cardinal Archbishop of Westminster from the Church of England website www.chpublishing. co.uk © The Archbishops' Council of the Church of England site; p154–5 exert from *The Historical Roots of Our Ecological Crisis*, Lynn White, 1967. Published by Science 155: 1203–1207 www.sciencemag.org. Reproduced with permission from AAAS; p178–9 exert from *The Land Ethic*, Aldo Leopold, 1948, reprinted with permission of Oxford University Press Inc.

Every effort has been made to contact the copyright holders and we apologise if any have been overlooked. Should copyright have been unwittingly infringed in this book, the owners should contact the publishers, who will make corrections at reprint.

Contents

For R, H and M

Tolstoy once said that the only important question for us is
'What shall we do and how shall we live?'
This book explores religious and philosophical answers to these two questions.

AQA introduction

Nelson Thornes has worked in partnership with AQA to ensure this book and the accompanying online resources offer you the best support for your GCSE course.

All resources have been approved by senior AQA examiners so you can feel assured that they closely match the specification for this subject and provide you with everything you need to prepare successfully for your exams.

These print and online resources together **unlock blended learning**; this means that the links between the activities in the book and the activities online blend together to maximise your understanding of a topic and help you achieve your potential.

These online resources are available on *kerboodle!* which can be accessed via the internet at **http://www.kerboodle.com/live**, anytime, anywhere. If your school or college subscribes to this service you will be provided with your own personal login details. Once logged in, access your course and locate the required activity.

For more information and help visit
http://www.kerboodle.com

Icons in this book indicate where there is material online related to that topic. The following icons are used:

🔆 Learning activity

These resources include a variety of interactive and non-interactive activities to support your learning.

✔ Progress tracking

These resources include a variety of tests that you can use to check your knowledge on particular topics (Test yourself) and a range of resources that enable you to analyse and understand examination questions (On your marks…).

📄 Research support

These resources include WebQuests, in which you are assigned a task and provided with a range of web links to use as source material for research.

How to use this book

This book covers the specification for your course and is arranged in a sequence approved by AQA.

The book is split into two parts. Part I, Ethical theories has chapters covering Utilitarianism, Situation ethics, Kant and Natural moral law. Part II, Ethical issues has chapters covering Abortion, Euthanasia, Religion and the created or uncreated world and Environmental ethics. At the front of the book is a map to specification, showing you at a glance how to find the information you need.

The features in this book include:

Learning objectives

At the beginning of each chapter you will find a list of learning objectives that contain targets linked to the requirements of the specification. These are listed under 'By the end of this chapter you will:'

Key terms

Terms that you will need to be able to define and understand.

Key philosophers

Key philosophers and their relevant works, listed at the beginning of some chapters.

■ Activity

Activities to encourage you to think about and form opinions about what you have read.

Link

These highlight where material in a chapter is connected with other chapters.

AQA✓ Examiner's tip

Hints from AQA examiners to help you with your study and to prepare for your exam.

AQA✓ Examination-style questions

Questions in the style that you can expect in your exam.

AQA examination questions are reproduced by permission of the Assessment and Qualifications Alliance.

Extracts from key texts

Quotes from important texts that are relevant to the chapter you have just worked through.

Learning outcomes

At the end of each chapter you will find a list of learning outcomes that show what you should know having worked through the chapter. These are listed under 'In this chapter you have:'.

■ Web links in the book

As Nelson Thornes is not responsible for third party content online, there may be some changes to this material that are beyond our control. In order for us to ensure that the links referred to in the book are as up-to-date and stable as possible, the websites are usually homepages with supporting instructions on how to reach the relevant pages if necessary.

Please let us know at **kerboodle@nelsonthornes.com** if you find a link that doesn't work and we will do our best to redirect the link, or to find an alternative site.

Map to specification

Specification	In book	Page
AS Unit A Religion and Ethics 1		
Utilitarianism ■ The general principles of utilitarianism: consequential or teleological thinking in contrast to deontological thinking	Chapter 1: What is ethics? Three ways of 'doing' ethics	2–7
■ Bentham's utilitarianism, act utilitarianism, the hedonic calculus	Chapter 3: Utilitarianism The theory of utilitarianism	19–22
■ Mill's utilitarianism, rule utilitarianism, quality over quantity	Chapter 3: Utilitarianism John Stuart Mill	22–26
■ The application of Bentham's and Mill's principles to **one** ethical issue of the candidate's choice **apart from abortion and euthanasia**	Chapter 3: Utilitarianism Evaluating utilitarianism	26–29
Situation ethics	Chapter 2: Absolutism and relativism (background reading)	11–14
■ The general principles of situation ethics: the middle way between legalism and antinomianism, the idea of situation, conscience – what it is and what it is not; the emphasis on making moral decisions rather than following rules	Chapter 4: Situation ethics The theory of situation ethics	36–37
■ Fletcher's six fundamental principles and the understanding of Christian love	Chapter 4: Situation ethics The theory of situation ethics	37–38
■ Fletcher's four presumptions: pragmatism, contextual relativism, positivism, personalism	Chapter 4: Situation ethics The theory of situation ethics	39
■ The application of situation ethics to **one** ethical issue of the candidate's choice **apart from abortion and euthanasia**	Chapter 4: Situation ethics The application of situation ethics	43
Religious teaching on the nature and value of human life. Candidates will be expected to have studied the teaching of **one** of the six major world religions, but, where appropriate, may refer to more than one religion in their answers.	Chapter 7: Religious teachings on the nature and value of human beings	

Map to specification

Specification	In book	Page
Environment, both local and worldwide		
■ Threats to the environment: pollution and its consequences, especially global warming; conservation of living environment, e.g. forests, animals, sea creatures	Chapter 11: Environmental ethics Threats to the environment	159–161
■ Protection and preservation of the environment	Chapter 11: Environmental ethics Conservation, preservation and protection	161–164
■ Developing countries and attempts to restrict this development	Chapter 11: Environmental ethics Developing countries	165–166
■ Religious teachings about human responsibility for the environment	Chapter 11: Environmental ethics Religious and philosophical perspectives	166–174

I Ethical theories

This first part contains an introduction to ethics and chapters that cover the major ethical theories. Usually, one or two important philosophers are closely related to the theory, as are a few important philosophical works. Some chapters are divided between two opposing theories, as with absolutism and relativism. At the beginning of each chapter there are lists of the key philosophers and key terms associated with the theories under scrutiny. There are also activities designed to illustrate the kind of problems that the theories address and to initiate the topic. At the ends of most chapters there are important extracts from key texts that are closely associated with the theory.

1 Introduction to ethics I: what is ethics?

By the end of this chapter you will:

- have explored some of the major kinds of ethical questions

- be familiar with the key aspects of deontological and teleological approaches to ethics, and how metaethics differs from these

- have begun to consider different ways of exploring ethical issues and ethical theories.

 Examiner's tip

This is important background information which you may be able to use effectively in the examination even though it is not required by the specification.

Introduction

One of the things that distinguishes humans from other animals is our ability to make moral decisions. We deliberate before making choices. Afterwards we may feel guilt when we do things that we feel are wrong or satisfied that we did the right thing. Sometimes we are motivated to take great risks because of what we believe is right. We disagree passionately with each other over how we should live. Humans have a moral dimension. This book explores how human beings decide what is right and wrong, good and bad. It examines the ways in which different thinkers have tried to define what it means to be a good person. It also investigates some of the most prominent ethical issues of our time.

The big questions in ethics

There are a number of big ethical questions that commonly interest philosophers. You will learn how different philosophers try to answer them, but consider them here for yourself:

- If I do a good thing for a bad reason, does it matter?
- Is it sometimes right to do a bad thing for a good outcome?
- Do the needs of the many outweigh the needs of the few or the one?
- Is what's wrong for you necessarily wrong for me?
- Does the rightness or wrongness of an action vary according to the situation?
- Are we free to make moral choices?
- Is being moral about following rules?
- Should we use our heads or our hearts when deciding what's right?
- Can we have morals without religion?
- Should I help my father before I help a stranger?
- Is ethics a special kind of knowledge or are moral views just personal feelings?
- Does the environment have any value beyond its usefulness to human life?

■ Is killing an unborn human as immoral as killing a born human being?

■ Should people who want to die be helped to die?

■ Do animals have rights?

If you're going to study ethics seriously, you must be prepared to examine your views critically and be open to a range of ideas that may be quite different from your own. What you read may challenge your convictions. At the very least, it will require you to re-examine them.

Activities

Consider the following scenarios:

1. You witness a car crash. The wreckage is burning, but you may be able to save one of the two passengers. To your horror, you realise that one is your father and the other is a famous cancer specialist on the brink of a breakthrough. Who do you save?

2. Your mother comes home with an appalling hat and asks you what you think. She's clearly delighted with her purchase. Do you tell the truth?

3. You're close to a breakthrough with a new medical treatment, but to complete your work you must carry out some particularly slow and painful experiments on animals. What do you do?

4. Your ship goes down and you are lost at sea with two others, in a life raft. You have no food. Without a supply of food there's no hope of rescue before you starve to death. Two would survive by eating the third: otherwise, all three will die. What do you do?

5. The parents of a car crash victim allow their son's body to be used for transplants, but only if the parts go to white patients. Do you accept their condition?

6. One night in a concentration camp a boy is raped and some of his uniform is taken away by the rapist. Prisoners who are incorrectly dressed are shot at dawn by the guards. Should he accept his fate or steal from someone else?

7. Conjoined twins are born, attached at the abdomen and sharing several major organs. If nothing is done, both will die. If the twins are separated, one will die and one will live. What should be done?

8. A railway drawbridge operator is closing the bridge for the express train that is about to arrive when he sees his son trapped in the machinery. To close the bridge will kill his son but save the train. To open the bridge will save his son, but the train will not be able to stop in time. What should he do?

9. An unattractive man offers to give a million pounds to the charity of your choice if you spend one night with him. What do you do?

Key terms

Ethics: the principles by which people live.

Morality: concerned with which actions are right and wrong, rather than the character of the person.

Ethical theory: covers religious and philosophical systems or methods for making moral decisions or analysing moral statements.

Practical (or applied) ethics: focuses on debates about specific dilemmas, such as abortion or euthanasia.

Normative ethics: decides how people ought to act, how moral choices should be made and how the rules apply.

■ What is ethics?

The term **ethics** comes from the Greek word *ethikos*, meaning 'character'. It may be translated as 'custom' or 'usage'. It refers to the customary way to behave in society. The term **morality** comes from the Latin word *moralis*, and is concerned with which actions are right and which are wrong. Today, the two terms are often used interchangeably.

Ethics can be broadly divided into **ethical theory**, and **practical (or applied) ethics**.

■ Three ways of 'doing' ethics

There are three main ways of 'doing' ethics:

■ the normative approach

■ the descriptive approach

■ metaethics.

Normative ethics was prevalent until the end of the 19th century. It begins by asking what things are good and what things are bad, and what kind of behaviour is right and wrong. These decisions may come from an established group or culture, such as the Christian tradition, or they may be based on some philosophical or ideological way of thinking. This is the traditional way of doing ethics. A normative ethical question would be: 'Is sex before marriage right?' Many of the theories in this book are normative theories.

Descriptive ethics describes and compares the different ways in which people and societies have answered moral questions. It can be described as moral sociology or moral anthropology. A descriptive ethical question would be: 'What do the Christian and Muslim traditions teach about sex before marriage?'

Metaethics, sometimes called **philosophical ethics**, attracts a great deal of interest today. What, if anything, do we mean when we use words such as 'good' or 'bad', 'right' or 'wrong'? A metaethical question is: 'What do we mean when we say that sex before marriage is good?' Theories important to the metaethical debate include **ethical naturalism (definism)**, **ethical non-naturalism (intuitionism)** and **ethical non-cognitivism (emotivism)**.

> ### Activities
>
> Identify the kind of ethical approach that these phrases fit best:
>
> **1** Adultery is wrong because God's law forbids it.
>
> **2** When you say euthanasia is wrong, you're only saying you don't like euthanasia.
>
> **3** In some Muslim communities men may take a number of wives, while in most Christian communities only one wife is permitted.
>
> Now think of a new statement of your own for each ethical approach.

Normative ethics

There are two main ethical systems within normative ethics.

Teleological ethics is concerned with the ends or consequences of actions. The word *telos* is Greek for 'end'. Teleological theories, sometimes known as **consequentialist**, hold up the link between the act and the consequence as extremely important in moral decision-making. A teleological theory maintains that the rightness or wrongness of an action is decided by the consequences that it produces. For a teleological ethical thinker, the end justifies the means. If my action causes pain and suffering, then it is bad. If my action causes happiness and love, then it is good. The action isn't good in itself (not **intrinsically good**), but good by virtue of the result. You decide the rightness of an action by judging the end it produces so this is the key issue in moral decision-making.

In this type of ethical formation stealing or lying is right if it leads to a better situation afterwards – for example, if the theft feeds a starving family, or the lie conceals a secret from a spy. Qualities such as love, honesty and kindness are not good in themselves. They are only good in an instrumental way because they cause good results. Two teleological theories are **utilitarianism**, which values actions that produce the greatest amount of happiness and well-being for the most people, and **situation ethics**, which values actions that produce the most love-filled result.

There are some weaknesses with teleological approaches: How can you be sure what the result will be? Do ends justify all **means**? Aren't there some things, such as rape and the murder of children, that can never be justified by a noble result and simply shouldn't be done?

> ### Key terms
>
> **Descriptive ethics:** looks at how different people and societies have answered moral questions.
>
> **Metaethics/philosophical ethics:** explores the meaning and function of moral language.
>
> **Definism:** or ethical naturalism is the theory that ethical facts are known in the same way as mathematical or scientific facts.
>
> **Intuitionism:** or non-naturalism disagrees with ethical naturalism, stating that moral properties cannot be reduced to entirely non-ethical properties; they are not like mathematical facts.
>
> **Emotivism:** A. J. Ayer's theory, which argues that moral choices are based on emotional reactions to what we see. If we dislike the sight of blood, for example, then our emotional reaction to it will make us predisposed to outlaw murder.

> ### AQA Examiner's tip
>
> This is information that might be examined.

> ### Key terms
>
> **Teleological ethics/teleological thinking:** a description applied to utilitarianism. It stresses that an action is right or wrong depending on its purpose/intended outcome.
>
> **Consequentialist/consequential thinking:** thinking, in this case, about the rightness or wrongness of an action, that takes only the consequences of an action into consideration. Contrasted with deontological thinking.
>
> **Intrinsically good:** intrinsic good is 'built-in' good, e.g. one does not have to ask why health is good. Intrinsic good for Kant is in the good will – duty for duty's sake.

AQA Examiner's tip

In exams, bear in mind that although the *theory* of deontological approaches to ethics ignores the consequences of actions, in practice consequences *are* important. In Judaism, Christianity and Islam, for example, following the rules has the consequence of a life with God. Even in Kantian ethics, the categorical imperative insists that people should act as law-abiding members of a kingdom of moral *ends*. The right consequences are a *product* of the right intentions.

Key terms

Utilitarianism: a philosophical system concerned with consequences rather than motives and in which the happiness of the greatest number should be the result.

Situation ethics: the moral theory proposed by Joseph Fletcher which requires the application of love to every unique situation.

Means: in any action, we distinguish between the end result to be achieved, and the way in which it is achieved – the means.

Deontological/deontological ethics: in contrast to consequential thinking – this is only concerned with the moral law, or duty, that makes a particular action right or wrong regardless of the consequences.

Duty: the central plank of Kant's ethics. Good will's only motive is to act for the sake of duty. Duty is based on moral obligation as shown by the categorical imperative, and it must not be confused with desire.

Ethical theories that concentrate on moral rules that can't be broken are **deontological**. For **deontological ethics**, the important thing isn't the result or consequence of the action, but the action itself. Deontological ethics is concerned with the nature of the *acts* themselves and it is the action which is the defining feature of importance in moral decision-making. Deontologists maintain that acts are right or wrong in themselves (they are intrinsically right or wrong) because of some absolute law perhaps laid down by God, or because they go against some **duty** or obligation. A deontologist might say that murder is wrong because the very act of murder is intrinsically evil. Pacifists claim that all physical violence is wrong, and many religious groups maintain that certain acts are inherently sinful. Deontologists have the advantage of being able to take strong moral positions on certain actions, as illustrated

Activities

1 Which statements show teleological thinking and which show deontological thinking?
- We should permit the abortion because she's too young and too poor to look after the child.
- You should help your mother because it's your duty.
- Do what your father says.
- It's okay to steal if you're starving.
- If you tell her the truth she'll be really upset.
- Whatever you say, just tell the truth.

Now add two statements of your own to each of the two categories.

2 Make a list of deontological moral statements and teleological moral statements. Read them to your partner to see if he or she can correctly identify which is which.

3 A naval warship is in a battle. It receives a severe hit to the engineering section and a fire breaks out. If the fire continues, the ship's munitions could explode, killing the whole crew. The captain can use a fast-acting extinguisher that would result in blasts of steam putting out the fire, but this will kill the men trapped in the engineering section. What should he do? What would a teleological thinker do? How would a deontological thinker respond?

4 Can you think about the sort of criteria that you would have to use to judge the ends of an action? What things would you want to consider when deciding whether or not a result or consequence was morally acceptable?

by anti-abortion campaigners. On the other hand, they aren't flexible enough to take into account special circumstances, or culture groups with different religious perspectives on life. Examples of deontological theories investigated in this book are **absolutism**, **natural moral law** and **Kantian ethics**.

Consider torture from both teleological and deontological perspectives. A deontologist may argue that torturing prisoners is always wrong, no matter what the situation. On the other hand, a teleologist will want to look at the consequences of either choosing to torture or not choosing to torture before deciding whether or not it is right. Let us suppose that the prisoner has secrets that, once revealed, will save the lives of many innocent people. The prison guards know he has this information. The teleological thinker will maintain that it is right to go ahead and torture to discover the truth, as it will save the lives of many innocents.

Metaethics

The language of ethics: what does good mean?

Metaethics is a complex but important modern development in ethical studies. It is concerned with the meaning (or meanings) of the language of ethics. The philosopher G. E. Moore thought that there is a difference between good things and goodness itself. An action may be good because it is a generous action, but good isn't identical to generosity.

When we add 'good' to a sentence about a person it has a different effect from that of other adjectives. If we call a hat 'a red hat' then it adds a quality, or aspect, to the description. If we call a person 'a good person', however, the word good adds a moral dimension. A good knife is better than a bad knife, but here when we use the word 'good' we're probably talking about sharpness or shininess. A good knife isn't *morally* better than a bad knife. In fact, a person may use a good knife to stab someone
 a morally bad thing to do. Another may drink good coffee that has been produced by farmers who aren't fairly paid for their work, a process which can be perceived as morally bad.

Key terms

Absolutism: in ethics, the view that moral rules have a complete and universal authority that derives either from God, or from the internal authority/consistency of the rule.

Natural moral law: the name of Aquinas's ethical system, derived partly from Aristotle, in which the good is defined by acts which are within our common human nature. Good actions are those which help us become fully human, whereas bad actions are those which hinder us from being fully human.

Kantian ethics: the ethical theory defined by Immanuel Kant, consisting of the primacy of duty, good will and the categorical imperative.

Activities

1. We use the word 'good' in many different ways. Try to describe in different words what 'good' means in each of these sentences:
   a. He was a good dog.
   b. It was a good film.
   c. We gave it a good shot.
   d. They made us a good breakfast.
   e. It was good that we double-checked the time of the flight.
   f. She had a good soul.
   g. This car's as good as any other.

2. Different philosophers explain the word 'good' in many different ways, according to their preferred ethical theory. Consider these examples and decide which you most and least agree with. Good means:
   a. In accordance with the will of God.
   b. The thing that produces the greatest good for the greatest result.
   c. Following the moral rules.
   d. The thing that produces the most loving result.
   e. Doing your duty.
   f. Becoming a virtuous person.
   g. Things you like.

3. Describe, in no more than 20 words, a good person – someone who helps others, follows the Commandments, has good intentions …?

4. Write definitions for each of these words: right, wrong, good, bad, moral, immoral, amoral.

5. Is there any difference between good things and goodness?

6. Are pleasurable things always good?

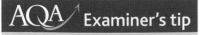

However, when we call someone a '**good**' person we're saying something very different than when we call them 'tall' or 'short', or 'old' or 'young'. We may be referring to the nature of their character, the kind of things that they do or the way in which they weigh up a situation.

Metaethical theories

By thinking about the language of ethics, we can focus on two important questions in ethics. First, *how* we come to moral knowledge and, second, *what* we think that moral knowledge is. Some moral thinkers argue that when we make moral statements we think that those statements refer to facts about the world, which are just as real as other kinds of facts. Others think that moral knowledge comes to us in a different way, perhaps through our intuition. Some argue that moral statements are a kind of moral cheer or emotion and don't actually mean anything more, while others think they have something to do with our beliefs and values. Some argue that moral statements are things which lead to certain kinds of behaviour and that we want others to agree with us and do the same thing.

Ethical naturalism

With the rise of modern science in the 17th century, a view of ethics emerged that tried to link morals with this new scientific knowledge. This was known as ethical naturalism, and was based on the idea that by observing the natural world we can deduce the correct moral order. The naturalist F. H. Bradley, writing in his book *Ethical Studies* (1876), believed that knowledge of our own place in society would lead to an understanding of our moral duties. He wrote: 'we have found the end, we have found self realisation, duty, and happiness in one – yes, we have found ourselves, when we have found our station and its duties, our function as an organ of the social organism.' Ethical rules in this formulation can be deduced by an understanding of our place and role in society.

Naturalism is not a metaethical theory itself, but it gave rise to them. Metaethics describes a movement which challenged the kind of thinking found in naturalism and other theories. Metaethical thinkers propose quite different kinds of ways of thinking morally and here we shall note just three of them.

The philosopher G. E. Moore criticised naturalism in his work *Principia Ethica* (first published in 1903). He held that moral judgements are not based on scientific knowledge but an infallible intuitive knowledge of good things. Being moral means doing things which bring about these good things. The idea that you can analyse in detail what these good things are is preposterous. Moore said: 'If I am asked "What is good?" my answer is that good is good, and that is the end of the matter. Or if I am asked "How is good to be defined?" my answer is that it cannot be defined, and that is all I have to say about it' (Moore, 1993, p6). To try to define good is, for Moore, a **naturalistic fallacy**, because such a definition isn't possible. Good is indefinable. Moral judgements are not like scientific or mathematic judgements as the naturalists think. The way in which we understand what is moral, is through our intuition. Moore maintained we know by intuition that 'the most valuable things which we know or can imagine … are certain states of consciousness, which may roughly be described as the pleasures of human intercourse and the enjoyment of beautiful objects' (p188).

The intuitionist H. A. Prichard, in his 1912 article 'Does moral philosophy rest on mistake?', also thought that moral obligations presented themselves directly to our intuitions: 'This apprehension is immediate, in precisely the same sense in which a mathematical apprehension is immediate' (Prichard, 1949). He thought that reason worked through any factual information and then intuition weighs up the value of the different possible moral responsibilities and works out a moral course of action.

Emotivism

Naturalists claimed that we can examine morals in the same way as we examine other features of the universe and intuitionists thought we have a special intuitive faculty which weighs up the moral knowledge and tells us the best course of action. Some metaethical thinkers rejected the possibility of moral knowledge entirely. In his book *Language, Truth and Logic* (1936), the emotivist A. J. Ayer argued that when we say a thing is wrong we are not making a factual statement at all. We are simply expressing a moral sentiment, a moral feeling or emotion that has no basis. People have different moral feelings about things, but none them are right, over an above the others. Another emotivist was C. L. Stevenson and in his book *Ethics and Language* (1945), he argued that while moral statements were not factual ones, they were based on something more than just expressing feelings. They actually had something to do with our fundamental beliefs and values, not just emotions, and described this belief in some way.

This drift away from moral certainty among the metaethical thinkers turned with R. M. Hare who, writing in his books *The Language of Morals* (1952) and *Freedom and Reason* (1963), argued that moral language was much more important than just expressing an emotion or describing a belief. He argued that moral judgements were both **prescriptive** and universal. A moral statement prescribed a course of action that we should follow and that we would want others to agree with and follow. If I say that lying is wrong, I am implying that we should not lie. What is more, it is only sensible to prescribe things which are always right or wrong. In other words we can't say lying is wrong one day and right another day. Moral statements are universal, because they apply on all occasions.

■ Tools for examining ethical theories

Here are some suggestions for questions to think about which are useful in unpacking ethical theories in particular.

We can analyse theories in an attempt to try to make sense of them. Initially we can ask, what kind of family of theories does this fit into – normative, descriptive, or metaethical? If normative, is it teleological or deontological? Does it have absolutist or relativistic tendencies?

Beyond these we can ask another set of helpful questions around the exercise of authority and judgement in the theory.

- How is the theory oriented towards moral knowledge?
- How does the theory pose the question 'what should I do'?
- How can an action be determined to be right by the theory?
- What sort of character trait does the theory uphold?
- How does the theory resolve disagreement?
- To what extent does the theory offer specific moral guidance on given acts?

AQA Examiner's tip

Don't underestimate the importance of understanding metaethics before you get to grips with the normative theories like those of the utilitarians and Kant:

- Does 'good' refer to something cognitive (factual) or non-cognitive (non-factual)?
- Ethical naturalism holds that good is factual. Moral facts can be analysed in terms of things like happiness, or doing God's will. For non-naturalists moral facts are unanalysable, like 'yellow' – they just 'are'.
- Ethical non-cognitivism says that values are not about facts at all, but are about *approval* or *disapproval* (as in Ayer's emotivism), for example, or the *will* (as in Hare's prescriptivism).

Key terms

Prescriptivism: the moral theory of R. M. Hare, that moral statements have a prescriptive quality about them (meaning that we want them to apply to others) and in that sense are universalisable (which Hare imports from Kant).

AQA Examiner's tip

This information will help you to explore ethics and you may be able to use it effectively in the examination even though it is not required by the specification.

Activity

1 Is knowing right and wrong different from other kinds of knowing? If so, in what way(s)? Does it make it a less reliable kind of knowledge? If so why, if not, why not?

2 Moore argues that we can't define moral things, and the way in which we get moral knowledge is through something called intuition.

■ Do you have intuitive feelings about moral situations – have you ever felt something was wrong or right intuitively?

■ If, when making a moral decision, your intuition tells you something different than my intuition, what should we do?

■ Do things other than intuition have anything to do with moral decision-making? For instance, intelligence, instinct, experience, thoughtfulness?

3 When someone makes a moral statement which of these things is going on and which isn't?

Are they:

■ expressing an emotive response

■ expressing a belief or attitude

■ expressing a moral fact

■ expressing something to guide behaviour and influence others?

Give reasons for your answer(s).

4 Should a 'proper' moral statement be one that applies to all situations?

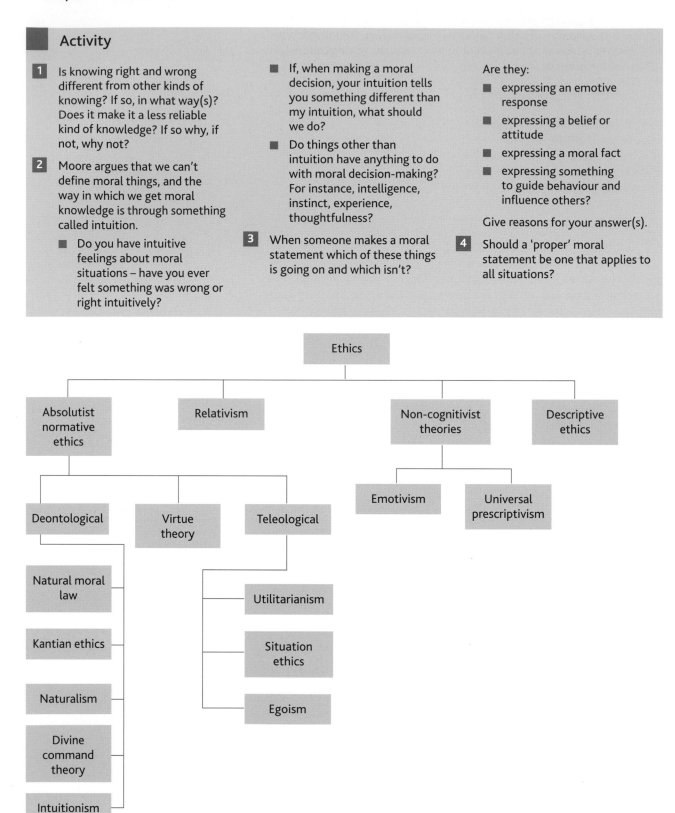

You can ask these questions of an ethical theory to analyse the elements and workings of the theory in specific and applied ways. This should throw up useful pieces of information about the workings of the theory and its presuppositions, revealing areas of strength and weakness. We can also ask a number of questions to see if they seem to hold up. These are evaluative questions.

- Are any assumptions that the theory rests on true? Some theories make suggestions about human nature – are these suggestions true or can they be challenged?
- Does the theory fit together – does one thing flow from the other? Has something important been left out?
- Does the theory seem to work in practice? Is it usable as a theory?
- Does it work on its own or does it rely on other theories?
- Does it work well in theory but is unmanageable in practice (or vice versa)?
- Does it only work in certain kinds of situations and not others?

We can, of course, use examples of situations and ethical issues to evaluate moral theories and there are many examples contained in this book. Ethical examples can be grouped in three ways:

1 Ostensive examples are taken from real life to be worked through using a theory. An example of an ostensive example would be an evaluation of the decision to drop the atom bomb on Hiroshima and Nagasaki.

2 A hypothetical example enables you to consider your decision on what to do in a plausible moral dilemma – whether to give some change to a beggar, whether using a weapon is justified in self-defence.

3 An imaginary example is an unreal scenario, such as the situation illustrated by the balloon game where one must decide to save one of, for instance, the Pope, a pregnant single mother and Mozart, for instance.

You might like to consider which of these kinds of examples you think presents a better test for an ethical theory. When looking at the ethical examples in the book, check to see what kind of example they are. This might help you improve your evaluation of a theory working in practice.

Chapter summary

- The term 'ethics' comes from *ethikos* – a Greek word meaning 'character'.
- The term 'morality' comes from *moralis* – a Latin word concerned with which actions are right and which are wrong.
- Ethics is a branch of philosophy concerned with morality.
- Ethical theory explores philosophical systems or methods for making moral decisions or analysing moral statements.
- Practical, or applied, ethics focuses on debates about specific dilemmas, such as abortion or euthanasia.
- Ethics is studied in three ways:
  - Normative – a traditional approach that asks what is right and what is wrong, and how we know.
  - Descriptive ethics – a form of anthropology that compares differing ethical beliefs without making value judgements.
  - Metaethics – a 20th-century approach that explores the meaning of ethical language such as 'good', 'bad', 'right' and 'wrong'.
- Normative ethical theories are divided into two broad kinds:
  - Deontological theories, according to which acts are intrinsically right or wrong (such as absolutism or natural moral law).

- Teleological theories, according to which the consequences (or ends) of an act are the defining features of whether something is moral.

- Metaethics is concerned with the meaning of the language of ethics.

- When we use words like 'good', sometimes it is meant in a moral sense, but not always.

- Ethical naturalism holds that moral facts can be deduced from the scientific order of the world, like any other empirical fact.

- Intuitionists argue that we know moral things using intuition, and that moral facts are different from other kinds of facts.

- Emotivists argue that moral statements are expressions of emotion or belief.

- Prescriptivists think that moral statements encourage people to perform certain moral behaviours and imply a hope that others will do the same. In addition they hold that these statements are universal.

Further reading

There are a number of good ethics books which provide different introductions to the moral ballpark. Here are some favourites which also go a little further (in different ways) to identify the landscape of debate:

Glover, J., *Causing Death and Saving Lives*, Penguin, 1990, pp22–38
Pojman, L., *Ethics: Discovering Right and Wrong*, Wadsworth, 1998, pp1–23
Rachels, J., *The Elements of Moral Philosophy*, McGraw-Hill, 1993, pp1–14

and an old favourite of mine:

Frankena, W., *Ethics*, Prentice-Hall, 1969, pp11–28

This is my favourite anthology, which has a wonderful collection of original sources gathered together covering many theories. It is also remarkably priced for the weight of wisdom it contains.

Singer, P., *Ethics*, in the Oxford Readers series, Oxford University Press, 1994

In this chapter you have:

- considered the major kinds of questions with which ethics is concerned

- considered deontological and teleological approaches to ethics, and how metaethics differs from these

- considered different ways of exploring ethical issues and ethical theories.

2 Introduction to ethics II: absolutism and relativism

Key philosophers

Aristotle (384–322 BC): *Nicomachean Ethics*

Plato (c.429–c.347 BC): *The Republic*

Protagoras (490–420 BC): only fragments surviving

J. L. Mackie (1917–81): *Ethics, Inventing Right and Wrong*, 1977

William Graham Sumner (1840–1910): *Folkways*, 1906

Key questions

1 Do moral rules really exist?
2 Should moral rules ever be broken?
3 Are there times when an action might be right and other times when the same action is wrong? What are they?
4 Are there any actions which are always wrong?
5 Is one culture's view of morality as good as another?
6 Are all moral opinions equally valid, or are some moral opinions better than others?

Absolutism

Consider the following:

- A man has an affair with his secretary.
- A gang leader murders a member of a rival gang.
- A youth mugs an old lady and takes her purse.

Many people would say that each of these examples shows someone doing wrong. It is wrong to have affairs, wrong to murder and wrong to mug old ladies. To help an old lady across the road is right, just as it is to remain faithful to your partner. People make moral judgements about right and wrong all the time. Some organisations are quite vocal about what is right and wrong. Christian churches preach the Commandments as a guide to knowing what one should not do: 'Do not murder', 'Do not steal', 'Do not bear false witness', and so on. Islamic law gives clear guidelines on morally good and bad behaviour. Politicians often make statements about right and wrong. In ethical terms, to maintain that some things are right and other things are wrong, and that these things are fixed for all time and all people, is called absolutism.

An ethical absolute is a moral command or prohibition that's true for all time, in all places and in all situations. Absolutists hold that some things are wrong from an objective point of view, not just wrong from your or my perspective. In the Middle Ages, the principle 'follow the good and avoid the evil' expressed an absolutist perspective. It implies that the moral way of living is to do things that are objectively good and avoid things that are objectively bad. In ethical absolutism, things that are right or wrong can't change. They aren't affected by mitigating circumstances. They don't depend on the situation. For example, absolutists might say that torturing children, rape and murder are always wrong. They don't change according to the culture in which you live. What is right and wrong for you is the same for me and for every other person in the world. Immoral acts are intrinsically wrong, which means wrong in themselves. The thing isn't made wrong by the situation or the result it causes. It is wrong because the act, in itself, breaks a moral rule.

Plato

Plato and the forms

Ancient Greek philosopher Plato (c.429–c.347 BC) was an ethical absolutist. He thought that moral absolutes such as goodness and justice really existed in some way, beyond our normal perceptions of the world, and are fixed. This other world was inhabited by the forms or ideas, which were the true reality. What we perceived around us was a shadow of this truth.

We might find a piece of music beautiful. We might use the word 'beautiful' to describe a statue or painting, or the way a mother holds her baby, or the sound of a bird. Plato believed that a beautiful painting had 'form beauty' participating in it. Without the form beauty there would be no beautiful things. He held that there were many forms. The form 'green' participated in the grass, the form 'red' participated in wine, and so on. The highest of all the forms was goodness itself. While another ancient Greek philosopher Protagoras (490–420 BC) thought that you could only ask the question, 'What is good for you?', Plato thought that you could ask the question 'What is goodness itself?' Goodness itself was the highest form of reality – an objective or absolute thing that existed eternally, beyond our limited world. It is this belief that makes Plato an absolutist.

Plato described his view of reality using similes. In the simile of the Sun (see Table 2.1), he illustrated the importance of the form good for truth by drawing an analogy with the importance of the Sun.

He felt that we must escape from the mistake of believing that our perceptions of reality were the truth. Our mind was distorted by pleasure and pain, and so the search for truth was a struggle to get beyond our physical perceptions and sensations. He described this journey in *The Republic*, in the simile of the cave. An extract from that book is given at the end of this chapter.

Table 2.1 *Plato's simile of the Sun*

Visible world	Intelligible world of the forms
The Sun Source of growth and light, which gives visibility to the objects of sense and the power of seeing to the eye. The faculty of sight.	The good Source of reality and truth, which gives intelligibility to objects of thought and the power of knowing to the mind. The faculty of knowledge.

Relativism

People don't always agree about what is right and what is wrong. Some people feel that it is acceptable for a man to marry more than one wife, while others feel that such a practice is a crime. Different cultures express different moral codes of conduct. An ancient observer of this cultural diversity was King Darius of Persia (c.549–485 BC). In a story recorded by the 5th-century Greek historian Herodotus in the *Histories* (Herodotus, 1996, Book 3, p38), Darius observed that while certain Greeks burnt the bodies of their fathers, a different people called Callations ate the bodies of their fathers. He brought the two groups together and asked each how much he would have to pay them to adopt the practice of the other. In both cases, the groups were outraged at the suggestion and refused to follow the practice of the other for any amount of money. What was right for one tribe was wrong for the other.

Activity

Working in small groups, write down nine different things on pieces of paper which people might say are wrong (e.g. killing, stealing, etc.).

Quickly and randomly, arrange them into a diamond shape with one at the top and one at the bottom.

Now, in a group, try to come to agreements on which are 'most likely to be always wrong' and 'least likely to be always wrong'. Then, put those which are more likely to be always wrong at the top of a new diamond and those which are less likely at the bottom.

Try to give a plausible exception for the three at the top of the new diamond – those you as a group feel are most likely to be always wrong.

From this activity do you feel yourself inclined towards believing there are some things that are always wrong or not?

Protagoras held that there's no truth in anything beyond the way it seems. There's no objective knowledge, because all knowledge depends on the perceptions of the person. There's no objective truth. Truth is only true for you, or true for me. Man is the measure of all things. Things are good or bad relative to our perspective. A sick person eating food may find that it tastes horrible, while a healthy person eating the same food will find it delicious. Each view is true relative to each person's perspective. If I say I don't like spaghetti and you say you do like spaghetti, both of us are right. Protagoras thought that moral statements were like this: so if I say 'abortion is wrong' and you say 'abortion is right', we're both saying things that are true, because what we're saying is true for you, and true for me.

A debate between an absolutist and a relativist might go something like this:

Sam: Abortion is wrong. It's killing and killing is wrong. It's something that should not be done. People should not ask for abortions and they should not carry out abortions. Killing is wrong. It's one of those rules that can't be broken.

Ben: Who says it's wrong? Maybe it's wrong for you, perhaps because of your religion, but just because you feel it's wrong doesn't actually mean it is wrong, except in your eyes. It's just your view. I have a view that's different – and who is to say that your view is better or more accurate than my view? How do you know for sure that abortion is wrong? You can't tell me what to think. There isn't just one set of morals that everyone agrees with or follows.

Another ancient Greek philosopher thought to be more relativistic was Plato's pupil Aristotle (384–322 BC), whose ethics were collected into a book called *Nicomachean Ethics* in the 4th century BC. Aristotle did not believe in universal forms which are absolute and beyond our world. He felt that the forms were in the world, and therefore not absolute. He believed in a rule-of-thumb approach to moral characteristics, whereby we should seek a midway approach of behaviour between two extremes. Virtue is the mean between two extremes. For example, we should not be rash in our behaviour or cowardly but should choose a 'midway' courageous approach. Human circumstances are infinite and it is not possible to have a general rule which will cover every situation. Moral rules hold for the most part, but there are times when they won't. This makes Aristotle more relativistic than Plato. We shall learn more about Aristotle's ethics in Chapter 10.

Cultural relativism

Modern anthropologists have observed cultural differences and some have concluded that the existence of diverse moral codes implies that morality is not absolute. Morality simply means 'socially approved habits'. The anthropologist William Graham Sumner (1840–1910) expressed this view in 1906:

> The 'right' way is the way which the ancestors used and which has been handed down. The tradition is its own warrant ... The notion of right is in the folkways. It is not outside of them, of independent origin, and brought to test them. In the folkways, whatever is, is right. This is because they are traditional, and therefore contain in themselves the authority of the ancestral ghosts. When we come to the folkways we are at the end of our analysis.

Sumner, 1906

Activities

1. What, in your view, does Darius's experiment prove, if anything?

2. In Christian cultures it is almost always believed that monogamy is the only acceptable way of arranging marriage. In Islamic law, husbands have the right of polygamy and may be validly married at the same time to a maximum of four wives. The nomadic Masai of East Africa practise polygamy and wife-lending between men of the same age group. Some Westerners practise open marriages whereby husbands and wives engage other husbands or wives in sexual relations openly. What are the arguments that:

   - these are different but equally valid ways of arranging marriage or
   - one way is right (or morally better) and the others are wrong (or morally worse)?

3. Think of any other examples of cultural moral difference, and consider the arguments for in each case.

4. Construct an argument against the claim that views about moral issues are similar to views about chocolate – some prefer dark chocolate, others prefer milk, others still prefer white, but all are equally valid.

This approach to ethics is **cultural relativism**. Moral rules are expressions of the culture and nothing more. There is no set of moral rules that applies to all. There is nothing absolute or universal about morality; when in Rome, do as the Romans do. This theory directly challenges ethical absolutism. Cultural relativism celebrates the variety of beliefs and values held by different peoples. There's no way of deciding between one set of morals and another, because there's no objective measure. What is right and wrong depends upon the perspective of the group. That is the only measure you can apply as there is nothing else 'out there' against which it can be measured.

Cultural relativism would maintain if you're in a strict Islamic country, the women are right to cover themselves. In a Western country, conversely, the women are right to expose more skin. This ethical theory suits the multicultural nature of the world, as it gives equal measure to the different ethnic and religious groupings. It doesn't raise one particular cultural expression to supremacy over others, as happened during the period of European colonial expansion, and more recently in Nazi Germany. Cultural relativism seems a more modern and open ethical system than the early absolutist view.

Relativism also explains other differences. What is right and wrong not only differs from culture to culture, but also from one time to another. In the past, it was considered acceptable to leave highwaymen in hanging cages to starve and rot. Today, that form of punishment is considered morally unacceptable. In the past, women didn't have the vote or the same property rights as men. Today, many countries grant men and women equal status. Moral points of view vary from time to time, from culture to culture, from religion to religion and from place to place. Relativism allows for moral improvements.

Relativism and J. L. Mackie

A modern relativist, J. L. Mackie (1917–81), writes that 'There are no objective values' (Mackie, 1977, p15). He maintains that values, the good, rightness and wrongness, aren't part of the fabric of the world; they don't exist. He sees the existence of diverse ethical values expressed in different times and cultures as evidence that no moral absolutes exist. An absolutist might argue that there are common values beneath many of these cultural expressions, but Mackie thinks that a more convincing argument is to assume that people participate in different ways of living because they actually follow different codes. Mackie agrees with Plato that if moral rules existed they would have to be entities of a strange sort, uniquely different from all other things, but he finds this idea unconvincing.

Evaluating relativism and absolutism

Relativism

Moral relativism has several attractions. It explains the different values that people hold and it encourages diverse cultural expressions. It prohibits a dominant culture from enforcing itself over others simply because 'we're right and they're wrong'. Relativism is a flexible ethical system that can accommodate the wide diversity of lifestyles found in the modern world. However, it does have some weaknesses. Cultural relativism observes that as different value systems exist, there can't be one moral truth. However, the existence of different views doesn't mean that they are all equal, and the existence of many views doesn't mean that all views are equally true.

In a dialogue written by Plato between ancient Greek philosopher Socrates (c.470–399 BC) and his friend Crito, Socrates argues that 'one should not regard all the opinions that people hold, but only some and not others … one should regard the good ones and not the bad'. He goes on to illustrate his point by observing a male athlete who doesn't take all the praise or criticism that he receives to be equally important. He only listens to the comments of a qualified person such as his trainer, and he disregards anything said by people who do not have any expertise in athletics (Plato, 1979, Crito 46B–47C).

For Plato, not all views are of equal worth. This is quite apparent when we consider the Nazi Reich. To argue that the Nazi ethic was 'right for them' seems very dangerous. Most people today consider an ideology that justified the extermination of millions of innocent people to be morally corrupt and utterly wrong. Many people see the Second World War as a battle against evil, but this is an absolutist perspective. Cultural relativists are unable to criticise a different culture; relativists cannot prefer one moral opinion rather than another.

Another problem is that a cultural relativist cannot condemn any practices that are accepted by society, because there's no objective measure by which those practices can be judged. Ultimately, cultural relativism reduces the meaning of 'good' to 'that which is socially approved'. If a culture endorses wife-beating, then wife-beating is morally acceptable.

There's also a paradoxical consequence of adopting relativism. If the relative belief that differing moral codes should all be supported was adopted universally, relativism itself would become an absolute moral code. Put another way, to say that the statement 'what is right is what is approved by the culture' is always true is to make an absolute claim about relativism.

Absolutism

Ethical absolutes overcome some of these problems. Absolutism provides a fixed ethical code by which to measure actions. An ethical absolutist can condemn Nazi Germany or the wife-beater. Absolutism gives people clear guidelines of behaviour that reinforce a global view of the human community. One country may judge the actions of another country as wrong and act on that judgement. The United Nations Declaration of Human Rights suggests a universal set of absolutes that apply to all people, no matter where they live. Absolutism can support the Declaration, while relativism might have difficulty when the Declaration differs from a particular culture's way of doing things.

Absolutism also has its weaknesses. It can't take into account the circumstances of the situation. An absolutist might consider stealing to be wrong. If the thief is a starving child who needs money for food, and the victim is a rich tourist, the absolutist must still condemn the thief, while the relativist could tolerate the action. An absolutist with strong beliefs about the treatment of animals might find the Islamic practice of ritually killing a lamb immoral, while a relativist can recognise the religious significance and the importance of the activity to that community. Absolutism can seem intolerant of cultural diversity in the way in which colonial nations were in the past.

Despite various limitations, relativism remains a popular ethic, although it is rejected by most religions, which remain staunchly absolutist. However, it has been accommodated by one Christian ethic in situation

AQA Examiner's tip

Make sure you understand the difference between moral relativism and moral scepticism. Moral scepticism holds that there are no valid moral principles *at all*, whereas moral relativism holds that all the different moral principles that you see in the world are valid relative to the culture you live in. Avoid, therefore, the kind of negative evaluation that candidates often dole out to Mackie, seeing him as some kind of moral anarchist who wants us to go around eating babies. Holding that moral values are relative does not mean you don't *have* any moral values.

ethics. Other ethical theories – such as utilitarianism, which defines goodness relative to the amount of happiness created, and emotivism, which takes relativism to an extreme individualistic position – have relativistic aspects.

Extracts from key texts

Plato, The Republic

Imagine an underground chamber like a cave … in this chamber are men who have been prisoners there since they were children, their legs and necks being so fastened that they can only look straight ahead of them and cannot turn their heads. Some way off, behind and higher up, a fire is burning, and between the fire and the prisoners and above them runs a road, in front of which a curtain-like wall has been built, like a screen at puppet shows between the operators and their audience … Imagine further that men are carrying all sorts of gear along behind the curtain-wall, projecting above it and including figures of men and animals made of wood and stone and all sorts of other materials, and that some of these men, as you would expect, are talking and some are not … Then if they [the prisoners] were able to talk to each other, would they not assume that the shadows they saw were the real things? … that whenever one of the passers by on the road spoke, that the voice belonged to the shadow passing before them? … And so in every way they would believe that the shadows of the objects we mentioned were the whole truth …

… Suppose one of them were let loose, and suddenly compelled to stand up and turn his head and look and walk towards the fire … and if he was forcibly dragged up the steep and rugged ascent and not let go till he had been dragged out into sunlight … he would need to grow accustomed to the light before he could see things in the upper world outside the cave. First he would find it easier to look at the shadows, next at the reflections of men and other objects in water, and later on at the objects themselves. After that he would find it easier to observe the heavenly bodies and the sky itself at night, and to look at the light of the moon and stars … The thing he would be able to do last would be to look at the sun itself … Later on he would come to the conclusion that it is the sun that produces the changing seasons and years and controls everything in the visible world, and is in a sense responsible for everything that he and his fellow prisoners used to see.

… Now my dear Glaucon, this simile must be connected throughout with what preceded it. The realm revealed by sight corresponds to the prison, and the light of the fire in the prison to the power of the sun. And you won't go wrong if you connect the ascent into the upper world and the sight of the objects there with the upward progress of the mind into the intelligible region. That at any rate is my interpretation, which is what you are anxious to hear; the truth of the matter is, after all, known only to God. But in my opinion, for what it is worth, the final thing to be perceived in the intelligible region, and perceived only with difficulty, is the form of the good; once seen, it is inferred to be responsible for whatever is right and valuable in anything …

The Simile of the Cave, Book VII

Activities

1. If you believe that a certain thing is wrong, should you try to persuade others not to do it?

2. Explain the view that there are objective moral truths.

3. Explain the view that all moral statements are relative.

4. What are the strengths and weaknesses of relativism and absolutism?

5. What is the most plausible argument for and the most plausible argument against moral absolutism?

Chapter summary

Table 2.2 *Absolutism and relativism – the essentials*

Absolutism	Relativism
Moral truth is objective Moral actions are right or wrong intrinsically (in themselves) Moral truth is universal and unchanging in all circumstances, cultures, times and places Absolutists: Plato, Aquinas, Bradley	There is no objective moral truth, or if there is we cannot know it What is morally true for you is not necessarily true for me Morals are subject to culture, religion, time and place Relativists: Protagoras, Aristotle, Sumner, Mackie

Absolutists:
- Believe in moral truths that are fixed for all time and all people.
- Believe that moral actions are right or wrong in themselves, irrespective of circumstance, culture or opinion.
- Deontological thinkers are concerned with acts, not ends.
- 'Follow the good and avoid the evil' (a saying from the Middle Ages).

Examples of ethical absolutists:
- Plato, believing that goodness itself really exists beyond this world.
- St Thomas Aquinas (see Chapter 6), believing in a fixed divine law.
- F. H. Bradley (see Chapter 1), believing that morals are fixed, part of a concrete universe.

Relativists:
- Believe that moral truth varies depending on culture, time, place and religion.
- Believe that there's no fixed objective moral reality – or if there is, that it can't be discovered.
- Believe that morals are subjective – subject to the culture, religion, time and place.

Examples of ethical relativists:
- Aristotle believed that forms were in the world and therefore not absolute. Differing human circumstances mean we cannot have a general rule for all situations.
- Protagoras: 'Man is the measure of all things' (attributed).
- William Graham Sumner: 'The "right" way is the way which the ancestors used and which has been handed down.' Sumner was an anthropologist who investigated and appreciated cultural diversity.
- J. L. Mackie: 'There are no objective values' – different cultures' ethics are evidence against the existence of moral absolutes, and people participate in different ways of living, or codes.

Evaluate:
- Relativism explains the existence of the different values that people hold.
- Relativism supports diverse cultural expressions.
- Relativism prohibits the dominance of a single culture.
- Relativism is a flexible ethical system that can accommodate the wide diversity of lifestyles found in the modern world.

However:

- The existence of different views doesn't mean that they are all equal.
- The Nazi culture was morally wrong, not 'right for them'.
- Cultural relativists are unable to criticise a different culture.
- Cultural relativists can't condemn any cultural practices – if a culture endorses wife-beating, then wife-beating is morally acceptable.
- If the relative belief that differing moral codes should all be supported was adopted universally, relativism itself would become an absolute moral code.

On the other hand:

- Absolutism provides a fixed ethical code to measure actions.
- Absolutism gives clear guidelines of behaviour.
- The UN Declaration of Human Rights suggests a set of absolutes that apply to all people, no matter where they live.

However:

- Absolutism can't take into account the circumstances of the situation.
- Absolutism can seem intolerant of cultural diversity in the way European nations were in the past.

Further reading

For a brief visual guide to Greek thinkers see:

Robinson, D. and Garratt, C., *Ethics for Beginners*, Icon Books, 1996, pp3–47

and for a longer readable study try:

Williams, B., *Plato*, Phoenix, 1998, pp1–57

If you have even more time then this book is excellent:

Melling, D., *Understanding Plato*, Oxford University Press, USA, 1987, pp96–113

For a detailed exploration of relativism try:

Pojman, L., *Ethics, Discovering Right and Wrong*, US Military Academy, 2002, pp24–41

Rachels, J., *The Elements of Moral Philosophy*, McGraw-Hill, 1993, pp15–143

and the classic and essential:

Mackie, J., *Inventing Right and Wrong*, Penguin, 1977, pp30–41

As well as my favourite anthology:

Singer, P., *Ethics*, in the Oxford Readers series, Oxford University Press, 1994

In this chapter you have:

- considered the idea of absolutism in general, and in particular the Platonic form, and applied absolutist thinking to some ethical statements
- considered the theory of relativism, and the contributions of Protagoras, Sumner and Mackie and applied relativist thinking to some ethical statements
- identified and commented on respective strengths and weaknesses of absolutism and relativism.

3 Utilitarianism

Key philosophers

Jeremy Bentham (1748–1832): *Principles of Morals and Legislation*, 1789; *A Fragment on Government*, 1776

John Stuart Mill (1806–73): *Utilitarianism*, 1863

Peter Singer (1946–): *Practical Ethics*, 1993

Key terms

Hedonism: the belief that pleasure is the chief 'good'.

Key questions

1 A moral world is one in which as many people as possible are as happy as they can be. Do you agree?

2 When making a moral decision, is it more important to think about the action you are performing, or the consequence of that action?

3 'The good of the many outweighs the good of the few, or the one.' Is this true or false?

The theory of utilitarianism

Jeremy Bentham

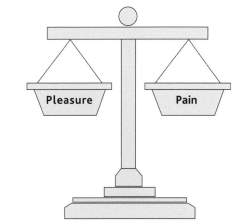

The theory of utilitarianism was devised by the English philosopher Jeremy Bentham (1748–1832). He was born in London and lived at a time of great scientific and social change. With revolutions in France and America, demands were being made for human rights and greater democracy. Bentham worked on legal reform and wrote *The Principles of Morals and Legislation* (1789), in which he put forward his ethical theory. We can divide his theory into three parts:

1 His view on what drove human beings, and what goodness and badness was all about.

2 The principle of utility (from the Latin *utilis*, meaning 'useful'), which is his moral rule.

3 The hedonic calculus, which is his system for measuring how good or bad a consequence is.

The motivation of human beings

Bentham maintained that human beings were motivated by pleasure and pain, and so he can be called a **hedonist** (*hedone* is Greek for 'pleasure'). He said, in *Principles of Morals and Legislation*, 'Nature has placed mankind under the governance of two sovereign masters, pain and pleasure. It is for them alone to point out what we ought to do, as well as to determine what we shall do' (Bentham, 1988, Chapter 1).

Link

For an introduction to teleological and deontological ethics, see Chapter 1, pp3–5. For an introduction to absolutist and relativistic thinking, see Chapter 2, pp11–14.

Key term

Utility principle: the rightness or wrongness of an action is determined by its 'utility' or usefulness.

Key terms

Hedonic calculus: created by Bentham, this is a utilitarian system whereby the effects of an action can be measured as to the amount of pleasure it may bring.

Bentham believed that all human beings pursued pleasure and sought to avoid pain. He saw this as a moral fact, as pleasure and pain identified what we should and shouldn't do. As a hedonist, Bentham believed that pleasure was the sole good and pain the sole evil: hence Bentham's utilitarianism is called hedonic utilitarianism.

The principle of utility

Once Bentham had established that pleasure and pain were the important qualities for determining what was moral, he developed the **utility principle**. The rightness or wrongness of an action is determined by its 'utility' or usefulness. Usefulness refers to the amount of pleasure or happiness caused by the action – hence it is a teleological ethical theory which determines a good act by the ends it brings about. The theory is known as the greatest happiness principle, or a theory of usefulness:

> By the principle of utility is meant that principle which approves or disapproves of every action whatsoever, according to the tendency which it appears to have to augment or diminish the happiness of the party whose interest is in question: or, what is the same thing in other words, to promote or to oppose that happiness. I say of every action whatsoever; and therefore not, only of every action of a private individual, but of every measure of government.

Bentham, 1988, Chapter I, II

This can be shortened to 'An action is right if it produces the greatest good for the greatest number', where the greatest good is the greatest pleasure or happiness and the least pain or sadness, and the greatest number are the majority of people. Good is the maximisation of pleasure and the minimisation of pain. The ends that Bentham's theory identifies are those with the most pleasure and least pain. His theory is democratic, because the pleasure can't be for one person alone. When faced with a moral dilemma, Bentham argued that one should choose to act in such a way that brings about the maximum possible happiness for the most people. However, the possible consequences of different possible actions must be measured clearly to establish which option generates the most pleasure and the least pain. To measure the results, Bentham proposed the hedonic calculus.

The hedonic calculus

The **hedonic calculus** weighs up the pain and pleasure generated by the available moral actions to find the best option. It considers seven factors:

1 Its intensity.
2 Its duration.
3 Its certainty or uncertainty.
4 Its propinquity or remoteness
5 Its fecundity, or the chance it has of being followed by, sensations of the same kind: that is, pleasures, if it be a pleasure: pains, if it be a pain.
6 Its purity, or the chance it has of not being followed by, sensations of the opposite kind: that is, pains, if it be a pleasure: pleasures, if it be a pain …
And one other; to wit:
7 Its extent; that is, the number of persons to whom it extends; or (in other words) who are affected by it.

> Sum up all the values of all the pleasures on the one side, and those of all the pains on the other. The balance, if it be on the side of pleasure, will give the good tendency of the act upon the whole, with respect to the interests of that individual person; if on the side of pain, the bad tendency of it upon the whole.

Bentham, 1988, Chapter IV, II

In the hedonic calculus Bentham considers how strong the pain or pleasure is, whether it is short-lived or life-long and how likely it is that there will be pain or pleasure. He considers how immediate the pain or pleasure is and how likely it is to lead to more of the same, the extent to which there might be a combination of pains and pleasures, and lastly, the number of people affected. The balance of pleasures and pains is compared with those of other options and the best result determined. The action that leads to this best consequence is the morally correct one to pursue.

Act utilitarianism

Utilitarianism is also described as being either act or rule. Bentham's approach is closer to act utilitarianism. **Act utilitarians** maintain that, whenever possible, the principle of utility must be directly applied for each individual situation. When faced with a moral choice, a person must decide what action will lead to the greatest good in a particular situation. If that person is in a situation in which lying will create the greatest pleasure, then they should lie. If, in the next situation, lying brings about a lesser result than telling the truth, then they should tell the truth. According to act utilitarians, when determining whether the act is right, it is the value of the consequences of the particular act that counts. A person may break any law if, in that situation, greater happiness will result.

Act utilitarianism has the benefit of flexibility, being able to take into account individual situations at a given moment, although the actions that it justifies can change.

There are a number of criticisms of act utilitarianism. First, it has the potential to justify virtually any act if, in that particular case, the result generates the most happiness. A second problem is that it is impractical to suggest that we should measure each and every moral choice every time, especially as we may not have all the information required by the hedonic calculus. A third difficulty is that act utilitarianism can have some quite extreme results.

For example, an act utilitarian goes out to see a film. On the way to the cinema, she sees someone collecting money for charity. She gives her money to the collector instead of buying the ticket, and then goes home. A week passes and she sets out to the cinema again. She meets the collector again, hands over her money and again returns home. In each case, giving up her money to help the greatest number generates the greatest happiness. However, taken to extreme, all leisure activity would end – which seems a little hard to stomach. The other form of utilitarianism – rule utilitarianism – addresses this difficulty.

Jim finds himself in the central square of a small South American town. Tied up against the wall are a row of Indians, mostly terrified, a few defiant, in front of them several armed men in uniform. A heavy man in a sweat-stained khaki shirt turns out to be the captain in charge and, after a good deal of questioning of Jim which establishes that he got there by accident while on a botanical expedition, explains that the Indians are a random group of the inhabitants who, after recent acts of protest against the government, are just about to be killed to remind other possible protestors of the advantages of not protesting. However, since Jim is an honoured visitor from another land, the captain is happy to offer him a guest's privilege of killing one of the Indians himself. If Jim accepts, then as a special mark of the occasion, the other Indians will be let off. Of course, if Jim refuses, then there is no special occasion, and Pedro here will do what he was about to do when Jim arrived, and kill them all. Jim, with some recollection of schoolboy fiction, wonders whether if he got hold of the gun, he could hold the Captain, and the rest of the soldiers to threat, but it is quite clear from the set-up that nothing of that kind is going to work: any attempt at that sort of thing will mean that all the Indians will be killed and himself. The men against the wall, and the other villagers, understand the situation, and are obviously begging him to accept. What should he do?

Williams, 1973, pp98–99

Activities

1 Suggest an example where a desirable consequence justifies an undesirable action, and another example when it does not. What distinguishes one from the other? Try to come to agreement within a small group on precisely what those distinctions are and how they are measured. How easy or difficult is this to do and what does this say about the usefulness or the morality of the theory?

2 The following questions raise challenges for the theory. Consider each one and decide which are more significant problems and which are less significant challenges, justifying your decisions:

■ How can we perform the hedonic calculation if we are unsure or unable to know what is going to happen in the future? How can we be sure that we are sure about what is going to happen?

■ Are there some pains that are good and some pleasures that are bad?

■ Are affection or honesty only good because they have good results or is there something inherent in them which makes them good?

■ How can the interests of minority groups be protected under utilitarianism?

3 One contemporary utilitarian, Peter Singer, goes as far as to consider animals in the equation 'the greatest good for the greatest number'. When making moral decisions, should you include the happiness and well-being of non-humans?

4 Why does Bentham's theory pose a problem for those who believe we have a special obligation to certain people (parents, family, children and so on)?

5 Sadistic guards torture a wrongly imprisoned innocent man. What difficulty does this example pose for Bentham's theory?

6 Read the extract opposite then consider the following questions:

■ On what grounds would a utilitarian kill the single prisoner?

■ Would you agree with a utilitarian that the action of choosing and killing the single prisoner was good? If so, why – and if not, why not?

7 Bernard Williams thinks that utilitarians find the decision to kill one too easy to take. What might he mean by this?

■ John Stuart Mill

John Stuart Mill (1806–73) was a child prodigy who was able to read several languages at an early age; his father, Scottish philosopher James Mill (1773–1836), was a follower of Jeremy Bentham. Perhaps the greatest British philosopher of the 19th century, John Stuart Mill was an administrator for the East India Company and a Member of Parliament. Among his other works, he wrote *On the Subjugation of Women* (1869), one of the inspirations behind modern feminism. His works concerning ethics were *On Liberty* (1859) and *Utilitarianism* (as a series of articles in 1861 and as a book in 1863).

Mill maintained that the well-being of the individual was of greatest importance and that happiness is most effectively gained when individuals are free to pursue their own ends, subject to rules that protect the common good of all. While Mill accepted the utility principle of the greatest good for the greatest number, he was concerned about the difficulty raised in the example of the sadistic guards (see p22). If the greatest good for the greatest number was purely **quantitative**, based on the quantities of pleasure and pain caused, what would stop one person's pleasure from being completely extinguished if the majority gained pleasure from that act? Mill was aware that utilitarianism was being criticised as promoting nothing other than desire and the pursuit of pleasure and that it lowered human nature to that of swine because of its baseness.

Higher and lower pleasures

To address this difficulty, Mill distinguished between higher and lower pleasures, and the higher pleasures were **qualitatively** better and more important than the lower pleasures. He argued that, 'Human beings have faculties more elevated than the animal appetites and, once made conscious of them, do not regard anything as happiness which does not include their gratification' (Mill, 1979, Chapter 1).

Some kinds of pleasures are more desirable than other kinds and what is more, it is not just that we should prefer the higher pleasures to the lower ones, but that a happiness which did not include a higher pleasure was not considered a happiness by human beings. A higher, qualitatively better, pleasure should be preferred over a lower, more quantitative, gratification, even if in seeking the higher pleasure we find ourselves with a greater level of dissatisfaction because we have forgone quantity. He writes: 'It is better to be a human being dissatisfied than a pig satisfied; better to be Socrates dissatisfied than a fool satisfied' (Mill, 1979, Chapter 2).

Key terms

Quantitative: concerned with the amount.

Qualitative: concerned with the value and nature.

AQA Examiner's tip

Remember that some of the background to this view lies in Mill's reading of the Greek philosophers. For Plato, philosophical thinking is the highest activity for humans, because Plato's Forms are non-physical – they are ideas, and unlike physical things, ideas cannot rot or decay or change, hence they are perfect. When you do Activity 1 at the end of this section, consider how much of this is really true and, in particular, think what religious ideas might follow from these views. This is an important issue, and will help to clarify your thinking on ethical matters.

■ Activities

1 Are bodily pleasures lower than intellectual pleasures?

2 Working on your own arrange the following pleasures in qualitative order, from higher to lower quality:

- eating
- listening to music
- making music
- drinking alcohol
- watching a good movie
- viewing beautiful artwork
- spending time with your partner
- spending time with your friends
- attending family gatherings
- eating chocolate
- reading or hearing poetry
- playing sport
- achieving fame.

Now compare your list with that of a partner or group, and try to come to an agreement.

3 Is it possible to enjoy both the opera and promiscuous sex? If so, does this present a problem for Mill?

4 Why might Mill's formulation of utilitarianism offer more protection to individuals and minority groups than Bentham's?

■ Key terms

Rule utilitarianism: a version of utilitarianism in which general rules are assessed for the happiness-making properties rather than individual decisions. Often associated with John Stuart Mill. Actions are therefore 'right' or 'wrong' depending on whether they conform to a happiness-making rule, not because of their individual effects.

Mill maintained that the pleasures of the mind were higher than those of the body. There's a link between the two, as to be able to enjoy poetry or art, we need to eat and drink in order to survive. Nevertheless, Mill clearly believed that to pursue purely bodily pleasures – food, drink, drugs and sex – was not as high an objective as those that are intellectually demanding. When confronted with a choice between a pleasure of the body or a pleasure of the mind, that of the mind is to be preferred.

Mill is aware of the challenge presented by the fact that many people do seem to pursue the more bodily pleasures, over the higher mental ones, and he accepts that temptation leads some people this way. It is not that the intrinsic superiority of the higher pleasure is not recognised, but that people may lack the character to forgo the nearer bodily pleasure over the higher one: 'They pursue sensual indulgences to the injury of health, though perfectly aware that health is the greater good' (Mill, 1979, Chapter 2). Mill is concerned that in some cases a person acting in such a way can sink into a state where they no longer recognise higher pleasure. Through bad habits they become incapable of recognising its value. Mill writes:

> Capacity for the nobler feelings is in most natures a very tender plant, easily killed, not only by hostile influences, but by want of sustenance; and in the majority of young persons it speedily dies away if the occupations to which their position in life has devoted them, and the society into which it has thrown them, are not favorable to keeping that higher capacity in exercise.

Mill, 1979, Chapter 2

By failing to nurture an appreciation of the higher pleasures, they become inaccessible, and then the decline into more base gratifications can happen.

In Mill's view, according to the greatest happiness principle the ultimate aim is life as far away from pain, and as rich as possible in enjoyments, both qualitatively and quantitatively. Judging the mix of these things is difficult but it can be done. Experienced people who are habitually self-conscious and self-observant will have a preference towards a certain balance of qualitative and quantitative, and they can provide a benchmark standard of morality.

To further distance his form of utilitarianism, which may be near-sighted, or in the interest of the individual rather than the whole, Mill goes on to stress that utilitarian morality does recognise that there are times when the greatest good is served by self-sacrifice, though of itself sacrifice is not good. Resisting claims that utilitarianism was godless, he argues that the concern for others that utilitarians must show in the pursuit of the greatest good for the greatest number is similar to the Christian teaching of loving your neighbour as yourself.

Rule utilitarianism

Rule utilitarianism focuses on general rules that everyone should follow to bring about the greatest good for that community. Rule utilitarianism establishes the best overall rule by determining the course of action which, when pursued by the whole community, leads to the best result. This form of utilitarianism is associated with John Stuart Mill and British legal philosopher John Austin (1790–1859), particularly in his book *The Province of Jurisprudence Determined* (1832). In a particular situation, I must obey the rule even if it doesn't lead to the greatest pleasure for me in this particular situation. A rule utilitarian will maintain that a person must always drive on the left-hand side of the road in the UK, even in situations in which that does not bring about the greatest pleasure for that person – such as when they are in a traffic jam – because that will ensure the greatest good when everyone acts in such a way. A person should never lie because, as a general community rule, lying doesn't bring about the greatest good for the community. In each case, the rule takes priority over the person's immediate situation.

Rule utilitarianism seems to overcome some of the difficulties encountered in act utilitarianism. Whereas in the example of act utilitarianism above (with a woman trying to go to the cinema but never getting there because she keeps giving her money to charity), under rule utilitarianism the woman would be able to see a film, because a rule that allows people leisure time would be acceptable. On the other hand, it creates difficulties of its own. The British philosopher R. M. Hare (1919–2002) notes a weakness with rule utilitarianism. Suppose that a maniac is chasing someone who hides in a shop. The maniac runs into the shop and asks the shopkeeper where the person is. In this situation, our gut feeling would be to lie. A rule utilitarian would state that the shopkeeper has to be honest, because he or she is not allowed to break a rule even though, in this instance, the result is not the greatest good (Hare, in Childress and Macquarrie, 1986, p642). In addition, it's possible that a rule utilitarian could still permit certain practices, such as slavery, that appear to be morally unacceptable. There's no guarantee that minority interests will be protected. As long as the slaves are the smaller proportion of the people, the greatest good might be to keep them enslaved, because of the benefits that this would give to the majority.

Preference utilitarianism

The modern, Australian ethicist Peter Singer (1946–) argues in *Practical Ethics* (1993), for a modified view of utilitarianism, commonly called **preference utilitarianism** or best consequence utilitarianism. Singer declares that the clearest way in which preference utilitarianism differs from classical utilitarianism is that best consequences is understood to mean what furthers the best interests of those affected, rather than what creates the most pleasure and least pain. Singer argues that our ethical decisions should benefit the best interests (or preferences) of those affected, rather than create the most pleasure (be it mental or bodily pleasure) and that everyone's interests must be given equal consideration. Singer writes:

> This other version of utilitarianism judges actions, not by their tendency to maximize pleasure or minimize pain, but by the extent to which they accord with the preference of any beings affected by the action or its consequences.

Singer, 1993, p94

What matters in preference utilitarianism is the satisfaction of an individual person's interests or desires. Sacrificing an individual because it benefits the majority becomes more problematic according to Singer, who continues:

> According to preference utilitarianism, an action contrary to the preference of any being is, unless this preference is outweighed by contrary preferences, wrong. Killing a person who prefers to continue living is therefore wrong, other things being equal.

Singer, 1993, p94

Preference utilitarianism tries to maximise the satisfaction of people's preferences. This requires considerable thought. When a person thinks ethically they must try to weigh up all of the interests of the affected parties, recognising that their own interest is not worth any more than anyone else's. In that kind of moral reasoning a person must do their best to take account of all these interests and, in Singer's words, 'choose the course which brings about the best consequences, on balance, for all affected' (Singer, 1993, p13). This kind of deliberation should not take place on every occasion, but is reserved for very special occasions, such as when a person is trying to decide by what principles they should live their life. Singer gives the example of whether we should share the fruit we have picked. It seems to have better consequences for all as many preferences are satisfied, and if everyone did that then the best consequences would be achieved – a fair and just distribution of resources. However, if some decided to stop gathering fruit then things would not go well and a fair and just distribution of fruit would not be achieved.

Activities

1 Consider the following examples and map out all the possible affected individuals and what preferences each of those individuals might have:

   a A middle-aged mother suffering from an incurable and slowly deteriorating mentally and physically debilitating disease, wanting to end her life sooner rather than later.

   b A policeman trying to decide whether or not he should torture a terrorist suspect in the hope of gaining information about the bomb which is believed to have been planted in a public place somewhere in the city.

   c A drug addict desperate for the next fix.

2 Identify where there might be clashes of interest. How might Singer resolve these clashes?

3 Identify where there is uncertainty over the nature of the interests or particular affected people.

■ Evaluating utilitarianism

Consequences

Jeremy Bentham's theory has a number of clear benefits. It seems reasonable to link morality with the pursuit of happiness and the avoidance of pain and misery, and this connection would receive popular support. It also seems natural to consider the consequences of our actions when deciding what to do. Utilitarianism offers a balanced, democratic morality that promotes the general happiness. Utilitarianism does not support individual pursuits that are at the expense of the majority. It is a common sense system that is practically applicable to real-life situations. It has no need for a special wisdom.

These benefits are considerable, as they signify a working morality that can be brought into operation in organisational rather than simply individual matters. One could envisage the benefits of using utilitarianism in the management of hospitals, where fixed budgets must be best used to alleviate the suffering of the many.

However, there are a number of difficulties with utilitarianism. One difficulty concerns all theories that rely on the consequences for deciding which actions are good. I need to be sure that what I think will come about as a result of a particular action *will* actually come about. Utilitarianism depends upon accurate predictions of the future but human beings don't always display accurate foresight. The consequences of actions may not become apparent until years into the future and it is unclear how far into the future one must look when evaluating a choice. There is also what is sometimes referred to as the law of unforeseen consequences where an action begins to affect lots of things in unexpected, unpredictable ways.

Justice v happiness

We might feel that a theory which only really looks at consequences might ignore some pretty nasty acts that get carried out for some idea of a greater good. This raises the questions of whether some individuals can be 'used' for some greater good of the majority which might lead to unpalatable conclusions. Having a minority as a slave class could serve the majority's interests well but it would be at a cost of the slaves losing everything. Utilitarianism ensures a maximum-pleasure result but it doesn't set out how that pleasure is distributed. It ensures that the most people receive pleasure, but it guarantees nothing for minorities. There is nothing in utilitarianism that prevents the total sacrifice of one pleasure for the benefit of the whole: five bullies get pleasure from torturing a single boy; his pleasure is sacrificed for the greater benefit of theirs.

In his book *A Short History of Ethics* (1966), Scottish philosopher Alasdair MacIntyre (1929–) notes that utilitarianism could justify horrendous acts as being for the pleasure of the many. The Nazi policy of persecution and, eventually, extermination of Jews could be considered good if the greater population thought it pleasurable (MacIntyre, 1966, p238). He identifies the focus on happiness as the cause of the problem: 'That men are happy with their lot never entails that their lot is what it ought to be. For the question can always be raised of how great the price is that is being paid for the happiness' (MacIntyre, 1966, p239). Perhaps the pursuit of justice is as important as the pursuit of happiness.

High and low pleasures

Mill seems to offer some solutions to Bentham's theory in that he differentiates between high pleasures and low pleasures and seeks to rule out some of the possible applications of Bentham's theory which might allow an injustice to be done to an individual if the majority is best served. Mill was far more conscious of the threat that the majority might pose to individuals.

Nevertheless it is not clear that Mill's views about what is high pleasure and what is low pleasure would be universally held. One might argue that base sexual appetite is a lower pleasure than the refineries of excellent opera, and yet passionate and tender lovemaking could be much more important for a couple than a visit to Madam Butterfly. Indeed a person might attend opera frequently and without much thought and treat encounters with their lover in the same way. Are peoples' intentions about these actions and attitudes towards them rather more important than utilitarianism gives credit for?

Questions about pleasure and pain

A second general area of difficulty is found in the issue of pleasure and pain as understood by utilitarianism. This falls into different areas. Measuring pleasure is less straightforward than it might at first appear. The balancing process brought about using the seven criteria of the hedonic calculus appears straightforward. However, can different pleasures and different pains be so easily quantified? Can someone compare the pleasure of seeing children grow up into adults with the pleasure of eating a chocolate bar? How would that person quantify those two pleasures? What about pain that's good for you? When we hurt ourselves, the pain is a reminder that we have the injury and must take care of it. People who suffer from conditions that prevent their sensation of pain are at risk of serious injury.

Some pain is good for us – it's there for a reason. This raises further questions about weighing pleasure against pain. If some pleasures can only be reached through some suffering (training hard to excel in sport for instance) is it better not to have them so as to not suffer? Should we try to eliminate all pain, even if some gains are lost as a result? In some instances pain is a very natural and human response to an emotional wound – for instance the death of a loved one or the end of a relationship. Surely the removal of such pain would make us less human? In these cases is not the pain there because of the love we feel? The hedonic calculus formula is not as simple as it at first appears. It is questionable whether all actions can be declared good or bad by an empirical test in the way the hedonic calculus suggests.

Utilitarianism seems not to consider different views on what happiness is. It asserts that there is common agreement about what brings pleasure and what brings pain. This can be challenged on many levels. Not only do people have different tastes with regards to art, music and literature, but there are even extreme exceptions with regard to physical sensations – there are people who find pleasure in experiencing pain. If human beings don't have the same idea of what gives them pain and pleasure, then the premise on which utilitarianism is built is severely weakened. The identification of one's interests with those of others becomes artificial. There seems to be an assumption that everyone shares a similar human nature but is this assumption proven? For instance, do people simply desire happiness? What about material goods, economic stability, success in business or the arts? These things may lead to happiness, but not necessarily. Some of the most talented people are also very unhappy, and rich people can also be unhappy, but that does not mean they do not pursue their talents or seek to increase their wealth as an aim in life. What about spiritual fulfilment as understood in the religious traditions? This is not the same as happiness, and in some cases embracing suffering is seen to be part of living a religious life.

More recent forms of utilitarianism

Despite these weaknesses, utilitarianism has proved popular and useful in the centuries since its original formation. In *The Methods of Ethics* (1874), the English philosopher Henry Sidgwick (1838–1900) produced a more complex account of utilitarianism. He rejected Bentham's view that people pursued their own pleasure and replaced it with ethical hedonism – the view that individuals should seek general happiness.

We have seen above that another popular form of utilitarianism, called preference utilitarianism, has also emerged and is illustrated by Peter Singer in *Practical Ethics*. Does this resolve some of the difficulties identified above? There is clearly some exploration of what is meant by preference or interests. Is it clear that we would be able to make a moral decision knowing what everyone's preference would be? Is it possible for someone to prefer something which is not in their best interest, such as gambling their money instead of putting it in a savings account? In this case how should the preference utilitarian respond? Beyond this we might also ask questions about the people whose preferences are considered. Are all people's preferences to be considered, even those of a dangerous criminal?

Elsewhere in his book Singer makes it clear that newborn babies are not persons as, like the unborn baby, they are not autonomous, and they do not see themselves as having a future. In effect they have no interests to take into account. The issue of what defines a person who has interests is central to preference utilitarianism. Consider a heroin addict, who lives to find the next fix by any means possible. He has no concept of long-term future and is driven by his addiction, not any familiar kind of rational autonomy. He certainly has desires and would express his preferences in terms of getting the next fix. But, under Singer's classification, is he really a person whose interests can be taken account of, and what exactly are those interests? Finally when preferences come into direct conflict, on what basis should a decision be made about what to do? Singer uses phrases such as 'on balance', and 'all things being equal', but how does one come to a decision of what is balance, and when are all things equal?

Modern formulations of utilitarianism don't fully address all its opponents' criticisms. The current concern for justice and minority issues in the light of human rights abuses raises powerful arguments against adopting a classical utilitarian stance. Nevertheless, utilitarianism will remain a persuasive ethical theory owing to its practical dimension, which provides organisations with clear-cut systems for making decisions.

Utilitarianism and the religious life?

To what extent is utilitarianism compatible with living a religious life? Utilitarians do not seem to be particularly close to religion. Peter Singer has had major disagreements with religious believers over his application of his theory to unborn children, and John Stuart Mill seems to have had no personal faith. Utilitarian theories do not make reference to religious rules and principles, and seem more pragmatically driven by focusing on the outcome. Many religions express absolutes in terms of things which should or should not be done, as well as principles to apply, while utilitarianism suggests an overriding principle, rather than any absolute moral norms. Religions sometimes express strong ideas that self-sacrifice and suffering are part of the spiritual life and are not evils to be avoided, which seems to contradict some of the assumptions underpinning utilitarianism. Religions also look beyond the immediate world of happiness and suffering to some greater end. This is teleological in a sense, a focus on some eternal goal, rather than a worldly one, but not in the kind of immediate terms that could be used to apply utilitarianism in the world. However, utilitarianism is often used as a way of maximising welfare (something John Stuart Mill was very concerned about) to bring about improvement in the lives of people. This is an aim of many religious people who, out of compassion for others and in response to religious commandments, seek to improve the world as an expression of their love of others. This concern of utilitarianism is more broadly in line with some religious aspirations.

AQA Examiner's tip

Have a look at 'multi-level' utilitarianism, a sophisticated version of utilitarianism that employs both a rule-utility feature and an act-utility feature. The rule-utility feature covers general classes of acts which we are generally happy to have embedded as rules (e.g. for promise-keeping, telling the truth, and so on). Where the rules won't produce the best results (as with telling the maniac the location of her victim), the act-utility feature overrides the rule. You could look at the examples in L. P. Pojman's *Ethics: Discovering Right and Wrong*, Wadsworth, 1998, pp121–5.

Activities

1. Explain what is meant by the definition 'Goodness means the greatest happiness of the greatest number.'

2. Explain the distinctive features of utilitarianism.

3. Identify and evaluate three strengths of utilitarianism.

4. Identify and evaluate three weaknesses of utilitarianism.

Application

When applying a theory to an issue, remember that your choice of issue is significant if you are going to evaluate the theory on the basis of how well it deals with your issue. Re-read the 'Tools for evaluating ethical theories' section in Chapter 1 to remind yourself of some of the tools you have available.

Use the following questions when applying Bentham's version of utilitarianism to an ethical issue. In the issue you are addressing:

1 What are the pleasures and pains and is it appropriate to avoid the pains and seek the pleasures?

2 Consider each of the options available taking account of all of the factors in the hedonic calculus.

3 Which option leads to the greatest amount of pleasure and least amount of pain?

4 Does the option identified in number 3 seem reasonable or unreasonable?

5 If unreasonable why is this?
- Is it because of some other moral factor which utilitarianism doesn't account for and, if so, which factor?
- Is it because you value different moral factors than those expressed in the theory (such as virtue, the moral law, etc.)?
- If so can you justify why you value those factors over and above the ones which are important in the theory?
- Is this a factor which is likely to be found in many ethical issues? In other words does this flag up a more major problem with the theory as a whole, or just a problem with this particularly difficult issue?

6 If the solution seems reasonable, how adequate do you think this moral example is in testing the theory? Might there be different kinds of examples which the theory has more trouble with?

You can draw up a set of questions like the ones above but adjusted for the components of Mill's version of utilitarianism and Singer's version and run the example you looked at past each of these.

Extract from key text

John Stuart Mill, Utilitarianism, 1863

Chapter 2: What Utilitarianism Is

The creed which accepts as the foundation of morals, Utility, or the Greatest Happiness Principle, holds that actions are right in proportion as they tend to promote happiness, wrong as they tend to produce the reverse of happiness. By happiness is intended pleasure, and the absence of pain; by unhappiness, pain, and the privation of pleasure …

To suppose that life has (as they express it) no higher end than pleasure – no better and nobler object of desire and pursuit – they designate as utterly mean and grovelling; as a doctrine worthy only of swine, to whom the followers of Epicurus were, at a very early period, contemptuously likened; and modern holders of the doctrine are occasionally made the subject of equally polite comparisons by its German, French, and English assailants …

It is quite compatible with the principle of utility to recognize the fact, that some kinds of pleasure are more desirable and more valuable than others. It would be absurd that while, in estimating all other things, quality is considered as well as quantity, the estimation of pleasures should be supposed to depend on quantity alone …

Now it is an unquestionable fact that those who are equally acquainted with, and equally capable of appreciating and enjoying, both, do give a most marked preference to the manner of existence which employs their higher faculties. Few human creatures would consent to be changed into any of the lower animals, for a promise of the fullest allowance of a beast's pleasures; no intelligent human being would consent to be a fool, no instructed person would be an ignoramus, no person of feeling and conscience would be selfish and base, even though they should be persuaded that the fool, the dunce, or the rascal is better satisfied with his lot than they are with theirs. They would not resign what they possess more than he for the most complete satisfaction of all the desires which they have in common with him. If they ever fancy they would, it is only in cases of unhappiness so extreme, that to cscapc from it they would exchange their lot for almost any other, however undesirable in their own eyes. A being of higher faculties requires more to make him happy, is capable probably of more acute suffering, and certainly accessible to it at more points, than one of an inferior type; but in spite of these liabilities, he can never really wish to sink into what he feels to be a lower grade of existence …

It is indisputable that the being whose capacities of enjoyment are low, has the greatest chance of having them fully satisfied; and a highly endowed being will always feel that any happiness which he can look for, as the world is constituted, is imperfect. But he can learn to bear its imperfections, if they are at all bearable; and they will not make him envy the being who is indeed unconscious of the imperfections, but only because he feels not at all the good which those imperfections qualify. It is better to be a human being dissatisfied than a pig satisfied; better to be Socrates dissatisfied than a fool satisfied. And if the fool, or the pig, are of a different opinion, it is because they only know their own side of the question. The other party to the comparison knows both sides.

■ Chapter summary

Jeremy Bentham:

- Jeremy Bentham devised the utilitarian theory. Human beings are hedonists; they pursue pleasure, which is good, and seek to avoid pain, which is bad.

- The utility principle: the rightness or wrongness of an action is determined by its 'utility', or usefulness.

- Usefulness refers to the amount of pleasure or happiness caused by the action.

- An action is right if it produces the greatest good for the greatest number.

- The hedonic calculus: this weighs up pain and pleasure based on intensity, duration, certainty or uncertainty, propinquity or remoteness, fecundity, purity and extent.

Act utilitarianism:

- Act utilitarians maintain that the good action is the one that leads to the greatest good in a particular situation.

- Act utilitarianism is flexible, being able to take into account individual situations at a given moment.

- However, it has the potential to justify virtually any act.

- It may be impractical to suggest that we should measure each moral choice every time.

John Stuart Mill:

- The well-being of the individual is of greatest importance, and that happiness is most effectively gained when individuals are free to pursue their own ends, subject to rules protecting the common good.

- Focused on qualitative pleasures – some pleasures are higher (mind) and more desirable and others lower (body) and less desirable.

- 'It is better to be a human being dissatisfied than a pig satisfied; better to be Socrates dissatisfied than a fool satisfied.'

- Higher and lower pleasures are related but higher pleasures are more important.

- People may, in error, seek the lower pleasure over the higher while still recognising the higher is a greater pleasure.

- An appreciation of higher pleasures must be cultivated or there is a danger that a person declines into gratuitous pursuit of bodily pleasures.

- For those who are experienced, self-consciousness and self-observance provide a benchmark standard of morality.

Rule utilitarianism:

- Rule utilitarians establish the best overall rule by determining the course of action which, when pursued by the whole community, leads to the greatest result.

- Rule utilitarianism overcomes some of the difficulties of act utilitarianism.

- However, it may still permit certain practices, such as slavery, that appear to be morally unacceptable, because minority interests are not protected.

Preference utilitarianism:

- Peter Singer's *Practical Ethics*.

- Preference or best consequences means what furthers the best interests of those affected, rather than what creates the most pleasure and least pain.

- What matters is the satisfaction of all affected individuals' interests.

- An individual cannot be sacrificed for others, as their interest must be respected as much as anyone else's.

- Preference utilitarianism maximises the satisfaction of people's preferences.

- People should deliberate on the general principles of how they should live, rather than consider each situation every time.

Evaluating utilitarianism:

- It's reasonable to link morality with the pursuit of happiness and the avoidance of pain and misery.

- It's natural to consider the consequences of our actions when deciding what to do.

- Utilitarianism offers democratic morality that promotes general happiness and opposes individual pursuits.

- It's a common sense system that doesn't require special wisdom.

Difficulties:

- Utilitarianism relies on knowledge of consequences, but predictions may be mistaken or not apparent until years into the future.

- It is difficult to quantify pleasure.

- Some pain is good for us and some pleasure may be bad.

- The problem of justice: utilitarianism doesn't set out how pleasure is distributed.

- Utilitarianism fails to consider different views on what happiness is.

- Utilitarianism has proved popular and useful in the centuries since its original formation, with updated versions suggested by Henry Sidgwick and Peter Singer.

- Singer's preference utilitarianism raises questions about the criteria for granting a person interests and resolving clashes of interests.

- Utilitarianism remains persuasive because of its practical dimension, which provides organisations with clear-cut systems for making decisions.

■ Further reading

Again, a readable exploration and evaluation of utilitarianism is:

Rachels, J., *The Elements of Moral Philosophy*, McGraw-Hill, 1993, pp127–138

and a more recent exploration is found in:

Pojman, L., *Ethics, Discovering Right and Wrong*, US Military Academy, 2002, pp104–133

For those who find visuals helpful this is good:

Robinson, D. and Garratt, C., *Ethics for Beginners*, Icon Books, 1996, pp68–79

For some classic, well-written explanations, try:

Foot, P., *Theories of Ethics*, Oxford University Press, 1970, pp128–144
Frankena, W., *Ethics*, Prentice-Hall, 1969, pp29–46
Mackie, J., *Inventing Right and Wrong*, Penguin, 1977, pp125–149

A great book if you can find it which is entirely devoted to arguments for and against utilitarianism is:

Smart, J. J. C. and Williams, B., *Utilitarianism: For and Against*, Cambridge University Press, 1973

And my favourite anthology:

Singer, P., *Ethics*, in the Oxford Readers series, Oxford University Press, 1994

In this chapter you have:

- explored utilitarianism, including the utility principle, the hedonic calculus, and act and rule utilitarianism

- applied different kinds of utilitarian thinking to different ethical issues

- explored the distinctive contributions of important utilitarian philosophers, including Jeremy Bentham, John Stuart Mill and, as a contemporary example, Peter Singer

- explored and considered strengths and weaknesses of utilitarianism.

4   Situation ethics

By the end of this chapter you will:

- have an understanding of how situation ethics differs from traditional approaches to moral decision-making

- be able to explain both the assumptions underpinning situation ethics and the principles by which the approach is applied

- have explored the application of situation ethics to moral dilemmas

- be able to identify key weaknesses and strengths in the theory and application of situation ethics.

Key philosophers

Joseph Fletcher (1905–91): *Situation Ethics, the New Morality,* 1963

Paul Lehmann (1906–96): *Ethics in a Christian Context,* 1963

Link

For an introduction to tcleological and deontological ethics, see Chapter 1, pp3–5. For an introduction to absolutist and relativistic thinking, see Chapter 2, pp11–14.

The morality of an action depends on the situation.

Joseph Fletcher, Situation Ethics, 1963

Key questions

1 Is moral behaviour about following rules or working things out for ourselves?

2 Are there unbreakable laws to govern moral behaviour, or should we make our own moral decisions?

3 Are there ever situations when you should ignore established moral rules?

4 When deciding what is right, how much weight should be given to the actual people involved and the consequences the moral judgement brings them?

A radical Christian ethical approach

There is only one ultimate and invariable duty, and its formula is 'Thou shalt love thy neighbour as thyself.' How to do this is another question, but this is the whole of moral duty.

Temple, 1923, p206

The law of love is the ultimate law because it is the negation of law; it is absolute because it concerns everything concrete ... The absolutism of love is its power to go into the concrete situation, to discover what is demanded by the predicament of the concrete to which it turns. Therefore, love can never become fanatical in a fight for the absolute, or cynical under the impact of the relative.

Tillich, 1951, p152

Joseph Fletcher (1905–91), an American professor who founded the theory of situational ethics in the 1960s, starts his book *Situation Ethics* by noting the words of Bishop Robinson, 'there is no one ethical system that can claim to be Christian' and of Rudolf Bultmann, who argued that Jesus had no ethics apart from 'love thy neighbour as thyself', the ultimate duty. Ethics has traditionally been seen by Catholics as something defined by natural moral law. Protestants tended to deduce morality from the moral laws in the Bible. In *Situation Ethics*, Fletcher offers different ethical principles that he maintains are true to Christian beliefs. His work is a radical departure from rule-based Christian ethics and has been condemned and castigated by traditional Christian moralists. In his foreword, Fletcher writes:

Let an anecdote set the tone. A friend of mine arrived in St. Louis just as a presidential campaign was ending, and the cab driver, not being above the battle, volunteered his testimony. 'I and my father and grandfather before me, and their fathers, have always been straight-ticket Republicans.' 'Ah,' said my friend, who is himself a Republican, 'I

Before you go into an exam, it's useful to remind yourself of the different elements that make up 'Christian ethics'. Broadly speaking, these include:

1   Old Testament ethics (e.g. the law of Moses, centred on the 10 commandments).

   New Testament ethics: primarily

   a   the ethics of Jesus, e.g. in Matthew 5–7, and

   b   the ethics of Paul.

   Both demand very high standards (sometimes called 'Kingdom Ethics' since they hopefully get you into God's kingdom).

2   The Roman Catholic tradition based on Aquinas' natural law ethics.

3   The Protestant tradition, which includes situation ethics.

Activities

A rich man asked a young woman if she would spend the night with him. She said 'No.' He then asked if she would do it for $100,000. She said 'Yes!'

1   Is it wrong to have sex for money:

   a   To survive?

   b   For luxury purchases?

   c   To fund a life-saving operation for a friend or relative?

   In each case, explain your answer.

2   Why might your answers for a, b and c differ?

take it that means you will vote for Senator So-and-So.' 'No,' said the driver, 'there are times when a man has to push his principles aside and do the right thing.'

Fletcher, 1963, p13

For Fletcher, that St Louis cabbie is the hero of *situation ethics*. To understand the theory, we need to look at the detail.

The theory of situation ethics

Three kinds of ethical theory

Fletcher maintains that there are essentially three different ways of making moral decisions. **Legalistic ethics** has a set of prefabricated moral rules and regulations. Judaism and Christianity both have legalistic ethical traditions. Pharisaic Judaism has a law-based approach to life, founded on the Halakah oral tradition (the full collection of Jewish religious law); Christianity has been focused either on natural law or biblical commandments. According to Fletcher, legalistic ethics runs into problems when life's complexities require additional laws. For example, once murder has been prohibited, one has to clarify killing in self-defence, killing in war, killing unborn human beings and so on. The legalist must either include all of the complex alternatives in the law or create new laws to cover the result. This can produce a choking web of laws, a kind of textbook morality that requires people to check the manual to decide what is right and wrong. For Fletcher this error has been made by Catholics through their adherence to natural law, and by Protestants through puritanical observance of the sayings of the Bible. The fanatical, rigid, sticking to the moral laws is not, in the end, morally good, or morally good enough. Fletcher rejects legalistic ethics.

Antinomian ethics is quite the reverse of legalistic ethics. The term 'antinomian' literally means 'against law'. A person using antinomianism doesn't really use an ethical system at all. He or she enters decision-making as if each occasion was unique. Making a moral decision is a matter of spontaneity. According to Fletcher, 'it is literally unprincipled, purely *ad hoc* and casual. They follow no forecastable course from one situation to another. They are, exactly, anarchic – i.e. without a rule' (Fletcher, 1963, p23). Fletcher is critical of antinomianism as an acceptable approach to ethics, because it is unprincipled.

The third approach to ethics is the situational approach, a different way of thinking about ethics which is more concerned with love and people than rules for rules' sake. The situationist enters into the moral dilemma with the ethics, rules and principles of his or her community or tradition. However, the situationist is prepared to set aside those rules in the situation if love seems better served by doing so. The situation itself is an important factor in moral decision-making processes and influences whether the rules should be set aside. Situation ethics agrees that reason is the instrument of moral judgements, but disagrees that the good is to be discerned from the nature of things (as natural law suggests). In Fletcher's words, 'The situationist follows a moral law or violates it according to love's need' (Fletcher, 1963, p26). For the situationist, all moral decisions are hypothetical. They depend on what best serves love. The situationist doesn't say that 'giving to charity is a good thing'; they only ever say 'giving to charity is a good thing if …'. In addition to the particulars of the situation, love is a crucial idea for the situationist.

An insane murderer who asks you the whereabouts of his next victim should be lied to; in that situation, a legalist must tell the truth. A situationist must best serve love but he or she does not deduce rules from that principle. In the words of William Temple (1881–1944), who was both Archbishop of York and subsequently Archbishop of Canterbury: 'What acts are right may depend on the circumstances … but there is an absolute obligation to will whatever may on each occasion be right' (Temple, 1923, p27). Situation ethics identifies its roots in the New Testament, and turns away from legalistic interpretations. As St Paul writes, 'Christ Jesus … abolished the law with its commandments and legal claims' (Ephesians 2:13–15).

Situation ethics is sensitive to variety and complexity. It uses principles to illuminate the situation, but not to direct the action. Fletcher divides his principles into two categories: the six fundamental principles and the four presumptions (properly known as four working principles).

The six fundamental principles and Christian love

First proposition

Only one thing is intrinsically good; namely love: nothing else at all.

Fletcher, 1963, p56

Only love is good in and of itself. Actions aren't intrinsically good or evil. They are good or evil depending upon whether they promote the most loving result. They are **extrinsically** good, depending on their circumstances and consequences.

Second proposition

The ruling norm of Christian decision is love: nothing else.

Fletcher, 1963, p69

Jesus replaced the Torah with the principle of love. Take, for example, his decision to heal (work) on the Sabbath day, rejecting the obligations of Sabbath observance. The Commandments are not absolute. Jesus broke them when love demanded it. Love replaces law. It isn't equalled by any other law.

Third proposition

> Love and Justice are the same, for justice is love distributed, nothing else.

Fletcher, 1963, p87

Love and **justice** can't be separated from each other. Fletcher writes, 'Justice is Christian love using its head, calculating its duties, obligations, opportunities, resources … Justice is love coping with situations where distribution is called for' (Fletcher, 1963, p95). Justice is love at work in the whole community, for the whole community.

Fourth proposition

> Love wills the neighbour's good, whether we like him or not.

Fletcher, 1963, p103

The love that Fletcher is concerned about isn't a matter of feeling, but of attitude of the will towards the other person. It isn't sentimental or erotic but, rather, a desire for the good of the other person. This is the New Testament **agape love**. Your neighbour is anybody and agape love goes out to everyone; not just those we like but those we don't like as well. Agape love is unconditional; nothing is required in return.

Fifth proposition

> Only the end justifies the means, nothing else.

Fletcher, 1963, p120

To consider moral actions without reference to their ends is a haphazard approach. Actions acquire moral status as a means to an end. For Fletcher, the end must be the most loving result. When weighing up a situation, one must consider the desired end, the means available, the motive for acting and the foreseeable consequences.

Sixth proposition

> [L]ove's decisions are made situationally, not prescriptively.

Fletcher, 1963, p134

Jesus reacted against the kind of rule-based morality that he saw around him. There were Jewish groups that lived within rule-based moral systems, but Jesus distanced himself from them. Whether something is right or wrong depends on the situation. If an action will bring about an end that serves love most, then it's right. Fletcher believed that if people do not feel that it is wrong to have sexual relations outside marriage, then it isn't, unless they hurt themselves, their partners, or others (although they have to really feel this is the case).

It is clear from these six propositions that Fletcher's moral theory differs from traditional Christian ethics. It embraces a form of relativism as actions are not intrinsically right or wrong. Actions are right or wrong depending on their result. For Fletcher, the good result is that which serves agape love best. Any action that leads to that end is right: 'Whether any form of sex is good or evil depends on whether love is fully served' (Fletcher, 1963, p139).

■ **Key terms**

Justice: not principles underpinning law and their relationships to those laws

Agape love: in Christian terms, the unconditional love that they must show their neighbours.

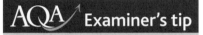 **Examiner's tip**

The early Christians used agape in the sense of God's self-sacrificial love, to which the appropriate response is that agape must, in turn, be shown to all other members of the community. In other words, Christians are not required simply to love others, but to do so to the extent that they sacrifice part of themselves in doing so. Research Fletcher's example of Mrs Bergmeier and try to identify the different sacrificial aspects of the story. This should also help to put your evaluation of situation ethics into a useful context.

■ **Activity**

Take a moral dilemma with which you are familiar and apply Fletcher's six propositions to the dilemma. How straightforward is it to apply them? What is the result of Fletcher's thinking? How morally satisfying do you think it is?

Four presumptions (also known as four working principles)

Fletcher's ethical thinking rests on some more general presuppositions: pragmatism, relativism, positivism and personalism.

1 **Pragmatism** – a practical or success posture. The proposed course of action must work, and must work towards the end, which is love.

2 **Relativism** – situation ethics is relativistic: 'The Situationist avoids words like "never" and "perfect" and "always" and "complete" as he avoids the plague, as he avoids "absolutely"' (Fletcher, 1963, p44). There are no fixed rules that must always be obeyed. However, nor is it a free for all! Fletcher maintains that all decisions must be relative to Christian love. Situation ethics 'relativizes the absolute, it does not absolutize the relative' (Fletcher, 1963, p45).

3 **Positivism** – religious knowledge or belief can only be approached by one of two ways. With natural positivism reason deduces faith from human experience or natural phenomena. Nature provides the evidence and reason grasps hold of it. With theological positivism faith statements are made and people act in a way that is reasonable in light of these statements. Reason isn't the basis for faith, but it works within faith. Situation ethics depends on Christians freely choosing the faith that God is love, so giving first place to Christian love.

4 **Personalism** – the legalist puts the law first. The situationist puts people first. He asks what to do to help humans best: 'There are no "values" in the sense of inherent goods – value is what happens to something when it happens to be useful to love working for the sake of persons' (Fletcher, 1963, p50). Whereas some ethical theories place a lot of weight on rules, situationists are much more interested in people. In a sense, people are more sacred than rules.

Some Christian writers have argued that **conscience** was the voice of God inside you, the way in which we understand what God's laws are. However, for Fletcher, conscience is not a bag of reliable rules and principles to tell you what to do. It in no way guides human action. For the situationist, conscience describes the weighing up of the possible action before it is taken.

Activities

1 In groups consider each of these presumptions. Do you think these presumptions are correct or can they be challenged? For instance, are there no absolute rules at all? Is it practical to have an approach to morality which puts people first and does not consider moral rules to be all that important?

2 Can you think of examples or arguments which seem to suggest the presumptions are true and others which challenge them?

Related ethical developments

Contextual ethics

In 1963 Paul Lehmann (1906–96) wrote *Ethics in a Christian Context*. He is associated with what is called contextual ethics. His thinking is similar to Fletcher's in that love is central, and Christian behaviour cannot be generalised. He is, according to R. M. Crook in his 2002 book *Introduction to Christian Ethics*, more concerned with faith in Christ

Key terms

Pragmatism: any theory of ethics must be practical and work towards the end that is love.

Relativism: in moral terms, moral relativism is the view that there are no moral absolutes, so that our moral judgements relate to upbringing, milieu, psychology, society, and so on. Philosophers have sought to justify relativism culturally, meta ethically and normatively. Cultural relativism simply notes that moral values vary between societies, and so assume that this reflects the fact that moral values are relative. Meta ethical relativism argues that the discussion about the meaning of moral language cannot reach an agreed conclusion between the competing theories of naturalism, non-naturalism and non-cognitivism; so in the absence of such an agreement, it seems safest to conclude that this is because values are indeed relative and not factual. Normative relativism is the view that right and wrong are defined by the situation.

Positivism: the situational principle that Christians freely choose to believe that God is love and then act in a way reasonable with this faith statement.

Personalism: the ethic that demands that human beings come first and are not treated as 'means'.

Conscience: used in a special sense in situation ethics. Fletcher rejects the idea that conscience is (1) intuition, (2) a channel for divine guidance, (3) the internalised values of the individual's culture, or (4) the part of reason that makes value judgements, because all of these treat conscience as a thing, which Fletcher believes is a mistake. Rather, for him, conscience is a verb rather than a noun – it is something you do when you make decisions, as he puts it, 'creatively'.

and the involvement of a Christian community than Fletcher. Lehmann writes that Christian ethics can be defined as:

> disciplined reflection upon the question and its answer: what am I, as a believer in Jesus Christ and as a member of his church, to do? … Christian ethics is not concerned with the good, but what I, as a believer in Jesus Christ, and as a member of his church, am to do. Christian ethics, in other words, is oriented toward revelation and not toward morality

Lehmann, 1963, p45

The importance of the Christian community to Lehmann is a significant difference from Fletcher who has a more individually orientated moral view. Lehmann writes that, 'the church … is the fellowship-creating reality of Christ's presence in the world' (Lehmann, 1963, p49). Decision-making for Lehmann is made within the Christian fellowship, not by an individual on his or her own. The Church is the moral space where decisions should be considered. The Church offers a maturity which is valuable when making moral decisions as it offers a view to what is believed to be God's work in the world by the community.

Proportionalism

Situation ethics opposes natural moral law on several grounds. Natural law states that actions are intrinsically good or bad according to the law of nature, while situationists maintain that actions are extrinsically good or bad according to whether they produce the most loving result. Natural law is deontological and situation ethics is teleological.

There is a midway position between the two theories, which tries to combine elements of both. Bernard Hoose's **proportionalism** modifies both theories to come up with the maxim: 'It is never right to go against a principle unless there is a proportionate reason which would justify it' (Hoose, 1987). Proportionalism isn't an entirely new ethical theory. It can be found in St Thomas Aquinas's understanding of a 'just war'. The just war theory makes it possible for a Church that opposed killing to justify a certain amount of killing in particular circumstances. In other words, the basic rule of 'Do not kill' usually applies, but there are certain proportionate circumstances when it can be right to overrule the moral principle.

Proportionalism may be a way forward for Christian morality to resolve the different approaches currently adopted. However, it is not clear when it is acceptable to put moral laws aside or how proportionalism can produce a consistent ethical theory.

Evaluating situation ethics

Situation ethics is flexible and practical. It takes into account the complexities of human life, and can make tough decisions where, from a legalistic perspective, all actions seem wrong. This gives it a dynamism that can free up deadlocked moral dilemmas. It's able to take the least bad of two bad options, which legalistic approaches cannot. A legalist may always feel bound to tell the truth, but when faced with a murderer seeking his victim the legalist is in an impossible position. The situationist can lay aside the rule of not lying for the better outcome of saving a person's life.

Key terms

Proportionalism: a modification of natural law ethics which seeks to take account of the consequences of actions. It suggests that moral rules may sometimes be broken if there is a proportionate reason. Where this happens, the act remains objectively wrong but is morally right: e.g. contraception is an objective wrong which can be morally right in order to prevent the damaging effects of over-population.

William Barclay in his book *Ethics in a Permissive Society* (1980) feels that the freedom situation ethics presents us with is terrifying. When faced with a situation there is no 'prefabricated judgment; *you* – just *you* – have to make the right decision' (Barclay, 1980, p80). There is no ready-made decision, no easy answer, even for the most ordinary day-to-day things. Barclay warns that freedom can become licence, selfishness or even cruelty.

Christianity and situation ethics

Traditional Christian thinkers rejected situation ethics. In 1952, Pope Pius XII called situation ethics, 'an individualistic and subjective appeal to the concrete circumstances of actions to justify decisions in opposition to the natural law or God's revealed will.' The Roman Catholic Church hasn't abandoned St Thomas Aquinas's natural law approach and views situation ethics as a subjective and individualistic moral approach.

Many religious views of ethics are based on rules-based systems of thinking, either because it is believed that these rules are good for us, or simply because they are God's rules there to be obeyed. A relativistic, situational way of thinking about morality seems a long way from traditional Christian ethics.

However, it is also true that Jesus seemed to be prepared to set aside some rules in some cases, usually because a person mattered more than the rule. So he was prepared to associate with and touch people traditionally viewed as unclean – sinners, the sick, etc. Situation ethics provides an alternative Christian ethic that is consistent with the Gospel representation of Jesus. Traditional Christianity today often seems to take on the legalistic character of the kind of Pharisaic Judaism that Jesus opposed. Situation ethics develops a principle from Jesus's action of breaking the law when the situation demanded it for reasons of love. In this sense, it could be argued that situation ethics is more consistent with the New Testament than natural moral law ethics, providing a corrective to that and other legalistic approaches.

There are situations where, for what are called 'pastoral reasons' local ministers differentiate how they apply laws to particular people in certain situations. In other words there is a recognition that sometimes, heavy rule-based approaches to people in complex and difficult situations may not be the most helpful way of ministering to people.

Practicality

Situation ethics is subjective, because decisions must be made from within the situation as it's perceived to be. It is not easy to be certain that one's perception of the situation is correct. How can individuals safely decide which is the most loving action? We don't have an objective perspective, a bird's eye view of morality and could end up justifying unloving actions on the basis of loving results that never emerge. Situation ethics could prove unworkable because it is not easy to determine all the consequences of an action.

Situation ethics depends on the assumption that human beings are free to act morally. In his book *Moral Responsibility*, Joseph Fletcher writes: 'Nothing we do is truly moral unless we are free to do otherwise. We must be free to decide what to do before any of our actions even begin to be moral. No discipline but self discipline has any moral significance … morality is meaningless apart from freedom' (Fletcher, 1967, p136). But are we in fact as free as Fletcher suggests? Are we not influenced by our upbringing, surroundings, traditions, character traits? William Barclay asks whether in fact we are heavily influenced in all sorts of ways and need the law to push us in the direction of what is right.

The limits of love?

Situation ethics seems to be prepared to accept any action at all if it fits the required criteria. After a century of some of the most horrendous acts of genocide and the rise of a concern for the absolute protection of human rights, there is a common sense that there are some things that are just wrong and can never be right on any grounds. What is believed to be a loving end could justify actions that many people regard as simply wrong.

Moreover, situation ethics is individualistic, because humans see things from their own perspective. There's a danger that the ideals of unconditional love may be polluted by a selfish human tendency or human bad habits. Agape love is an extraordinary ideal. How many parents can show equal love to strangers as to their children? Attaining and living out agape love is fundamental to situation ethics. How do we judge when love is unconditional and when it isn't? How can we be sure when an action comes from agape love, and who is to decide whether the motive is pure?

The future of situation ethics

These criticisms show why situation ethics has not been adopted by mainstream moral thinking in any of the major Christian Churches. Contextual ethics and proportionalism are two directions that situation ethics can follow. Contextual ethics with its Christian community dimension starts to satisfy some of the concerns about individualism without losing the wariness of legalistic ethics. Proportionalism also tries to come to a midway position but in this case it is with the more legalistically orientated natural law ethics.

However, both of these developments are to compromise on one or other aspect of the radical nature of situationist thinking. Situationist thinking does seem to have similarities with some more recent moral thinking that is beyond the exclusively Christian. The radical challenge of situationist thinking can be seen as a response to the collapse of many moral certainties, as well as the inadequacies of legalistic moral thinking.

There are many religious and philosophical claims to truth. Many old moral certainties seem to have been turned over and we now seem to be living in a much less certain age. Another strong critic of legalistic approaches to ethics is the sociologist Zygmunt Bauman in his book *Postmodern Ethics* (1993). He argues that legalistic approaches actually cripple our ability to make moral decisions in the moment when we face moral dilemma on our own. It undermines our ability to take responsibility for our moral agency. Our desire to pass on such responsibility to another masks the reality that it is only us who can make the decision.

The subjective perspective we have is the only one that matters in moral decision-making. In our modern, plural and uncertain world there is no certain position we can take. The claim that situation ethics is individualistic belies the total primacy given to the duty to show unconditional love for the other. While this is a challenging demand, it is not selfish or individualistic. It is profoundly moral as it is concerned directly and acutely with the human person. The claim that somehow

Activities

1. Explain what is meant by the term 'situation ethics'.

2. Try to think of the two most plausible examples whereby killing a human being could serve love. Then evaluate how convincing your arguments are.

3. In what sense is situation ethics relativistic?

4. What does it mean to take a personalist approach when considering a moral dilemma, and how does this differ from a legalistic approach? Use a moral dilemma to illustrate your answer.

5. Is the end the only thing that can justify the means?

6. Can humans act out of unconditional love for each other, or are they selfish?

7. Evaluate the strengths and weaknesses of situation ethics.

8. To what extent should religious approaches to moral decision-making be influenced by moral laws (such as the Ten Commandments) and to what extent should they be focused on human beings?

situation ethics could lead to atrocities because it has no limits fails to account for the centrality of the human being in all moral considerations.

Application

When applying a theory to an issue, remember that your choice of issue is significant if you are going to evaluate the theory on the basis of how well it deals with your issue. Re-read the 'Tools for evaluating ethical theories' section in Chapter 1 to remind yourself of some of the tools you have available.

Use the following questions when applying situation ethics to an ethical issue. In the issue you are addressing:

1 What options are available in this situation?

2 Which of these options gives most consideration to the person (or people) in the situation?

3 Pragmatically, how likely is each option to succeed?

4 Regardless of moral laws, how loving (in an unconditional agape sense) will the outcome or consequence of each option be?

5 To what extent does each option seem to reflect a love that supports the whole community (in other words, a just love)?

6 Which option best fits your considerations in 2–5?

7 Does the option identified in 6 seem reasonable or unreasonable?

8 If so why is this?

   – Is it because of some other moral factor which situation ethics doesn't account for and if so which factor?

   – Is it because you value different moral factors than those expressed in the theory (such as virtue, the moral law, etc.)?

   – If so can you justify why you value those factors over and above the ones which are important in the theory?

   – Is this a factor which is likely to be found in many ethical issues? In other words does this flag up a more major problem with the theory as a whole, or just a problem with this particularly difficult issue?

9 If the solution seems reasonable, how adequate do you think this moral example is in testing the theory? Might there be different kinds of examples which the theory has more trouble with?

Extracts from key texts

John A. T. Robinson, Honest to God, *1963*
The Teaching of Jesus

'The clear teaching of our Lord' is taken to mean that Jesus laid down certain precepts which were universally binding. Certain things were always right, other things were always wrong – for all men everywhere.

But this is to treat the Sermon on the Mount as the new Law, and, even if Matthew may have interpreted Jesus that way, there would hardly be a New Testament scholar today who would not say that it was a misinterpretation. The moral precepts of Jesus are not intended to be understood legalistically, as prescribing what all Christians must do, whatever the circumstances, and pronouncing certain courses of action universally right and others universally wrong. They are not legislation laying down what love always demands of every one: they are illustrations of what love may at any particular moment require of anyone …

… Jesus' teaching on marriage, as on everything else, is not a new law prescribing that divorce is always and in every case the greater of two evils (whereas Moses said there were some cases in which it was not). It is saying that love, utterly unconditional love, admits of no accommodation; you cannot define in advance situations in which it can be satisfied with less than complete and unreserved self-giving …

Jesus never resolves these choices for us: he is content with the knowledge that if we have the heart of the matter in us, if our eye is single, then love will find the way, its own particular way in every individual situation.

… Love alone, because, as it were, it has a built-in moral compass, enabling it to 'home' intuitively upon the deepest need of the other, can allow itself to be directed completely by the situation. It alone can afford to be utterly open to the situation, or rather to the person in the situation, uniquely and for his own sake, without losing its direction or unconditionality. It is able to embrace an ethic of radical responsiveness, meeting every situation on its own merits, with no prescriptive laws.

pp110–115

Joseph Fletcher, Situation Ethics: The New Morality, *1963*

For real decision-making, freedom is required, an open-ended approach to situations. Imagine the plight of an obstetrician who believed he must always respirate every baby he delivered, no matter how monstrously deformed! …

No wonder that Jesus, in the language of a French Catholic moralist whose concern is contemporary, 'reacted particularly against code morality and against casuistry,' and that his 'attitude toward code morality [was] purely and simply one of reaction.' Modern Christians ought not to be naive enough to accept any other view of Jesus' ethic than the situational one …

As we know, for many people, sex is so much a moral problem, largely due to the repressive effects of legalism, that in newspapers and popular parlance the term 'morals charge' always means a sex complaint! 'Her morals are not very high' means her sex life is rather looser than the mores allow. Yet we find nothing in the teachings of Jesus about the ethics of sex, except adultery and an absolute condemnation of divorce – a correlative matter. He said nothing about birth control, large or small families, childlessness, homosexuality, masturbation, fornication or pre-marital intercourse, sterilization, artificial insemination, abortion, sex play, petting, and courtship. Whether any form of sex (hetero, homo, or auto) is good or evil depends on whether love is fully served. The Christian ethic is not interested in reluctant virgins and technical chastity. What sex probably needs more than anything is a good airing, demythologizing it and getting rid of its mystique-laden and occult accretions, which come from romanticism on the one hand and puritanism on the other. People are learning that we can have sex without love, and love without sex; that baby-making can be (and often ought to be) separated from love-making. It is, indeed, for recreation as well as for procreation. But if people don't believe it is wrong to have sex relations outside marriage, it isn't, unless they hurt themselves, their partners, or others. This is, of course, a very big 'unless' and gives reason to many to abstain altogether except within the full mutual commitment of marriage.

Situation ethics always suspects prescriptive law of falsifying life and dwarfing moral stature, whether it be the Scripture legalism of Biblicist Protestants and Mohammedans or the nature legalism (natural law) of the Catholics and disciples of Confucius ... To learn love's sensitive tactics, such people are going to have to put away their childish rules.

pp138–140

William Barclay, Ethics in a Permissive Society, 1980

Thirdly, the situationist points out again and again that in his view there is nothing which is intrinsically good or bad. Goodness and badness, as he puts it, are not properties, they are predicates. They are not inbuilt qualities; they happen to a thing in a given situation. I am very doubtful if the distinction between goodness and badness can be so disposed of.

We may grant that Fletcher has shown that there can be situations in which a thing generally regarded as wrong could be the right thing to do. But that does not prove that it is good. There is a close analogy here with dangerous drugs which a doctor may have to prescribe. When he describes these drugs, he does not pretend that they are not poisons. Poisons they are and poisons they remain. They have to be kept in a special cupboard and in a special container. They can only be used under the strictest safeguards. There are indeed occasions when the doctor will not prescribe them at all, because he is not certain that the patient has the strength of mind not to misuse them. These things have a kind of in-built red light, and that red light is not taken away, for the dangerous drug is never called anything else but a Poison. So there are certain things. which on rare occasions may be used to serve a good end. But the red light should not be removed by calling them good things. They remain highly dangerous, and they should never be called, or regarded as, anything else.

p82

Chapter summary

- 'The law of love is the ultimate law because it is the negation of law'. (Tillich)
- '"Love thy neighbour as thyself" is the ultimate duty.' (Bultmann)
- Ethics is either legalistic, antinomian or situational.
- The situationist enters into the moral dilemma with the ethics and rules and principles of his or her community or tradition. However, the situationist is prepared to set aside those rules in the situation if love seems better served by doing so.
- 'The situationist follows a moral law or violates it according to love's need.' (Fletcher)
- Moral decisions are guided by what best serves love.

Six fundamental principles and love:

- First proposition: 'Only one thing is intrinsically good; namely love: nothing else at all.' (Fletcher)
- Second proposition: 'The ruling norm of Christian decision-making is love: nothing else.' (Fletcher)
- Third proposition: 'Love and justice are the same, for justice is love distributed, nothing else.' (Fletcher)
- Fourth proposition: 'Love wills the neighbour's good, whether we like him or not.' (Fletcher)
- Fifth proposition: 'Only the end justifies the means, nothing else.' (Fletcher)
- Sixth proposition: 'Love's decisions are made situationally, not prescriptively.' (Fletcher)

Four presumptions (four working principles) and conscience:

- Pragmatism, which is a practical or success posture.
- Relativism – situation ethics is relativistic: 'The situationist avoids words like "never" and "perfect" and "always" and "complete" as he avoids the plague, as he avoids "absolutely".'
- Positivism – situation ethics depends on Christians freely choosing faith that God is love, so giving first place to Christian love.
- Personalism – the legalist puts the law first, but the situationist puts people first.
- 'Conscience' describes the weighing up of the possible action before it is taken.

Related ethical developments:

- Contextual ethics places importance on the Christian community and acting in accordance with God's will, while keeping love at the centre and avoiding generalised laws.
- Proportionalism seeks to find a midway position between situation ethics and natural law by following the natural laws in the main but being prepared to set them aside in extraordinary situations.

Evaluating situation ethics:

- Situation ethics is flexible and practical. It takes into account the complexities of human life and can make tough decisions where, from a legalistic perspective, all actions seem wrong.

- Situation ethics presents people with a enormous amount of freedom and responsibility which Barclay thinks is terrifying.

- In 1952, Pope Pius XII called situation ethics, 'an individualistic and subjective appeal to the concrete circumstances of actions to justify decisions in opposition to the natural law or God's revealed will'.

- Religious moral thinking is traditionally rule-based and so rejects situational thinking.

- Situation ethics is subjective, because decisions must be made from within the situation as it is perceived to be.

- Situation ethics is individualistic, because humans see things from their own perspective. There is a danger of a selfish human tendency polluting agape love.

- What is believed to be a loving end could justify actions that many people regard as simply wrong.

- Situation ethics depends on humans being free to act morally but in fact we are conditioned by many things and need law to guide us in the right direction.

- Zygmund Bauman thinks legalistic approaches to ethics rob people of their ability to make moral decisions out in the world.

- Situation ethics provides an alternative Christian ethic that is consistent with the Gospel representation of Jesus.

- Situation ethics is well suited to work in a world were people are more uncertain about what is right and wrong, but does this by placing the unconditional love of the other person in the situation at the centre of a decision-making process.

Further reading

Fletcher and his critic Barclay are both well worth looking at and are both clearly written, so consider:

Fletcher, J., *Situation Ethics*, Westminster Press, 1963, pp17–40
Barclay, W., *Ethics in a Permissive Society*, Collins, 1980, pp69–91

For another readable examination of Fletcher see:

Vardy, P., *The Puzzle of Ethics*, Fount, 1992, pp133–142

And my favourite anthology:

Singer, P., *Ethics*, in the Oxford Readers series, Oxford University Press, 1994

In this chapter you have:

- considered how situation ethics differs from traditional approaches to moral decision-making

- explored both the assumptions underpinning situation ethics and the principles by which it is applied

- explored the application of situation ethics to moral dilemmas

- considered key weaknesses and strengths in the theory and application of situation ethics.

5 Kant

By the end of this chapter you will:

- be able to describe the key features of Kant's deontological ethics: reason and morality, his theory of the moral law, good will and duty, the categorical imperative

- have considered a number of key issues associated with Kant's thinking

- be able to apply Kant's theory to moral issues

- know a number of strengths and weaknesses of Kantian ethics.

Key philosophers

Immanuel Kant (1724–1804):
Groundwork for the Metaphysics of Morals, 1785; *Critique of Practical Reason*, 1788; *The Metaphysics of Morals*, 1797

Activity

'Training children to obey is morally wrong because it undermines their ability to make difficult moral decisions.'

Consider arguments for and against this view with examples to support your arguments.

Link

For an introduction to teleological and deontological ethics, see Chapter 1, pp3–5. For an introduction to absolutist and relativistic thinking, see Chapter 2, pp11–14.

Key questions

1 Where should moral authority lie? With human beings or some other source?
2 Should we pay attention to our emotions and feelings when making moral decisions?
3 Should the motivations for our actions be pure?
4 Are human beings so special that they should never be sacrificed for a greater end?
5 Should moral statements be universally true?
6 Is honesty always the best policy?
7 Is being good being brave enough to use our own thinking to decide what to do?

Radical moral enlightenment thinking

In 1784, German philosopher Immanuel Kant (1724–1804) wrote a magazine article, 'What is Enlightenment?' In it he gives us a clear impression of his distinctive approach to ethics:

> [Enlightenment is the] emergence of man from his self-imposed infancy. Infancy is the inability to use one's reason without the guidance of another. It is self-imposed, when it depends on a deficiency, not of reason, but of the resolve and the courage to use it without external guidance. Thus the watchword of enlightenment is: Sapere aude! Have the courage to use one's own reason!

quoted in the entry on 'Enlightenment' in the Oxford Companion to Philosophy, *1995*

In his book *The War for Children's Minds*, Stephen Law unpacks this quote and Kant's ethical thinking in a helpful way (Law, 2006, p6). He argues that Kant locates the responsibility for making moral judgements, not in an external authority of tradition (such as a sacred text or religious leader) but the individual – an individual who has the courage to apply his or her own powers of reason when making moral decisions, instead of deferring to some other authority. It is not just that individuals should decide what is right or wrong, but that pure reason offers a firm moral foundation.

> [I]n morals, the proper and inestimable worth of an absolutely good will consists precisely in the freedom of the principle of action from all influences

Kant, 1948, pp80–87

Kant believed that humans were free to make rational choices. If people were not free, the possibility of making moral choices would be denied. This ability to freely rationalise, or reason, is what distinguishes humans from animals, which lack this ability. It is this quality of rational autonomy which Kant identifies as the key element of what gives human begins their value, or dignity. It is this characteristic which sets his moral theory apart from systems which propose obedience to some other authority.

We have to be free to do our duty. Our duty is to follow the categorical imperative. But if our choices are not free, and our actions are controlled by factors beyond our control, then we cannot truly be **moral agents**. Kant thought that 'ought' implied 'can' – in other words, something that is impossible cannot be a moral option, and therefore every moral option must be possible. For example, two people are mugged one night. The attackers quickly overpower them, and one is tied up. The other is then seriously assaulted, before the gang runs off. The person who has been tied up can't defend his friend. He has no choice and so he hasn't done anything wrong. Human reason means that we're able to choose what to do: we can freely make moral decisions.

Kant's deontological ethics

Deontological theories are concerned with actions, not consequences. Moral value is conferred by virtue of the actions in themselves. If a certain act is wrong, then it is wrong in all circumstances and all conditions, irrespective of the consequences. This view of ethics stands in opposition to teleological views such as utilitarianism, which holds that the consequences of an action determine its moral worth. Kant's theory is deontological because it's based on duty. To act morally is to do one's duty, and one's duty is to obey the moral law. Kant argued that we should not be side-tracked by feeling and *inclination*. We should not act out of love or compassion. Kant also stated that it isn't our duty to do things that we are unable to do. For Kant, the fact that we ought to do something implies that it is possible to do it. Moral statements are prescriptive; they prescribe an action. **'Ought' implies 'can'**. If I say 'I ought to do *x*', it means 'I can do *x*'.

Kant maintained that humans seek an ultimate end called the supreme good, the **summum bonum**, a state in which human virtue and happiness are united. However, since it is impossible for human beings to achieve this state in one lifetime, he deduced that we had to have immortal souls to succeed. While Kant rejected theological arguments for the existence of God, his ethical theory assumes immortality and God's existence. Kant believed that the afterlife and God must exist to provide an opportunity for reaching this supreme good. So, for Kant, morality led to God.

The moral law

> Two things fill the mind with ever new and increasing admiration and awe ... the starry heavens above me and the moral law within me.

Kant, 1977, pp193 & 259

Kant believed that there is an objective moral law and that we know this law through reason operating within us. Moral rules exist and they are binding but they are established through the operation of reason within, not in an external authority. Kant argued that we know the moral law without reference to any consequences. We do not look to any externalities when determining right from wrong.

What kind of statements did Kant think moral ones are?

Statements of knowledge can be **a priori**, knowable without reference (or prior) to experience, or **a posteriori**, knowable through experience. An example of a priori knowledge would be '1 + 1 = 2'. You don't need experience to know that when you add two 1s together you get 2. An example of a posteriori knowledge is 'the squirrel is behind the tree'. You can only know for certain by looking, and this looking is experience.

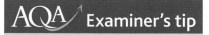

Activities

1 Why might Kant's thinking on the moral authority of human beings be challenging to some religious perspectives?

2 Do you think human beings can be trusted with such power? What are the risks in granting or not granting humans such power?

Key terms

Analytic: analytic statements are true by definition, e.g. a bicycle has two wheels. Here the predicate says something necessary about the subject. Since mathematical statements are also said to be true by the terms used, 1 + 1 = 2 is often said to be analytic a priori.

Synthetic: knowledge is said to be synthetic if it is based on observation/measurement/testing. Synthetic statements can be true or false. Statements like, 'Scooby is a dog' are synthetic, and since they are known after experience, they are a posteriori, so 'Scooby is a dog' is synthetic a posteriori (and given that Scooby can talk, it is probably synthetic a posteriori false).

Another division can be made. Knowledge may be **analytic**: the predicates (parts of the sentence) may say something that is necessarily true about the subject. For example, consider the sentence 'all spinsters are women' (the word 'spinster' refers to an unmarried woman). The statement needs no further facts from an exterior source – we don't need to go round checking! It is necessarily true – true by its own authority. The a priori example 1 + 1 = 2 is also analytic, as we do not need further information apart from the sum itself. It can be called 'a priori analytic'.

Alternatively, knowledge may be **synthetic**. It may require empirical tests, such as observations, measurements or experiments. The statement 'Jack is a butler' isn't necessarily true, because we need exterior information to support the claim that he's a butler. There's nothing inextricably linked to the word 'Jack' that means he must be a butler. Not all Jacks are butlers. It may in fact turn out that Jack isn't a butler at all. Synthetic statements may be true or false. The statement 'Jack is a butler' is also a posteriori, as it's knowable after experience. Therefore, we can call it 'a posteriori synthetic'.

Kant believed that statements of fact are either a priori analytic, such as 1 + 1 = 2 or all spinsters are women, or else they are a posteriori synthetic, such as 'Jack is a butler'. Moral statements, however, fall into a different category. We can't prove what people should do by looking, so moral statements must be a priori. Moral knowledge is gained by pure reason, not sense experience. However, as moral statements may be right or wrong, they are also synthetic, so moral statements are called 'a priori synthetic'.

To summarise, non-ethical statements are either:

- a priori analytic = necessarily true and knowable without experience (1 + 1 = 2), or
- a posteriori synthetic = possibly true and to be validated through experience (Jack is a butler).

Ethical statements are, however, a priori synthetic, which means they are knowable through reason, not sensation or experience, and may or may not be true. This places Kant in direct opposition to utilitarians, who consider the consequences of an action (experience) as fundamental in deciding what is moral.

It is in recognising Kant's universal law that you can suppose good people are motivated, in good will, to act according to their duty. It is to good will and duty that we must now turn.

Good will and duty

> Good will shines forth like a precious jewel. It is impossible to conceive anything at all in the world, or even out of it, which can be taken as good without qualification, except a good will.

Kant, 1948, p394

In Kant's book *Groundwork for the Metaphysics of Morals* (first published in 1785) he argues that the highest form of good is *good will*. To have a good will is to do one's duty. To do one's duty is to perform actions that are morally required, and to avoid actions that are morally forbidden. Doing one's duty is doing the right thing, not the wrong thing. Why do we do our duty? – because it's our duty to do it! Morality, at its heart, is an obligation to act.

To perform a moral action out of a desire for the good consequence it brings is to act in self-interest, and is not a morally good action. To tell the truth because it's in our interest to do so is not a moral action. We don't do our duty because of the consequences of doing it – we do it for duty itself. Duty is unconditional – it must be carried out irrespective of personal feelings or calculations of the consequences. Duty is good in itself.

Kant acknowledged that happiness is also good, and that it comes as a reward for acting through good will, but that duty is the highest good. Kant's theory directly opposes utilitarian ethics. If a murderer asked us whether our friend, who he was pursuing, was hiding in our house, Kant's theory insists we must be honest. The utilitarian would see greater happiness being caused by a lie, but Kant doesn't consider consequences, only the action, and to lie would be wrong.

Kant believed that we should act out of duty and not emotion. For him, a human action is not morally good because we feel that it is good, or because it is in our own self-interest. A human action is good when it is done for the sake of duty. A person may act out of kindness, generosity or compassion, but in these circumstances, the act confers no virtue on that person. Even if duty demanded the same action, but it was done for a motive such as compassion, the act would be a good act, but the person would not be moral for choosing it. If someone gives money to a beggar out of compassion, then that act may be good, but they are not virtuous for doing it. If they give to the beggar because duty demands it, then they are virtuous for doing so. For Kant, we are not moral for the sake of love – we're moral for the sake of duty. This makes Kant seem rather austere and uninterested in human emotions. In fact, he argued that duty and reason can help to guide our emotions, so that we are not ruled by them.

Kant is described as having produced a system of ethics based on reason and not intuition. A moral person must be a rational being. Being good means having a good will. A good will is when you do your duty for the

'Tell me where Jack is'

Activities

1 Do you agree that 'to tell a falsehood to a murderer who asked us whether our friend, of whom he was in pursuit, had taken refuge in our house, would be a crime'? How might you argue that this statement is true?

2 How significant is the example in Activity 1 in challenging Kant's theory?

3 Give an example where emotions and feelings encourage someone to do something wrong.

AQA Examiner's tip

Again, remember that consequences are indeed irrelevant to the theory, but not to the practice, where the consequences are important. This can be seen at two main points in Kant's argument:

1 The categorical imperative instructs people to act as *law-abiding members of a kingdom of moral ends*. Clearly, if people do act in such a way, then the end product is a stable and happy society.

2 As the supreme good, the *summum bonum* is the perfect match between duty and its expected reward – happiness.

■ **Activity**

What is wrong with moral laws that apply only to me?

■ **Key terms**

Categorical imperative: categorical imperatives are laws whose forces are absolute and undeniable, e.g. 'Do not murder', 'Honour your parents', etc. Their force is discernible by contrasting them with the weak command in hypothetical imperatives.

Hypothetical imperative: statements that take the form: 'If x, then y' are hypothetical, e.g. If you want to be happy, then you should take regular exercise. Statements such as this are hypothetical in that they describe instrumental good – good as a means to an end. An imperative is a command, so a hypothetical imperative is a weak command. Kant used hypothetical imperatives to illustrate the power of categorical imperatives, such as 'Do not murder', which he argues has a force that cannot be denied.

sake of duty alone. A person does their duty because it is right, and for no other reason. But what does it mean to act out of duty? Kant explained that to act out of duty is to perform actions that are morally obligatory and not to perform those that are forbidden.

There is an important link between duty and the moral community in which we exist, which Kant describes as the kingdom of ends. Recognition of duty is recognition of a universal law binding on every single member of the moral community. The universality of this law means that someone cannot create a law that is particular to themselves, serving their own interests. They must respect the law because respecting the law means respecting the dignity of other people. These ideas are expressed through his theory of the categorical imperative.

The categorical imperative

The **categorical imperative** helps us to know which actions are obligatory and which are forbidden. It tells us what we ought to do:

> All imperatives command either hypothetically or categorically … If the action would be good simply as a means to something else, then the imperative is hypothetical; but if the action is represented as good in itself … then the imperative is categorical.

Kant, 1996, p414

Kant argued that morality is prescriptive; it prescribes moral behaviour. Once you're aware of a moral requirement, your awareness is a reason for doing something. Moral statements are categorical in that they prescribe actions irrespective of the result.

A categorical imperative differs from a **hypothetical imperative**, which does not prescribe or demand any action. Hypothetical imperatives are conditional: 'If I want x, I must do y.' If you want to lose weight, do more exercise. If you want a sandwich, open the fridge. These imperatives are not moral. For Kant, the only moral imperatives were categorical: I ought to do such and such. For example, I ought to tell the truth. This makes no reference to desires or needs.

There are three principles of the categorical imperative, as follows.

The universal law

> There is … only one categorical imperative. It is: Act only according to that maxim by which you can at the same time will that it should become a universal law.

Kant, 1948, pp80–87

The categorical imperative is 'do not act on any principle that cannot be universalised'. Moral laws must be applied in all situations and to all rational beings universally, without exception. If an action is right for me, it is right for everyone. If it is wrong for one person, then it is wrong for all people. The categorical imperative means a person cannot maintain the proposal 'stealing is wrong for everyone, but because I haven't got enough to pay the rent this month I can steal'.

> For an action to be morally valid, the agent – or person performing the act – must not carry out the action unless he or she believes that, in the same situation, all people should act in the same way.

Kant, 1948, pp80–87

The moral law permits certain actions and forbids others. Why adopt such an emphatic absolutist stance? Kant argued that to allow exceptions would harm someone and have an eroding effect on society. He gave an example using the case of lying. In certain circumstances we might think that a lie is better than the truth. It might get us out of trouble! Kant argued that a lie always harms someone – if not the liar then mankind generally, because it violates the source of law. If everyone was to act in this way, society would become intolerable.

Kant gives another example. Let us imagine I want to get some money from someone by promising them I will pay it back, even though in truth I have no intention of paying it back. The maxim of such an act would be effectively impossible – something like: 'Make false promises whenever you want to.' The maxim is self-defeating and could never make for a universal law. Promises would quickly become meaningless and all trust would be lost.

Treat humans as ends in themselves

Kant's second principle in the categorical imperative is:

> So act that you treat humanity, both in your own person and in the person of every other human being, never merely as a means, but always at the same time as an end.

Kant, 1996, p428

According to Kantian theory you should never treat people as means to an end. You can never use human beings for another purpose, to exploit or enslave them. Humans are rational and the highest point of creation, and so demand unique treatment. Human beings have dignity and value, which sets them apart from all other things which simply have a price. There can be no price on a human being – they cannot be equated with some other material good. This guarantees that individuals are afforded the same moral protection. There can be no use of an individual for the sake of the many – as is the case with utilitarians, who can sacrifice the few for the greater good of the many. Kant argued that we have a duty to develop our own perfection, developing our moral, intellectual and physical capabilities. We also have a duty to seek the happiness of others, as long as that is within the law and allows the *freedom* of others. So we should not promote one person's happiness if that happiness prevents another's happiness.

Act as if you live in a kingdom of ends

The idea of the universal law and the idea that all humans are ends in themselves, together leads to the idea of a **kingdom of ends**; a union of all people acting rationally in accordance with a universal law. The third principle of Kant's categorical imperative is:

> So act as if you were through your maxim a law-making member of a kingdom of ends.

Kant, 1996, p74

Kant required moral statements to be such that you act as if you, and everyone else, were treating each other as ends. You had to imagine that you were living in an ideal society, even if that was not the case. You cannot act on a rule that assumes that others don't treat people as ends. You cannot create a *maxim* such as 'I may lie as all others lie'. If such rules were pursued, society would become intolerable. Moral behaviour must be in the direction towards the ideal society, the kingdom of ends, and not away from it.

Key terms

Kingdom of ends: Kant's term for the ethical community as a whole. One version of the categorical imperative is that humans should act always as if they were not just individuals but law-abiding members of a kingdom of moral ends.

Activities

During the Second World War, the Allies pursued a policy of bombing civilian targets (area bombing), in the hope that the Axis powers would be weakened by the loss of morale.

1 Explain the difficulties that Kant would have with this policy.

2 Do you agree with Kant's view?

3 What's the strength of never treating people as a means to an end?

The *Casablanca* example:

The film *Casablanca* is set in Morocco at the beginning of the Second World War. An anti-Nazi writer, Victor (played by Paul Henreid), and his wife Ilsa (Ingrid Bergman) arrive in Morocco as refugees. Victor needs to escape to America to continue the struggle, but he does not have the necessary documents. Ilsa meets a club owner, Rick (Humphrey Bogart), with whom she had been in love in the past. Towards the end of the film Rick persuades Ilsa to run away with him leaving Victor behind. In fact, he is making it possible for Victor and Ilsa to leave together to continue their anti-Nazi work. She only realises this at the last moment, and then he tells her that his feelings for her are an attachment to past and not present passion, which is also false. (And 'I'm not much good at being noble, but it isn't hard to see that the troubles of three little people don't amount to a hill of beans in this crazy world.') Rick has lied to Ilsa in order to be part of the struggle against something evil. And the motives are self-sacrificing ones. What stronger justification could be given?

Morton, 1996, p221

■ Activities

1 One day Callum's mother notices that he has a new football. She asks him where he got the money for it and he says he found it. When Callum's father discovers that some money is missing from his wallet, Callum owns up. His parents are very angry and give him a firm talking to about stealing always being wrong and lying always being wrong.

The next day there's a ring at the door. Callum opens it to see an agitated, angry man holding a large baseball bat. The man asks where his father is. Callum knows that his father is asleep in the back garden. What should he do?

Later on, in his adult life, Callum owns a small shop. He can see out into the street and he notices a very poorly looking beggar on the other side of the road. From time to time, Callum notices the beggar stealing fruit from the grocer's shop. Callum remembers his parents' words about stealing. One day, the police call by and ask Callum if he's noticed the beggar stealing, as the grocer has made a complaint. What should Callum do?

2 A friend of yours has, for some time, been going out with a local boy. She's besotted with him and believes that he's the perfect gentleman. One day, you discover that he's been two-timing your friend, but before you have a chance to say anything the boy is killed in a car crash. Your friend is devastated and decides to write a eulogy to him, to be read out at the funeral. She asks you to help. Should you tell her the truth or keep quiet?

3 Read the extract opposite and consider the following views about Rick's action:

■ Rick was dishonest, but for virtuous reasons.

■ Rick followed his head, not his heart.

■ The interests of the Resistance outweighed the interests of the lovers.

Which of these are true?

■ Rick used Ilsa as a means to the end of defeating the Nazis.

■ Rick was in a unique situation where a very special moral decision had to be made which is not likely to be duplicated, and certainly not faced again by the same people.

What would a Kantian thinker make of these views?

In what ways and to what extent does this example present difficulties for Kantian ethics?

■ Evaluating Kant

The categorical imperative is a powerful set of moral principles that prohibit acts that would be commonly considered wrong such as theft, murder, fraud, violence and sexual abuse. They bind us to set rules that apply to everyone and that command respect for human life. Through it Kant is seeking to show the way to a world in which the freedom of rational beings is expressed, as it should be, in accordance with necessary laws of morality; Kant once described this as bringing about a mystical body of all beings, free and united with the moral law. It is in this way that Kant gives supreme moral responsibility to the individual through their operation of reason.

Strengths

The contribution that Kant made is apparent in three ways. First, he makes a distinction between duty and inclination. We may be inclined to do what benefits ourselves individually, but morality is more than personal preference. Morality has a rational dimension. Second, he corrects the utilitarian presumption that the punishment of the innocent can be justified if the majority benefit. Kant insists you can't promote happiness if that happiness undermines another's happiness. The moral value of an action comes from its *intrinsic* rightness in itself. This means that justice is impartial, and that justice for individuals is safeguarded by the universal character of the categorical imperative. Finally, Kant's theory gives humans intrinsic worth, as the rational high point of creation. Humans can only ever be treated as ends in themselves, never as means. Therefore, humans can't be expended for some apparent greater good. They can't be enslaved or exploited. Human beings have a value and dignity which mean they cannot be bought, sold or disregarded. This sense of dignity or value, defined as rational autonomy, which Kant gives human beings has become extremely important in ideas about human rights which are frequently said to be based on and justified by the fact that humans have inherent dignity and that dignity includes an idea of freedom.

Weakness

However, there are a number of difficulties with Kant's deontological ethics. The refusal to allow exceptions in using people as a means to an end places severe restrictions on our behaviour. A government can't sacrifice the few for the many, and yet sometimes – as in war – such a sacrifice is politically necessary for the good of the majority. Arguably, Kant's theory is not well-suited to world politics, which occasionally requires hard decisions to be made. In some circumstances, duties conflict. If you run a hospital with a fixed budget, you have to make decisions about how many patients of each category of illness you can treat. There comes a point at which the money runs out, and so difficult decisions must be made as to who gets what treatment. Kant would find making such decisions very difficult.

A weakness with **universalisability** is the problem of different but similar moral dilemmas. Are any two moral dilemmas the same? How similar do they have to be to be covered by the same maxim? Are murder, self-defence and the defence of the realm all to be covered by one maxim about taking human life, or can some kinds of killing be justified and excluded because they are different? Does the desire for the union of all under universal law allow for all the particularities, special situations, special circumstances and general uncertainty which many people may feel they have when faced with dilemmas? Is the clarity of Kant's moral certainty actually possible in a confused world of moral uncertainty?

A further question can be raised about some of the examples Kant gives, for instance with regards to helping someone in distress. If I see someone in distress but refuse to give help even though I could easily do so, can I will a universal law from this of not helping people in distress? There is no inconsistency – I am saying that I won't ever help anyone in distress. Kant suggests that as we ourselves may one day be in distress we would not will such a law universally but that disregards the kind of thinking that places self-sufficiency above other qualities. What if the person in distress also values self-sufficiency such that they would not want help from a passer-by? Apart from the obvious cases where making a law produces a contradiction (as in the case of lying above), the moral law does not seem easily to provide guidance.

Activities

1 Do you agree with Kant that morality is more than personal preference? Can you think of arguments against Kant's view?

2 Do you think human beings are as special as Kant thinks they are? Think of specific examples of human greatness and human stupidity. Use these examples to build a case for or against Kant's belief in human nature.

3 'Kant's theory is a nice theory, but it's completely unrealistic and impractical for the tough decisions of life.' Discuss.

4 Do you think moral situations are different and difficult to solve using universal rules, or do they require overarching fixed rules to keep people on the straight and narrow?

Key terms

Universalisability: a central focus of Kant's ethical theory; a form of the categorical imperative, which states that reason is correct in holding a moral law to be true if it can be universalised, i.e. if the one who proposes to act on it is satisfied that it should apply to all humans – to everyone in the universe.

The role of reason and duty in ethics

For Kant, moral decision-making is a rational activity. However, other approaches to moral decision-making place much more importance on compassion or love in informing moral action. If I see someone in need I should feel an urge to give help. Love is considered by many to be a central dimension of humanity, a defining feature of what should motivate us and guide us in how we respond and treat others. Kant's emphasis on reason seems to come at the price of having to put love to one side. Kantian thinkers might respond by arguing that an emphasis on love could simply be an emphasis on emotion and emotions can be swayed by all sorts of factors. Love may be blind or foolish and not necessarily altruistic but self-serving, and it would be difficult to universalise the laws of love in the way Kant universalises the laws of practical reason. At the same time love can be self-sacrificial and is the basis of some religions and some ethical theories, such as situation ethics.

Kant's moral thinking does not give licence to selfish action or random decisions about when we should or shouldn't do something. He has a profound sense that we are compelled to act morally, that we have a duty to do so. This sense of moral compulsion is at the heart of moral conduct. While we need to be free to act to be morally required to do so, we do have a moral obligation to do good and avoid evil with that freedom. The freedom and power that Kant gives human beings are combined with a profound sense of responsibility which surely must be central to any idea of morality.

Kant's view of human beings and religious approaches to life

Some argue that giving individuals and the operation of their reason moral authority is a step too far. Writers such as Alasdair MacIntyre argue that tradition is a sound source of moral authority and other writers such as Soulen and Woodhead (for example, in their book *God and Human Dignity*, 2006) imply in their work that there is a danger that, by moving moral responsibility to the individual, this leads inevitably to a morality completely divorced from any external authority. In other words Kant is too optimistic about human moral autonomy and places far too much emphasis on human judgement. Is there not a danger that if humans are the authors of moral laws, then they can make whatever laws they like? Could this not lead to a break down in any sense of universal morality or commonly accepted moral code?

Kant's emphasis on the human being as the authority of moral law will seem, to some, removed from religious approaches to morality which tend to see moral law as something divine, beyond human authorship. In this way Kant seems out of step with religion. Giving human beings freedom to determine moral truth may seem quite the opposite to a view that religious traditions are the authorities in matters of moral truth.

Some religious perspectives suggest that individuals should defer their judgement and accept the moral teaching of religion or God, and yet other perspectives give great importance to the idea that people are given free will to decide how to live and have to live in good conscience with what they believe to be true.

Kantian thinking on the importance of human dignity, and repudiation of teleological thinking and the idea that an individual can be sacrificed for some greater end, is much more in keeping with religious ideas of the dignity of the human person, for instance the doctrine that humans are made in the image of God.

Application

When applying a theory to an issue, remember that your choice of issue is significant if you are going to evaluate the theory on the basis of how well it deals with your issue. Re-read the 'Tools for evaluating ethical theories' section in Chapter 1 to remind yourself of some of the tools you have available.

Use the following questions when applying Kantian thinking to an ethical issue. In the issue you are addressing:

1 Try to rule out feelings, preferences or consequences as factors in the workings.

2 Remember that freedom to reason through and act is important in moral decision-making.

3 Consider the options available:

   a Rule out any options which cannot be universalised and continue to (b).

   b Rule out any options which just treat human beings for some end or 'greater good' and only keep those which recognise the value and dignity of human beings involved, and continue to (c).

   c Rule out any options which throw up peculiar rules (such as those which are biased to you) which it would not be good if everybody was to follow.

   d Decide which option best satisfies each of these criteria.

4 Does the option identified in 3 seem reasonable or unreasonable?

5 If unreasonable why is this?

   a Is it because it ignores a moral factor which Kantian thinking doesn't account for, producing a problematic conclusion? If so which factor?

   b Is it because you value different moral factors than those expressed in the theory (such as the situation or the consequences, etc.)?

   c If so can you justify why you value those factors over and above the ones which are important in the theory?

   d Is this a factor which is likely to be found in many ethical issues? In other words does this flag up a more major problem with the theory as a whole, or just a problem with this particularly difficult issue?

6 If the solution seems reasonable, how adequate do you think this moral example is in testing the theory? Might there be different kinds of examples which the theory has more trouble with?

Activity

Consider a specific example of one of these situations and work through the situation using Kantian thinking: espionage, counter terrorism, the use of a weapon in self-defence, managing limited resources in a hospital. Try to address the key concepts of the theory in your application in the specific situation you have chosen. Show your workings to a partner and ask them to evaluate your application of the theory. Then discuss together whether you think the theory works well, and what weaknesses it may have.

Activities

1 What are the distinguishing features of deontological ethical theories?

2 'An act is morally good if it's done entirely from motives of duty.' What does Kant mean by duty? Consider the strengths *and* weaknesses of the claim.

3 a Can you explain the principle 'You ought to act in such a way that you would be willing to universalise the act'?

   b Why do some philosophers reject this view?

4 Does 'ought' imply 'can'? Explain Kant's view of freedom.

Extract from key text

Kant's Groundwork of the Metaphysics of Morals, *1948*

All imperatives command either hypothetically or categorically. Hypothetical imperatives declare a possible action to be practically necessary as a means to the attainment of something else that one wills (or that one may will). A categorical imperative would be one which represented an action as objectively necessary in itself apart from its relation to a further end. Every practical law represents a possible action as good and therefore as necessary for a subject whose actions are determined by reason. Hence all imperatives are formulae for determining an action which is necessary in accordance with the principles of a will in some sense good. If the action would be good solely as a means to something else, the imperative is hypothetical; if the action is represented as good in itself and therefore as necessary, in virtue of its principle, for a will which of itself accords with reason, then the imperative is categorical.

Chapter summary

- Kant presents a moral theory which gives moral responsibility to the individual, rather than an external authority.

- Humans are free to make rational choices. If people were not free, the possibility of making moral choices would be denied. Rational freedom means humans have dignity and this is what sets them apart from other animals and objects.

- Pure reason offers a firm moral foundation within individuals.

Kant's deontological ethics:

- Deontological theories are concerned with actions, not consequences.

- Kant's theory is deontological because it is based on duty. To act morally is to do one's duty, and one's duty is to obey the moral law.

- 'Ought' implies 'can'. If I say 'I ought to do x', it means 'I can do x'.

- Humans seek an ultimate end called the supreme good, the *summum bonum*, so, for Kant, morality led to God.

- 'Two things fill the mind with ever new and increasing admiration and awe … the starry heavens above me and the moral law within me.'

- Moral statements are 'a priori synthetic' (reason, not sense experience).

- 'Good will shines forth like a precious jewel' – the highest form of good is good will. To have good will is to do one's duty.

- To do one's duty is to perform actions that are morally required by the universal law.

- We should act out of duty, and not emotion; Kant's ethic is reason-based, not intuitive.

- Moral statements are categorical – they prescribe irrespective of the result.

- Universal law: 'Act only according to that maxim by which you can at the same time will that it should become a universal law.'

- Treat humans as ends in themselves.

- Act as if you live in a kingdom of ends.

Evaluating Kant:

- The categorical imperative prohibits acts that would commonly be considered immoral.

- Kant distinguishes between duty and inclination.

- Kant's theory gives humans intrinsic worth, which can't be sacrificed for the majority.

- Kant's system can't resolve conflicting duties.

- Universalisability generalises different but similar moral dilemmas.

- Kant focuses on reason in moral decision but human beings are also loving, emotional creatures motivated by feelings as well as thoughts.

- Kant's sense of duty places profound responsibility in human moral action, alongside the freedom and authority which he gives.

- Some argue that such authority to make moral laws is too much to trust for human beings and that an exterior source (such as religious code) is necessary.

- The centrality of the value of the individual human person not to be used for some other end in Kantian thinking is similar to religious ideas about the value of human life.

Further reading

Again I suggest, for his treatment of Kant:

Rachels, J., *The Elements of Moral Philosophy*, McGraw-Hill, 1993, pp117–138

as well as the readable:

Pojman, L., *Ethics, Discovering Right and Wrong*, US Military Academy, 2002, pp134–158

and the visual:

Robinson D. and Garratt, C., *Ethics for Beginners*, Icon Books, 1996, pp80–87
Vardy, P., *The Puzzle of Ethics*, Fount, 1992, pp74–83

Lastly, for a more demanding examination there is the indispensable:

Mackie, J., *Inventing Right and Wrong*, Penguin, 1977, pp149–168

And my favourite anthology:

Singer, P., *Ethics*, in the Oxford Readers series, Oxford University Press, 1994

In this chapter you have:

- explored the key features of Kant's deontological ethics: reason and morality, his theory of the moral law, good will and duty, the categorical imperative

- considered a number of key issues associated with Kant's thinking

- applied Kant's theory to moral issues

- considered a number of strengths and weaknesses of Kantian ethics.

Natural moral law

Key philosophers

St Thomas Aquinas (c.1225–74): *Summa Theologica*, 1273

Aristotle (384–322 BC): *Nichomachean Ethics*

Cicero (106–43 BC): *On The Republic*

John Finnis (1940–): *Natural Law and Natural Rights*, 1980

Key terms

Natural law: the name of Aquinas's ethical system, derived partly from Aristotle, in which the good is defined by acts which are within our common human nature. Good actions are those which help us become fully human, whereas bad actions are those which hinder us from being fully human.

Key questions

1 Is there a universal moral code within all people?
2 What makes a thing wrong, the nature of the act or the consequence of the action?
3 Are human beings essentially good or bad?
4 Do all humans have a common purpose and, if so, what is it?
5 Do you think our actions in life should be in line with our broader aims in life? Explain your view.

The roots of natural law

The roots of **natural law** can be found in the ancient Greek and Roman world. In the play *Antigone*, written in the 5th century BC by the great dramatist Sophocles, Creon, the ruler of Thebes, forbids the burial of Antigone's brother as punishment for his treason against Thebes. Antigone breaks Creon's law and buries her brother. She argues that the state cannot overrule the immortal laws of the Gods, which in this case require the dead to be buried. In *Nicomachean Ethics*, the Greek philosopher Aristotle (384–322BC) wrote that natural justice was not always the same as that which was 'just' by law. He observed that while laws may vary from place to place, natural justice is independent and applies to everyone no matter where they live:

> The natural is that which everywhere is equally valid, and depends not upon being or not being received … that which is natural is unchangeable, and has the same power everywhere, just as fire burns both here and in Persia.

Aristotle, 1980, Book V, Chapter 7

In ancient Greece, the Stoics – who, starting in the 3rd century BC, followed a school of philosophy called Stoicism – emphasised the importance of 'logos', or rationality, that governs the world and sees human nature as part of one natural order. They considered natural law a law of **right reason** which serves only its own ends and is not corrupted into serving special interests. In his letter to the Romans, St Paul wrote (Romans 2:14–15) about a law that is 'written in the hearts' of Gentiles. The Roman lawyer Cicero formulated the classic description of natural law in his work *On the Republic*:

> True law is right reason in agreement with nature; it is of universal application, unchanging and everlasting; it summons to duty by its commands, and averts from wrongdoing by its prohibitions … We cannot be freed from its obligations by senate or people, and we need not look outside ourselves for an expounder or interpreter of it. And there will not be different laws at Rome and at Athens, or different laws now and in the future, but one eternal and unchangeable law will be valid for all nations and all times, and there will be one master and ruler, that is, God, over us all, for he is the author of this law, its promulgator, and its enforcing judge.

Cicero, 1928, III, xxii

💡 Aristotle, the ends of actions and practical reason

Aristotle is important in understanding the development of natural law, particularly because of his view that an action is judged right or wrong insofar as it leads towards or away from the good end which everyone seeks. It is the extent to which an action helps you attain your good end that indicates whether the act is good.

This means that the act is not good in and of itself, but good in so much as it accords with the human purpose, and so some (such as the Catholic philosopher Frederick Copleston) have actually called it teleological. At the beginning of Book 1 of *Nicomachean Ethics*, Aristotle writes: 'Every art and every enquiry, every action and choice, is thought to aim at some good; and for this reason the good has rightly been declared to be that at which all things aim.' All human actions should aim at a good.

Aristotle goes on to explore the different ends that people have according to their profession. Doctors aim at the end of health, seamanship is aimed at the end of a safe voyage and so on. Some ends are subordinate to other ends. For instance, the maker of bits and reins for the cavalry aims to the end of fine effective bits and reins, but there is a more important end of the cavalry which is to do with winning battles. The good end of taking a sleeping draught may be to help a sick person sleep but this is subordinate (and contributory) to the overall good end of health. Some ends have further ends in view. Aristotle argues that there is an ultimate aim which is good in and of itself, and is not subordinate to any other aim. This is *the* good.

Aristotle goes on to say that it is difficult to establish what the ultimate good is. It is not as straightforward as, for instance, mathematics, because human actions are not as precise as maths. In ethics, he says, we start from 'true but obscure judgments' (Aristotle, 1984, 1216 b 32 ff) or 'first confused judgments' (Aristotle, 1984, 1217 a 18 ff) but go on to formulate general ethical principles. We establish what those principles are by working through and comparing our judgements. Aristotle assumes that within us there are natural tendencies which we should follow, which help in making a moral judgement, and following those tendencies is living the ethical life. Ethics have a natural basis, rather than an arbitrary one and we use our reason in working out what those ethics are. This practical reason, or moral discernment, is our ability to read what is morally right in situations. We need to be emotionally balanced and that means having the virtues.

In Book 1 Chapter 7 of *Nicomachean Ethics*, Aristotle suggests that human beings have a number of activities, each of which depends on the preceding one: growing, reproducing, sensing, feeling emotions, thinking and choosing. These activities can be done well or badly. It is the higher thinking social activities, the things which differentiate humans from animals, which are most important. Aristotle believed that living a fulfilled life for a human being meant ensuring that all the activities are functioning well.

💡 St Thomas Aquinas's theory of natural law

St Thomas Aquinas (*c*.1225–74), an important Christian philosopher and theologian, developed a fuller account of natural law in the 13th century. His ethical theory is absolutist and deontological, which means that it is focused on the ethicality of actions. In his 1273 work *Summa Theologica* Aquinas described natural law as a moral code existing within

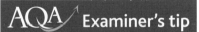

the *purpose* of nature, created by God: 'Law is nothing else than an ordination of reason for the common good promulgated by the one who is in charge of the community' (Aquinas, 1947, II.i Q. 90 art. 4). Aquinas took many aspects of Aristotle's thinking and added to it the idea of the Eternal Law of God.

This natural law exists to assist humans to direct their actions in such a way that they may reach their eternal destiny with God. This divinely inspired law covers both the outward external view of actions and the internal motivation for doing so. For Aquinas natural law evaluates both what you do and why you do it. Natural law affects all aspects of human behaviour, because, 'man needs to be directed to his supernatural end in a higher way' (Aquinas, 1947, II.i Q. 91 art. 4). Aquinas maintained that there was a basic law, or precept, within which all the other natural laws played a part: 'A certain order is to be found in the things that are apprehended by men … that good is to be done and pursued, and evil is to be avoided. All the other precepts of the law of nature are based on this' (Aquinas, 1947, II.i Q. 94 art. 2). This basic law is a formal principle of **practical reason**, an idea with which Aquinas has followed Aristotle.

Practical reason and human purpose

Aquinas borrowed Aristotle's idea that we can move from moral judgements to ultimate principles for ethical living. He argued that the eternal law of divine reason is perceived through revelation, in the form of the Word of God (the Bible), and through the use of human reason. A moral life is a life lived according to and in accordance with reason, and an immoral life is a life lived at odds with reason: 'To disparage the dictate of reason is equivalent to condemning the command of God' (Aquinas, 1947, II.i Q. 19 art. 4). Aquinas deduced that, fundamentally, humans should do good and avoid evil.

He held that reason determines that the ultimate purpose and destiny of human life is fellowship with God. Humans naturally tend towards this destiny and should live according to their design. They should avoid being enslaved by non-natural, non-rational desires. Very importantly, he, like Aristotle, did not think you could go the other way, from knowing general principles to specific judgements in moral situations.

For Aquinas, man's first precept (rule) is self-preservation. He established a series of **primary precepts** (rules) that are required to ensure this goal: the continuation of the species through reproduction, the education of children, to live in society and to worship God. These primary precepts don't change: 'Natural law is the same for all men … there is a single standard of truth and right for everyone … which is known by everyone' (Aquinas, 1947, II.i Q. 94 art. 4).

Whether or not acts lead towards God depends upon whether the action fits the purpose for which humans were made. We have seen that the main purpose of human nature is to preserve the self and the innocent, to reproduce, to acquire knowledge, to live in an ordered society and to worship God. These are called primary precepts. Acts that accord with the main human purpose are good. Acts not in accordance with human purpose are bad. **Secondary precepts** are rulings about things that we should or shouldn't do because they uphold, or fail to uphold, the primary precept.

The idea of primary and secondary precepts owes much to Aristotle's thinking on subordinate and ultimate ends and it is important to remember that it is from the moral situation we face that the final end is

Key terms

Practical reason: the consideration of basic human goods when deciding how to live.

Primary precepts: in natural law ethics, primary precepts are the 'first' level of rules which apply to all human beings by virtue of their common human nature, e.g. the primary precept of sexual behaviour is that all acts of sex should lead directly to the possibility of procreation, from which a number of interesting secondary precepts are then derived.

Secondary precepts: these are the rules which Aquinas derived from the primary precepts which are at the centre of his natural law theory. The set of secondary precepts most commonly referred to is that containing the rules for sexual conduct, which have caused much controversy.

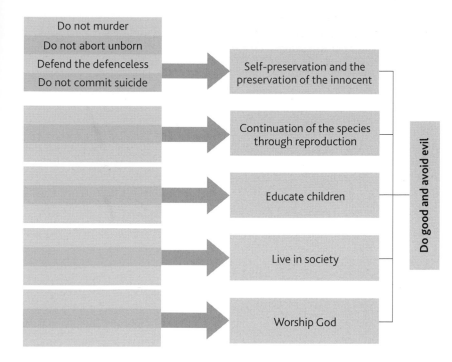

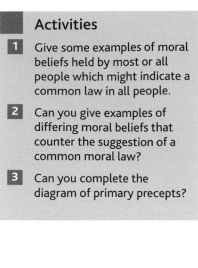

Activities

1 Give some examples of moral beliefs held by most or all people which might indicate a common law in all people.

2 Can you give examples of differing moral beliefs that counter the suggestion of a common moral law?

3 Can you complete the diagram of primary precepts?

deduced. It is from experience of moral dilemmas that we can reason the ultimate aims. In matters of ethics, both Aristotle and Aquinas believed moral decisions are made in the situation, as it is only in that position one can really reason what the good action is. Here conscience is very important. The person making the decision has to feel confident their action is something they believe is right, even though this will sometimes lead to mistakes, (which is acceptable). This kind of thinking, that ethical thinking should start with the issue and move from practical reasoning in the situation to principles, came to be called **casuistry** and was, and remains, an aspect of the practice of ethical thinking in the Roman Catholic Church.

Aquinas also held that a law that conflicted with the natural law was no law at all. This came to be known as probabilism, the view that laws are not binding if a solid probable arguments exists. If there are two probable opinions then either may be followed – this is called equiprobabilism.

Real and apparent goods

Aquinas believed that human nature was essentially good, as natural law is within everyone. He maintained that humans were oriented towards the achievement of perfection and that they could never knowingly pursue evil: 'No evil can be desirable, either by natural appetite or by conscious will. It is sought indirectly, namely because it is the consequence of some good' (Aquinas, 1947, 1.i Q. 19 art. 9). Human actions that are not in the pursuit of perfection can be explained as the pursuit of an *apparent* good – something that doesn't fit the perfect human ideal: 'A fornicator seeks a pleasure which involves him in moral guilt' (Aquinas, 1947, 1.i Q. 19 art. 9). Sin consists of falling short of God's intention for humans. To choose an apparent good is an error, because it is not really good for us. The adulterer or adulteress commits adultery because he or she believes that it is good. This is an error of reason, because adultery prevents a human from drawing close to what God intended. A parent advises a child to get as much education as

Key terms

Casuistry: casuistry is the practice of applying moral principles to particular cases, or types of case. It can be contrasted with situational approaches to ethics, which consider each moral situation as it arises.

Activity

Analyse your own life in terms of apparent and real goods. How straightforward is this to do? Are there any ambiguities?

Key terms

Exterior act/interior act: an interior act is an act of the will, which contrasts with an exterior act, which is what you do. In Aquinas's natural law system, both are important. The motive and purpose of an act is just as important as the exterior act, because its ultimate end is God.

Link

See the double effect example on pp106–7.

possible, but the child wastes time watching TV. The child thinks that watching TV in large amounts is good, although in fact less time should be given to such things, and more to learning. To correctly distinguish between apparent and real goods is to use reason rightly and to choose the right thing to do. It is not necessarily easy, as we are tempted by what we like doing, which may not be truly good for us.

Reason identifies 'natural' or 'cardinal' virtues: prudence, temperance, fortitude and justice. Scripture reveals theological virtues: faith, hope and charity (1 Corinthians 13:13). To adhere to natural law, an individual should seek to develop these virtues – this development requires practice. The virtues must become habitual. It is also possible for the very opposite to become habitual if people are not careful, and for a habit of sinful unnatural activity to develop.

Exterior and interior acts

For Aquinas, both the *intention* and the *act* are important. To act in a good way for the wrong reason is to perform a good **exterior act** but a bad **interior act**. For example, to help an old lady across the road (good exterior act) to impress someone (bad interior act) is wrong. It should be done out of charity and not for the sake of admiration by others. On the other hand, good intentions don't always lead to good actions. If I steal money to give it to a friend, the theft isn't made good by my intention to help my friend. The only end that Aquinas values is God. Physical pleasures can't be the final end, as animals can experience them. Academic pleasures aren't accessible to everyone, so the ultimate aim open to all humans is God. Aquinas believes that acts are intrinsically good or bad (good or bad in themselves) because when human beings act in accordance with their ultimate purpose, God is glorified. The act of helping the old lady across the road is good in and of itself, because it accords with the destiny of how humans should be and that glorifies God.

Activities

1. Suggest three apparent goods that aren't at all good, and explain your choices.
2. Aquinas believes that humans never choose evil, although they sometimes choose apparent goods which are in fact bad. Suggest examples that challenge this view; in other words, examples of evil actions that humans choose purposefully and knowingly. Are they convincing? Is Aquinas's view convincing?
3. Aquinas suggests that reason is the principal tool for making moral decisions. Can you suggest any alternative tools for making moral decisions? Can it ever be morally right to go against reason? Give a possible example.
4. Does it matter if someone does a good thing for a wrong reason, such as giving to charity for the admiration and praise that they will receive? Why might some say that this isn't the best way to act?

Modern developments: John Finnis

The Australian legal philosopher John Finnis (1940–) has been developing the natural law tradition since the 1960s. In his book *Natural Law and Natural Rights* (1980) he has adapted natural law so that it does not presuppose God's existence. He proposes that human beings desire to pursue a number of goods in life, and in so doing live a good life.

Seven basic goods

Like Aquinas and Aristotle before him, Finnis identifies a number of equally valuable basic goods or ends, given human nature:

Finnis suggests seven 'basic goods', which are as follows:

- Human life, including every aspect of vitality such as health and procreation.
- Knowledge.
- Play, or skilled performance.
- Aesthetic appreciation, which may be in the creation as well. So I may appreciate the art that I am painting as well as the painting I see in the gallery.
- Sociability, meaning at least peace and harmony but also, more than that, the full flowering of friendship.
- Practical reasonableness; that is bringing your intelligence to bear on the moral decisions that you face in life.
- Religion; the recognition that all the basic goods are made possible by a higher intelligence.

Like Aquinas he also agrees that these ends have intrinsic value in the sense that they should be valued for their own sake, and not merely for some other good they bring about. They are both the motivation and the goal of the action. For example, knowledge may have an instrumental value but it is also a good in and of itself. They are also universal, for all times, peoples and cultures. They are not relative or particular.

Nine principles of practical reasonableness

People exercise practical reason when making moral decisions in seeking out those goods. Finnis proposes nine principles of practical reasonableness that are the 'methods of operation' rather than 'ends sought'. These methods help in moral decision-making, guiding our actions to achieve the seven basic goods.

- The good of practical reasonableness structures our pursuit of good. We need skill and a thoroughgoing commitment to realise all of the seven basic goods.
- We must have a plan of life, with all our aims and attitudes in harmony; a commitment, not just a pipe-dream.
- A person must commit to all the basic goods, none can be left out.
- A person should not show arbitrary preference among people. In other words, the golden rule – do unto others as you would have done unto yourself.
- A person should not live completely in the moment, but act with a degree of detachment from the individual and specific situations. We should remember our commitment to all the aspects of a good life. We must not live completely in the moment or become fanatical so that we are only concerned about what is immediate to us.

Activity

Working alone or in groups, construct your own list of seven plausible basic goods. Try to come to an agreement as to what they are. Remember they should all be equally valuable. Explain your choices.

■ We should try to be efficient in our moral action. For instance where physical harm is inevitable such as in self-defence, stunning is preferable to wounding, or worse. It is reasonable to rescue the old lady from the burning house rather than her pet budgie.

■ In every moral act all basic values must be remembered. A utilitarian might justify killing one for the good of the many, (such as killing the hostage-taker to free the hostages) but this makes no sense in Finnis's thinking. The act of killing the hostage-taker does not lead to anything other than the death of the hostage-taker. There will always be consequences of actions.

■ We must foster the common good of one's community.

■ Following one's conscience. We should not do things which we feel all-in-all should not be done. We must act in accordance with our conscience. We might make mistakes with regards to following our conscience but this is acceptable.

For Finnis, moral principles give ethical structure to our pursuit of these basic goods. They help us to make decisions when there are competing goods and define what a human being ought to do in the pursuit of a basic good.

Like Aquinas, Finnis's natural law theory is both a theory of ethics and a theory of law. He believes that Aquinas's account of natural law provided an explanation of the moral force of law: 'the principles of natural law explain the obligatory force (in the fullest sense of "obligation") of positive laws, even when those laws cannot be deduced from those principles' (Finnis, 1980, pp23–24).

An unjust law may be legally valid, but it does not justify the use of coercive power of the state. It is not obligatory in the fullest sense as it does not realise the moral ideals which are implicit in the concept of law. While an unjust law may be legally binding it is not fully law.

■ Evaluating natural moral law

Strengths and weaknesses

The strengths of natural moral law are the strengths of an absolutist deontological view of morality. It enables people to establish common rules in order to structure communities. In a relativist era that is suffering from a breakdown in traditional social structures and moral uncertainty, this can be an attractive option.

Aquinas's view of reason as a tool for moral understanding and his idea of a common nature and morality for all people gives natural law a universality that goes beyond any one religion or culture. This is attractive in a world that suffers from intercultural strife and disharmony. Different cultures can all be seen to have the same basic principles of preserving life, continuing the species, education and building a society. A considerable portion of the human population still believes in God, even if in Western European countries such as the UK there is a decline in religious practice.

A reason to be moral

Natural moral law gives a concrete reason to be moral and a firm basis from which to refuse to step over moral boundaries. It provides justification and support for certain core ideas which are popular in modern times, such as human rights and equality. It judges actions, irrespective of consequences which seems right for some acts, such as rape. Natural moral law isn't simply a set of rules, but a way of living. It gives guidance on day-to-day questions of how to live and links them to the fundamental principles of life. It provides a complete system of moral living in step with what it is to be human.

Gerard J. Hughes adds a couple of strengths of the theory in his chapter in Bernard Hoose's book *Christian Ethics, an Introduction* (1998). For him, natural moral law is based on what human beings are really like. It is intimately related to human nature and how human beings relate to each other in their distinct environments and situations. In addition the theory allows for the possibility that we will make mistakes. We can lose sight of the really important ends, in and of themselves, in our daily lives and choices. We can get things right and we can get things wrong.

A natural good and a single human nature

Some have challenged Aquinas. They question whether there is a common natural law that is apparent and self-evident, whether there is a single 'one size fits all' human nature and whether day-to-day rules can be deduced from the fundamental laws (primary precepts).

In *God and the Grounding of Morality*, Kai Nielson argues against Aquinas's belief in a basic human nature that is present across all societies and cultures: 'From the point of view of science, there is no such thing as an essential human nature which makes a man man. The concept of human nature is a rather vague cultural concept; it is not a scientific one' (Nielson, 1991, p53). The challenge is that an essential human nature isn't as obviously self-evident as Aquinas claims – comforting, but not true. Nielson notes that anthropologists have investigated practices in other cultures. At one time, the Eskimos killed members of their families who would not make it through the winter, as well as newborn girls if there were no husbands to support them. Scandinavians killed their elderly family members to allow them into Valhalla (the place in Scandinavian mythology where heroes who have been killed feast for eternity). These differing moral standards challenge the idea of a common natural law within all human societies. Natural law obscures these basic moral differences. These differences challenge the possibility that there is a natural good at all.

Perhaps human beings have different or changeable natures, as indicated by people of different or variable sexual orientations. Homosexual men and women have had to argue for recognition as normal human beings. Their sexual acts are classed as unnatural by Aquinas as they can't lead to new life, but they themselves find love and purpose in life through the expression of their sexuality. Perhaps a common natural law does exist, but in a more complex form than Aquinas thought. Perhaps primary precepts differ in ways not fully understood yet.

The place of cause in the centre of life

In their book *The Puzzle of Ethics* (1994, p60), Peter Vardy and Paul Grosch challenge the way in which Aquinas works from general principles to lesser purposes. Aquinas maintains that as human beings must preserve the species, every sexual act should be associated with life generation. Other sexual acts are immoral. However, it isn't necessary that every discharge of semen should produce a new life to maintain the human species. Sexual acts could be justified on account of the benefits to the couple's relationship. Aquinas could be wrong about his deductions, as they may be based on an incorrect view of human life.

Holistic: characterised by the belief that the parts of something are intimately interconnected and explicable only by reference to the whole.

Vardy and Grosch also consider Aquinas's moral view of human nature as **unholistic**. Perhaps the genitals are for pleasure rather than reproduction, or some other purpose, or for a number of different purposes. Sexual activity isn't only found in the genitalia, so perhaps Aquinas has a far too nervous idea of what is involved in lovemaking. Psychologists have drawn much more complex pictures of human nature than Aquinas's simplistic account. Today, the human body is seen as one psycho-physical whole, not the fragmented collection of parts that Aquinas seems to believe in. Good lovemaking involves the whole body and mind. Perhaps Aquinas's idea of causes is simplistic.

Natural law and the religious life

Aquinas's natural moral law is a Christian ethic and yet Jesus opposes legalistic morality in the New Testament. He debated sharply with the moral legalists of his time, the Pharisees. Natural moral law appears to be similar to Pharisaic law, and some, such as Joseph Fletcher (see Chapter 4), argue that Jesus rejected this approach. Some Christian ethicists argue for a morality that is based more on the person involved than the acts committed. One such writer is Kevin T. Kelly. In his book *New Directions in Moral Theology* (1992), Kelly identifies two traditions found in Christian morality, one that is centred on acts, and another that is centred on the dignity of the human person. These different traditions are found in some other religions as well. Kelly sees both of these strands of morality at work in recent Christian thinking. The Constitution of the Roman Catholic Church, *Gaudium et Spes*, maintains that 'the moral aspect of any procedure is influenced by intentions and motives but also objective standards, based on the nature of the human person and his acts' (p29). Kelly argues for a morality based on the human person as author and director of any actions, and moves away from the idea that actions have moral value in themselves. A more extreme form of personalism is found in situation ethics, where 'a one size fits all' legalistic approach to morality is almost entirely abandoned. In situation ethics, the situation and the results of actions determine the goodness or badness of an action, not the action in itself.

John Finnis's proposal seems a more measured interpretation of natural moral law, which takes into account a wide range of aspects of moral decision-making, making his version of practical reason more attractive. He is also writing from a Catholic perspective but in a way that could be acceptable to atheists. It is not focused on a single way of measuring morality such as only looking at ends as utilitarians do. Of course it is possible to disagree that we are free to weigh up and make moral decisions – perhaps we are psychologically driven to make choices. Were this to be true Finnis's theory, and any other theory based on weighing up what to do rationally, would have difficulties. Another problem arises if the basic goods identified by Finnis are not correct. For instance, does the full flourishing of life always include reproduction? That might be able to be said in terms of the human species but in terms of an individual, many people are infertile for some or all of their lives. Some people have lifelong illnesses and disabilities which make universal definitions of health and natural life problematic when they include certain capacities. How specific should the ultimate goods be? Is the way in which an individual contributes to those goods to be differentiated?

Given these criticisms, it is worth noting that natural law may not be as rigid as it first appears. Aquinas observed that although the primary precepts were unchangeable, the secondary precepts may change in some particular aspects, or in a case in which special reasons make it

1 Make a case arguing that all humans share a common nature.

2 What benefits does this view have for society?

3 Consider the evidence against the claim in Activity 1.

4 Identify sexual issues affected by natural moral law and suggest what Aquinas's view of these issues would be.

5 Explain what it means to base morality on actions (deontology).

6 What does it mean to say that morality should be person-centred, and what are the merits of this approach?

impossible to observe them. Aristotle and Aquinas both thought it is much more difficult to work out moral decisions than other sorts of decisions and the fact that sometimes people following their conscience in good faith may still get things wrong. The conclusions of the Roman Catholic Church regarding the prohibitions of artificial contraception and homosexual acts may be challengeable in certain special cases. However, in the absence of guidelines to establish what is challengeable, this may equally render the whole of the natural moral law approach impossibly subjective. Vardy and Grosch (1994, pp62–63) note that this opens a door to the possibility of the proportionalist form of situationism, whereby rules apply to all proportionately extreme cases.

■ Application

When applying a theory to an issue, remember that your choice of issue is significant if you are going to evaluate the theory on the basis of how well it deals with your issue. Re-read the 'Tools for evaluating ethical theories' in Chapter 1 to remind yourself of some of the tools you have available.

Use the following questions when applying Finnis's version of natural moral law thinking to an ethical issue. In the issue you are addressing:

1 Try to rule out feelings, preferences or consequences as factors in the workings.
2 Remember that acting in good conscience is important, and making a decision in the situation is also important.
3 Remember that the actions involved in the options should aim for some end, the basic goods, which should be deducible from that action, rather than the other way round.
4 Consider the options available and consider which most closely satisfies the following criteria. Which option:
   ■ Is committed to all of the basic goods, without discounting or exaggeration?
   ■ Shows no arbitrary preference to one person in the situation over and against another?
   ■ Demonstrates that we are not focused exclusively on the situation but have the basic goods in mind?
   ■ Takes account of efficiency?
   ■ Pays attention to all the basic goods in the act, instead of some or one, at the expense of another or others?
   ■ Supports the common good of the community?
5 Does the option identified in 4 seem reasonable or unreasonable?
6 If unreasonable why is this?
   ■ Is it because it ignores a moral factor which natural law thinking doesn't account for producing a problematic conclusion? If so which factor?
   ■ Is it because you value different moral factors than those expressed in the theory (such as the situation or the consequences, etc.)?
   ■ If so can you justify why you value those factors over and above the ones which are important in the theory?
   ■ Is this a factor which is likely to be found in many ethical issues? In other words does this flag up a more major problem with the theory as a whole, or just a problem with this particularly difficult issue?

AQA Examiner's tip

Go for clear selection and sequence, e.g. for natural law:

In favour
■ The concept of a *common human nature* promotes fairness
■ so it leads to a strong *society*
■ and justifies our use of *punishment*.
■ It is *simple* to follow rules.

Other views
■ Humans have at least *three sexual natures*: heterosexual, homosexual and bisexual
■ so Aquinas could have been wrong about the *primary principles*
■ and therefore wrong also about the *secondary principles*.
■ Natural law ethics is *legalistic* rather than situational.
■ Natural law ethics involves *God* – pointless if you don't believe in God.

The words in italics should give you a reasonable sequence to memorise.

7 If the solution seems reasonable, how adequate do you think this moral example is in testing the theory? Might there be different kinds of examples which the theory has more trouble with?

Consider a specific example of one of these situations and work through the situation using Aquinas's or Finnis's version of natural law: the use of contraception, murder, homosexual sex, rape and adultery. Try to address the key concepts of the theory in your application in the specific situation you have chosen. Show your workings to a partner and ask them to evaluate your application of the theory. Then discuss together whether you think the theory works well, and what weaknesses it may have.

Extracts from key texts

St Thomas Aquinas, Summa Theologica

Of the Natural Law, II.i Q.94, art. 2

Now a certain order is to be found in those things that are apprehended universally … the first principle of practical reason is one founded on the notion of good, viz. that 'good is that which all things seek after'. Hence this is the first precept of law, that 'good is to be done and pursued, and evil is to be avoided'. All other precepts of the natural law are based upon this: so that whatever the practical reason naturally apprehends as man's good (or evil) belongs to the precepts of the natural law as something to be done or avoided …

Wherefore according to the order of natural inclinations, is the order of the precepts of the natural law. Because in man there is first of all an inclination to good in accordance with the nature which he has in common with all substances: inasmuch as every substance seeks the preservation of its own being, according to its nature: and by reason of this inclination, whatever is a means of preserving human life, and of warding off its obstacles, belongs to the natural law. Secondly, there is in man an inclination to things that pertain to him more specially, according to that nature which he has in common with other animals: and in virtue of this inclination, those things are said to belong to the natural law, 'which nature has taught to all animals', such as sexual intercourse, education of offspring and so forth. Thirdly, there is in man an inclination to good, according to the nature of his reason, which nature is proper to him: thus man has a natural inclination to know the truth about God, and to live in society: and in this respect, whatever pertains to this inclination belongs to the natural law; for instance, to shun ignorance, to avoid offending those among whom one has to live, and other such things regarding the above inclination.

The Catechism of the Roman Catholic Church

Chapter Three – God's Salvation: Law and Grace

Article 1 – the Moral Law

I. The Natural Moral Law

1954 Man participates in the wisdom and goodness of the Creator who gives him mastery over his acts and the ability to govern himself with a view to the true and the good. The natural law expresses the original moral sense which enables man to discern by reason the good and the evil, the truth and the lie:

The natural law is written and engraved in the soul of each and every man, because it is human reason ordaining him to do good and forbidding him to sin … But this command of human reason would not have the force of law if it were not the voice and interpreter of a higher reason to which our spirit and our freedom must be submitted. [Leo XIII, Libertas praestantissimum, 597.]

1955 The 'divine and natural' law [GS 89 §1] shows man the way to follow so as to practice the good and attain his end. The natural law states the first and essential precepts which govern the moral life …

> The natural law is nothing other than the light of understanding placed in us by God; through it we know what we must do and what we must avoid. God has given this light or law at the creation. [St Thomas Aquinas, Dec. praec. 1.]

1956 The natural law, present in the heart of each man and established by reason, is universal in its precepts and its authority extends to all men. It expresses the dignity of the person and determines the basis for his fundamental rights and duties:

> For there is a true law: right reason. It is in conformity with nature, is diffused among all men, and is immutable and eternal; its orders summon to duty; its prohibitions turn away from offense … To replace it with a contrary law is a sacrilege; failure to apply even one of its provisions is forbidden; no one can abrogate it entirely. [Cicero, Rep. III, 22, 33.]

1957 Application of the natural law varies greatly; it can demand reflection that takes account of various conditions of life according to places, times, and circumstances. Nevertheless, in the diversity of cultures, the natural law remains as a rule that binds men among themselves and imposes on them, beyond the inevitable differences, common principles …

1959 The natural law, the Creator's very good work, provides the solid foundation on which man can build the structure of moral rules to guide his choices. It also provides the indispensable moral foundation for building the human community. Finally, it provides the necessary basis for the civil law with which it is connected, whether by a reflection that draws conclusions from its principles, or by additions of a positive and juridical nature.

1960 The precepts of natural law are not perceived by everyone clearly and immediately. In the present situation sinful man needs grace and revelation so moral and religious truths may be known 'by everyone with facility, with firm certainty and with no admixture of error'. [Pius XII, Humani generis: DS 3876; cf. Dei Filius 2: DS 3005.] The natural law provides revealed law and grace with a foundation prepared by God and in accordance with the work of the Spirit.

Chapter summary

The roots of natural law:

- Aristotle wrote: 'The natural is that which everywhere is equally valid.'
- Stoics emphasised logos, or rationality, which governs the world.
- St Paul wrote about a law that is 'written in the hearts' of Gentiles.
- The Roman lawyer Cicero wrote: 'True law is right reason in agreement with nature.'

St Thomas Aquinas's theory of natural moral law (13th century):

■ His ethical theory is absolutist and deontological, which means that it is focused on the ethicality of actions.

■ Natural law exists to assist humans: 'man needs to be directed to his supernatural end in a higher way.'

■ There was a basic law: 'that good is to be done and pursued, and evil is to be avoided.'

■ Eternal law was perceived through revelation, in the form of the Word of God (the Bible) and human reason.

■ 'To disparage the dictate of reason is equivalent to condemning the command of God.'

■ The primary precepts are concerned with self-preservation, the continuation of the species through reproduction, the education of children, living in society and worshipping God.

■ The secondary precepts are deduced from the primary ones.

■ When humans do bad 'things' or 'acts' they are pursuing apparent goods, falsely believing them really to be good.

■ For Aquinas, both the intention and the act are important. To act in a good way for the wrong reason is to perform a good exterior act but a bad interior act.

■ Acts are intrinsically good or bad (good or bad in themselves) because when human beings act in accordance with their ultimate purpose, God is glorified.

John Finnis

■ A modern advocate of natural moral law.

■ There are seven basic goods which are intrinsically good ends and are universal: life, knowledge, play, aesthetic appreciation, sociability, practical reasonableness and religion.

■ There are nine principles of practical reasonableness that are 'methods of operation' which guide moral decision-making. These include having a rational plan, commitment to all basic goods, showing no arbitrary preference among people, detachment and commitment, efficiency within reason, respect for every basic value in every act, fostering the common good and following one's conscience.

■ Moral principles give ethical structure to our pursuit of these basic goods.

Evaluating natural moral law:

■ Natural moral law enables people to establish common rules to structure communities.

■ Different cultures can be seen to have basic principles of preserving life, continuing the species, education and building a society, so natural law seems reasonable.

■ Natural moral law gives guidance on day-to-day questions of how to live and links them to the fundamental principles of life.

■ Natural moral law is based on what human beings are really like.

■ The theory allows for the possibility that we will make mistakes.

However:

■ Some dispute the presence of a common natural law and whether humans have a single nature.

'It's a sign of respect in these parts...
rib or leg?'

- Humans may have different or changeable natures, as indicated by the different sexual orientations in society.

- Aquinas could be wrong about his primary precepts, his definition of human purpose.

- Natural moral law is a Christian ethic and yet Jesus's opposition to legalistic morality is apparent in the New Testament. Some, such as Joseph Fletcher, argue that Jesus rejected this approach.

- Finnis's account seems to balance a number of different important dimensions of morality, rather than just one, as helping to discern the ultimate good in actions.

- Natural moral law may not be as rigid as it first appears, as secondary precepts may change in some particular aspects.

Further reading

For a very good explanation see:

Vardy P., *The Puzzle of Ethics*, Fount, 1992, pp52–64

And for a more challenging discussion try:

Hoose B., *Christian Ethics*, Cassell, 1998, pp47–56

And my favourite anthology:

Singer, P., *Ethics*, in the Oxford Readers series, Oxford University Press, 1994

In this chapter you have:

- explored the ancient background of natural law and in particular the role of Aristotle

- examined the concepts of St Thomas Aquinas's natural moral law theory, including the importance of practical reason, the purpose of human beings, real and apparent goods, exterior and interior acts, and primary and secondary precepts

- identified the main features of John Finnis's version of natural moral law

- applied the theory to ethical issues

- considered significant strengths and weaknesses of natural moral law.

Ethical issues

This second part looks at religious perspectives of human life and the world around us, considering different responses from Judaism, Christianity, Islam, Hinduism, Buddhism and Sikhism. It then considers ethical issues which relate to both human life and the world around us. Religious traditions are diverse within themselves and the chapters try to capture something of that diversity, as well as identifying central ideas. Key terms are identified and defined beside the text when they appear for the first time. There are also activities to illustrate the kind of problems that arise from trying to deal with these issues, as well as some of the problems religious approaches produce. At the ends of some chapters there are important extracts from key texts that are closely associated with the theory.

7 Religious perspectives on the nature and value of human life

By the end of this chapter you will:

- be familiar with different religious teaching on human nature and the human condition, free will and fatalism, equality and the value of human life

- have evaluated some of these perspectives in terms of their ethical implications.

Key terms

Nirvana: a transcendent state in which there is neither suffering, desire, nor sense of self, and the subject is released from the effects of karma. It represents the final goal of Buddhism.

Activities

1 What is your place in the universe? Do you think you have a purpose, or a destiny? If so what is it?

2 Do you think human lives are special? If so why and in what ways?

Key questions

1 How do religions see human nature?
2 What is the human condition, according to the religions?
3 In religious thinking, are humans free?
4 What do religions say about equality?
5 How do religions value human life?

Introduction

In all of the religious traditions, there is a view of humanity and a claim for how humanity fits in the universe. In all of those traditions, human nature and human value is distinctive and special. Human beings have a special position in the universe distinct from other living creatures. In Western religious traditions that position is informed by an idea that a divine being has created the universe, known and unknown, and in that creation, human beings have a place (at the pinnacle).

In Eastern religious traditions there is not the creator with a will or purpose, but there is an idea that human beings have the possibility for reaching enlightenment, or **nirvana**, unlike all other animals, and therefore there is a possibility in human life of breaking from the otherwise endless cycle of rebirth.

This chapter has been organised in sections for each religion. Within those sections are themes for each of the aspects of religion explored. You can read the chapter through as it is arranged, but it is suggested that you then read through the material again thematically.

Warning! Some of the views expressed within this section may be considered controversial and are intended to stimulate thought and discussion. They do not necessarily represent the views of the author, the publisher or the examination board!

ℹ️ Jewish perspectives

Human nature and the human condition

When God created human beings, he created an image of God. No other creature was given such an honour. To underline this special status, Rabbi Joshua ben Levi said:

> A procession of angels pass before a human being wherever he or she goes, proclaiming – Make way for the image of God

Sherwin, 2001, p1, quoting Rabbi Joshua ben Levi

B. L. Sherwin, in his 2001 book *Jewish Ethics for the Twenty-First Century*, comments that human beings have the intelligence to understand this, and it is the purpose of Jewish ethics to work out how to live out their lives in a way which shows that they understand that they carry the image of God within them, that they are created 'in the image and likeness of God' (Genesis 1:26). There are different ways of understanding this. It is not thought that human beings are physically similar to God. On the one hand it might be that human beings have some divine quality within them (ontological). On the other hand it might be that human beings have the capacity to behave in a god-like way to each other (behavioural). In other words it might be that human beings are like God because of some holiness within them, irrespective of what they do, or because they have the capacity to do good rather than ill, to love rather than hate.

Free will and fatalism

Sherwin argues that some Jewish scholars have pursued an ontological idea of human Godliness and tried to define that quality of Godliness. The medieval Jewish philosopher Maimonides (1138–1204) argued that the way in which God and human beings were alike was that they were thinking creatures and this gave them the ability to discern good from evil (Sherwin, 2001, p3). Scholars stressed the moral dimension more than the intellectual. Animals lack the ability to make moral choices that humans, and God, possess. This places humans above all (other) animals. Maimonides wrote:

> The human species is unique in the world – there being not other species like it in the following respect; namely that a person by himself, and by the exercise of intelligence and reason knows what is good and what is evil …

Sherwin, 2001, p4, quoting Maimonides

Human beings have the capacity freely to choose between good and evil: they have a **free will**. Of course, the fact that human beings have the capacity to make moral choices does not imply that they will do good. They have freedom to act in a morally good or bad way. Human desire can lead to wrongdoing. The desire that human beings have to satisfy personal needs is not bad in itself. Hunger is not bad, nor is sexual desire, but both can lead to wrongdoing – stealing food or sexual assault, for instance. Ultimately it is human freedom and moral responsibility which determines whether or not the person does wrong. Maimonides rejects **fatalism**.

Beyond the moral capacity that humans have there is also the creative capacity that humans have. Just as God has creative powers, so human

Key terms

Free will: having the ability to choose or determine one's own actions.

Fatalism: the view that everything that happens is predetermined and that we have no control over it.

beings have these kinds of powers and this is an additional feature of the way in which human beings are like God.

Equality and difference

Equality is an important idea in Jewish thinking. Traditional Judaism sees women as separate but equal with different (but equal) duties. Judaism maintains that God is neither exclusively male nor female and has qualities of both. Many scholars agree that both man and woman were created in the image of God and that the 'man' that was created in Genesis 1:27 had dual gender. Only later was this separated into male and female. The difference between men and women is found in characteristics and this leads to their separate roles. Women are important in the Torah (there are matriarchs as well as patriarchs and female as well as male prophets), but in contemporary Judaism women's status varies and there have been important recent changes in the way different traditions of Judaism approach the issue of women's equality. Differences remain for instance over whether women should be allowed to be rabbis, what role they might have in synagogue, and what legal rights they have. There remains in some forms of Judaism the idea that women have distinctive qualities and have a different role in God's purpose than men. Some see this idea that women are different but equal as a way of retaining unacceptable inequalities.

The value of human life

In Jewish thinking the specialness of their humanity is underlined by the belief that they are God's chosen people. He has made a **covenant** with them which carries both obligations and blessings. They have to be a kingdom of priests and a holy nation. The covenant requires a response from the people to which it is offered and part of that response is in the recognition that human beings are precious.

These rational, moral and creative features of human beings (stemming from the image of God they reflect) means humans have a dignity or value which makes human life special. Judaism teaches that Jews should love their neighbour (Leviticus 19:18); the Ten Commandments teaches that murder is wrong. However, Jewish thinking goes further, arguing that we must protect our fellow man. Life must be preserved, so someone in danger should be helped and not abandoned.

■ Christian perspectives

Human nature and the human condition

The Bible teaches that people should love God, and love your neighbour as yourself. The basic rule of self-respect and respect of others is not simply a moral teaching, but a teaching that links to central Christian beliefs about the nature and value of human beings.

In Christian theology, human beings have a unique nature and value in all creation. They have a sanctity and this relates to their dignity which has both a natural dimension, in terms of rational thought and moral decision-making powers, and also a supernatural dimension, in terms of their ultimate purpose and destiny to be with God.

Christian ideas of dignity, the nature and value of human beings, are based on an understanding that God has given human beings a distinctive purpose. God had a purpose in creating the world and the human beings within it and the intention of saving humanity from sin

■ Activities

1 What is the difference between saying that human beings are special because they are like God in essence or because they can be loving and good?

2 Research conservative, reform and orthodox views on the role of women in synagogue and home. Compare and contrast your findings and relate them to the ideas discussed in the chapter.

■ Key terms

Covenant: an agreement which brings about a relationship of God and his people.

and death through the discovery of the image of Christ in every person. The early Christian thinker Lactantius (c.240–c.320) said that God had made humankind as a sacred animal and so humankind has dignity. This dignity means humans should not be sacrificed. So in the story of Abraham being ordered to replace his son with a ram (Genesis 22:3) for sacrifice, the practice of sacrificing a child to the gods in the hope that a good harvest will come is prohibited.

Human beings can reject God's love and fail to show love to others. They can choose to do ill, rather than good. They are imperfect and flawed with a tendency to sin, hence their need to be saved and redeemed by God. The power to think and act morally means there exists the possibility to make mistakes and do wrong.

Some Protestant traditions hold that the dignity that human beings had is largely lost due to sin (Cairns, 1973, pp127–133). Human beings do have the power of rational thought and will but it has become corrupted and lost. There is the possibility that it can be regained through a life focused on Christ. Even here the possibility of salvation makes the human being a being of value. God's intention for every person is salvation and so even if a person currently shows no feature of dignity because of their sinful conduct, they have the potential to be saved and so have a value.

Within Catholic Christianity the doctrine of original sin offers an important aspect of human nature. From St Augustine, and interpreting Romans 5:12, this was held to mean that since the **fall of man** human beings have the stain of original sin within them, the stain of Adam which he caused when he ate the forbidden fruit in the book of Genesis. Sin entered the world through his act. This led to the fall and then a much harder life for human beings where man had to work and women had to suffer pain in childbirth. This brought death into the world, as well and from early Christian times the baptism of children was practised to wash away this original sin. The human condition is one of hardship, suffering and death (Corinthians 15:21). Sin and the Devil have some influence over the world and human nature is tainted, weakened by its presence, and humans are inclined to sin though they are still free to act. There is hope of redemption and the possibility of goodness and love.

Free will and fatalism

St Augustine makes reference to the dignity of the human person with respect to its rational soul. Human beings have been created with thinking intellect and a will to act; they have the ability to act morally. The traditional Christian view is that human beings are free, **autonomous** agents, responsible for their actions. In Genesis, Adam and Eve exercise free will in choosing to eat the forbidden fruit. They are held responsible for their actions by God, who punishes them. St Thomas Aquinas, in *Summa Theologica*, wrote: 'man chooses not of necessity but freely' (*Summa Theologica*, I.i Q. 13 art. 6). Many Christian denominations hold to the view that we are free to choose to do good or sin. It is an important part of the idea of human dignity.

Furthermore, human beings who live their lives following Christ become Christ-like, or sons of God. This aspect of dignity can grow and takes human beings towards their final destiny with Christ. The specialness of human beings is also in the ongoing relationship between humanity and God. Human beings are in the image of God, ordained for God, redeemed by Jesus Christ and destined for unity with God. This is the supernatural dimension of human dignity (Soulen and Woodhead, 2006, pp1–7).

> ### Key terms
>
> **Fall of man:** when Adam and Eve ate of the fruit of the tree of knowledge of good and evil in the Garden of Eden, God punished them by driving them out of the Garden of Eden and into the world where they would be subject to sickness and pain and eventual death.
>
> **Autonomous:** free to make decisions.

Soulen and Woodhead argue then that the value of human beings, their dignity, is given to them by God, a gift given out of love (Soulen and Woodhead, 2006, pp1–7). That love and dignity then reaches out from human beings to other human beings in the care shown to one another. Instead of that dignity leading to kingly status, in the figure of Christ, dignity leads to service. The dignity of human beings, given by God, flows through and out through their love of others. This is the social dimension of the value of human life. Human beings are made free and able to choose and think for themselves. They are made special by virtue of this gift which God has given them and they grow in dignity in their use of these gifts to reflect the love of God to others around them.

Equality and difference

In principle, equality is a central idea within Christianity as all human beings are made in the image and likeness of God, and that, as St Paul says, in Christian fellowship social differences fall away: 'There is no longer Jew or Greek, there is no longer slave or free, there is no longer male and female, for all of you are one in Christ Jesus' (Galatians 3:28). Yet this must be set against many other references which are much more problematic for the modern idea of inequality. However, historically women have not been treated with this sort of equality within Christianity and there are many Christian denominations where women's roles are not considered to be the same as men's. In Roman Catholic ministry and priesthood are roles only men can adopt, even if women play essential parts in the life of the Church. The picture is mixed in Protestant Christianity.

The quote from Galatians is also a powerful assertion of race equality. Christian teachings challenge traditions which have excluded groups on account of race. For instance, in the story of the Good Samaritan Jesus uses a member of a community who were widely discriminated against as an example of moral goodness.

The Christian responses to disability are more complex. On the one hand there are strong mandates within Christianity to heal the sick and be concerned for those in need. Yet at the same time this does not seem to recognise the different worlds in which able-bodied and disabled people exist. John Hull has written about these worlds and the need for Christianity to recognise them in his book *A Spirituality of Disability*. The Bible describes Jesus as without blemish, God as perfect. Does that make able-bodied people closer to Jesus than disabled people? Jesus frequently heals the sick. Is the role of a disabled person to wait to be healed by the able-bodied? Hull argues that even as the world of the able-bodied is lost a new world replaces it:

> In the case of the person who has lost hearing, a new experience of living within vision appears, and communication becomes focused on the hands. The body builds up its new world, relating to it with new powers and functions for different parts of the body. In the case of the blind person, the hands are no longer mainly used to do things, but now to know things and finally to appreciate beauty.

Hull, 2003, pp21–35

Activity

If we see a disability as something to be 'cured', are we (a), undermining the dignity of a disabled person and (b), missing the value that a different perception of life brings? Consider different responses to these issues.

He goes on to draw on Paul who argued that the way of love is preferable to the way of miracles (1 Corinthians 12:31).

> The plurality of bodily parts is preferable to the domination of the uniform (1 Cor 12:12). The thorn in the flesh is a greater witness to the grace of God than the heavenly religious experience (2 Cor 12:1–9). In the four gospels, blindness is symbolic of lack of faith but in the letters of Paul and in Hebrews, it is faith that is blind (Rom 8:24, 2 Cor 5:7, Heb 11:1).

Hull, 2003, pp21–35

The Christian responses to equality are varied. While there is a profound sense of equality, how that is expressed in attitudes and approaches to the place of men and women, different races, and the place of disabled people in the Christian vision of life tends to vary.

Human value

In making human beings in the 'image and likeness of God' (Genesis 1:26) the dignity of humanity is evident. Human beings have the image of God within them – the *'imago dei'*. Christians hold that human beings are made for a relationship with God, and the Bible has many commandments about how human beings should treat each other and a requirement that human beings love each other as they are loved by God.

This informs Christian thinking about how important human lives are. The killing of life destroys the being made in God's image, and therefore good. It interrupts God's plan for that person and allows sin and the Devil to dominate. Nevertheless, there may be situations where a death is necessary. For instance, the preservation of life is important so self-defence can be justified. A **just war** may need to be fought when (among other conditions) all other alternatives have been ruled out, if there is some chance of success and if only proportionate force is used. Killing is nonetheless held to be wrong and indeed some Christians have adopted pacifist positions because they think it is such a strong prohibition there can be no exceptions. This forms the basis for the self-respect which all human beings have as well as the respect of others.

Self-sacrifice is also an important virtue in Christianity. Christ sacrificed himself for all humankind on the cross. In the Gospel he says that the greatest thing that someone can do is lay down their life for their friend. The giving of oneself for another is understood to be part of the life of discipleship, the way of Christ. In trying to be like Jesus Christians accept that the path may be difficult and they may be expected to give up their most valued possession, their life.

It is the possibility of such actions that sets human beings apart from all other creatures. This is not to say other animals have no value, but human beings especially have a divine destiny with God and a supreme responsibility to serve God and others. Of course, all of creation was made for God's purpose, so non-human life has some part to play in that purpose.

Activities

1. 'Killing humans is killing God.'

   Explain this view with reference to Christian beliefs about human value.

2. What would you say God-like behaviour is?

3. What characteristics might a God-like person have?

Key terms

Just war: a war that is deemed to be morally or theologically justifiable by established conditions.

Activities

1. There are many terrible things done by humanity. Do you think that human beings have lost their dignity or do they retain something sacred or holy despite the wrongdoing?

2. Examine what these texts suggest about the Biblical view of equality between men and women and what ethics might flow from them. Luke 8:1–3, Matthew 27:55–56, John 11:1–24, Matthew 5:25–33, 12:9–14, Luke 15, Acts 16:11–15, Philippians 4:2–3, Acts 18:2, Romans 16:1, Genesis 3:16, 1 Corinthians 11–14, Ephesians 5:23, 1 Timothy 2:8–15.

3. Research different Christian views of the role of women and relate these practices to the ideas expressed in this section.

Activities

1. Write your own definition of dignity. Working in groups, compare yours with others and agree on a common definition. Now compare that with different religious ideas of dignity.

2. Do you think dignity is something that should be earned by good deeds, or is it something that we have irrespective of what we do? Give reasons for your view.

Key terms

Hadith: the sayings of the Prophet Muhammad, as recounted by his contemporaries. The Hadith is a major source of Islamic law.

■ Muslim perspectives

Human nature and the human condition

In the Qur'an, which is commonly divided into 114 individually named chapters, or suras, sura 17:70 states:

> We have bestowed dignity on the progeny of Adam [...] and conferred on them special favours, above a great part of Our creation.

Sura 17:70, al-Isra

All human beings have dignity irrespective of who they are, what they are or what they do. Beyond this, as Mohammad Hashim Kamali argues in *The Dignity of Man*, God has also conferred reason (Kamali, 2002, p1). In other words, human dignity is not earned by moral behaviour, by doing good things, or behaving righteously, but is there from the moment of birth. Some Islamic scholars describe dignity as the right of every human being. It is a right which is conferred not by any honorific status in society (special role or position), but because of their human nature as children of Adam. Islam also specifically addresses the issue of religion. Dignity is conferred irrespective of the person's religion. To support this Kamali draws attention to the actions of the Prophet in rising at the passing funeral procession of a Jew. When challenged about this he refers to the humanity of the person emphasising the fundamental nature of the quality of dignity.

Equality and difference

While people are frequently referred to as God's servants, they are also described as God's beloved children in the **Hadith**. Kamali writes about dignity as, 'the basic unity in the creation of mankind, and its equality in the eyes of the Creator' (Kamali, 2002, p3).

The creation of human beings was unique in God's general act of creation of the heavens and the earth. His love for human beings is revealed in his command for the angels and Satan to bow down before Adam. A Muslim relates directly to God: 'Wherever you turn, there is the Face of God' (sura 2:115, al-Baqarah). Man is created in God's image and this is reflected in the higher powers given to man, such as speech.

Both men and women have an equal responsibility to follow Islam and women have many rights in Islam that Western women only received in the 20th century (for instance property ownership, right to make her own will, and keep her name after marriage). Nevertheless the status of women in Islam is a highly contentious topic. According the Dr Chris Hewer, Muslim women are entitled to education at all levels, entitled to engage in any business and may have control over their own earnings. While there seems to be permission for Muslim men to hit their wives (sura 4:34, an-Nisa) some schools of Islamic thought interpret the beating of women with any object as cruelty (Hewer, 2006, p130). Swiss Muslim academic Tariq Ramadan (b. 1962) argues that faithfulness to Islam has been misunderstood as meaning faithfulness to what was traditionally done in the culture or society, leading to discrimination towards women. Furthermore, some Muslim communities have remained silent about injustices carried out on women in the name of Islam (Ramadan, 2003, pp139–140). In other words, when people treat women differently in the name of Islam they are not in fact true to Islam, but confusing culture with religion.

Free will and fatalism

> The dignity of man is manifested, perhaps more than anything else, in his freedom of conscience, moral autonomy and judgement.

Kamali, 2002, p39

People's freedom of choice is a defining feature of their dignity and religious guidance, or laws, cannot overrule this freedom. That said certain caveats are attached. Words that amount to blasphemy, insult, slander or incitements to sin are punishable. Freedom is not without its consequences when used for the harm of others. This freedom is important as it empowers human moral autonomy. It gives people the authority to make a moral judgement on what they see and it is this faculty which then gives them the power to act or intervene where wrong is perceived to be done. Kamali writes that the teachings of the Qur'an and Sunnah …

> … confirm man's liberty of conscience as an inherent aspect of his dignity, and dignity as the basic right of every individual.

Kamali, 2002, p41

While human beings have freedom, God is all-powerful, all-knowing and intends for his will to be done. Hewer writes that there is an element of fatalism here. He notes the great **Sunni** scholar al-Ash'ari (874–936) developed a doctrine of attribution that said all power lies with God and God wills everything to happen. He has foreknowledge of everything. At the moment before a person acts he has responsibility over how that act is performed so is accountable to God. Muslims are taught to begin every act with the words 'In the name of God, the Merciful, the Compassionate' and believe that God will not allow them to be tempted beyond their means (Hewer, 2006, p83).

If a person is to be given responsibility then they must also be in a position to judge when to act. While the common good of the community is important in Islam, the individual is not 'totally subsumed by social purpose and interest', Kamali writes (Kamali, 2002, p43). Islam's teachings are addressed to the individual for the most part and while a person is instructed to obey those in government they are also required to dispute these rulers when deemed necessary.

The value of human life

Human beings, then, have infinite value in Islam and should not be harmed. If a single life is saved the whole of humanity is saved (Kamali,

Activities

1 Explain the different aspects of Muslim beliefs about freedom.

2 Compare your answer to Activity 1 with another religion's view of freedom.

Key terms

Sunni: one of the two main branches of Islam, commonly described as orthodox, and the most widely followed. The other main branch is Shia, with approximately 10 per cent of Muslims, though Shiites represent a majority in Iran.

2002, p21). Life is also sacred and for these reasons in times of war, great care should be shown to civilian life, especially those who are particularly vulnerable (children, the elderly, mothers, the sick, etc.). Life is God-given and only God can take life away without just cause. Physical abuse is also prohibited.

It is clear that the taking of life is not always completely prohibited as it may happen for instance in times of a just war or in self-defence, but even then only in proportion to that which is necessary. There is a moral responsibility to defend oneself, one's family and one's community, and this is known as a **lesser jihad**. The idea of human dignity and human status as having within it God's image prohibits the harm of a human in moral terms.

Activities

1 Do you think the most important thing about human beings is their ability to act freely? Give reasons for your answer.

2 Conduct research into the issue of equality in Islam and consider the extent to which it could be argued that cultural practices are undermining Islamic values.

Hindu perspectives

The value of human life

Hindu perspectives on the nature and value of human beings begin with an understanding of the divine or immortal soul within sentient life (the **Atman**) born and reborn in the cycle of rebirth. Every individual life – mineral, vegetable, animal or human – has a beginning and an end, a creation and a destruction which is part of the process of the world (Ramaswami Aiyar, 1965, p5). Every individual ego (*jivatman*) is at some stage of that process. The point at which a human is born is an especially important turning point. Human beings have, therefore, a special value.

There is something divine or immortal within human beings and other sentient creatures so they are special and the ultimate goal of all sentient creatures is union with God, the ultimate spirit. The value of the human body is instrumental and it makes possible the ultimate goal.

Free will and fatalism

Human beings are like other living creatures though they are sentient, that is to say they have higher mental faculties than other animals. In addition, they have moral freedom. They are able to choose whether to do good or evil and have responsibility for those decisions. This is an important feature of the law of **karma**. How they respond to their responsibility influences the nature of their rebirth through the law of karma. Good actions lead to pleasure and good things in the next life while bad actions lead to suffering and bad things in the next life. There is a sense of reciprocity: I may end up in your situation so I should care about you in your situation. Human beings then are both material and spiritual, but what matters most is the spiritual, the part that has been born before and will be reborn again. So human beings have special value or worth because they are an instrument by which the soul can be liberated from the body and the cycle of rebirth. Reincarnation into human form makes possible this transition.

The body has limitations as it seeks to regulate appetites and cravings. In fact the human body can lead to wrong or harm being done. In a very real sense the body can be made impure, abused by over-eating, drinking and sensual behaviour. Cleanliness and purity can be said to be part of Godliness. The cultivation of cleanliness leads to self-control and encourages virtuous behaviour. The body can encourage the pursuit of vices (such as gluttony, drunkenness or sensuality) and self-control is necessary to have power over the body's inclinations towards harm or wrong.

The belief that suffering is a part of life and that the life experienced now is the consequence of things done in the past, could suggest a kind of fatalism, a sense that everything now has been caused by what went before. However, human beings are fortunate to be in the position to determine how they respond to the current situation. They can choose how they act now.

Human nature and the human condition

The purpose of human beings is to seek as an end pleasure through good action, individual liberation and liberation of society, welfare and righteousness. Ultimately there is the possibility of gaining absolute freedom from the world and the merging of the individual immortal soul (Atman, or true self) with the universal absolute being or supreme soul (**Brahman** or **Paramatman**). Questions and disagreements remain within Hinduism about the extent to which the Atman of every human being is similar, or the same as Paramatman or the absolute soul of God. The human search for liberation is motivated by the unceasing cycle of birth and rebirth within which human beings are trapped. That existence is blighted then by suffering and death. The human condition is one from which to escape.

While there is much diversity within Hinduism the following general principles give an idea of the place of human beings in the universe. There is an overarching ethic which is the well-being of the human family and one must act for the good of that family. The self, then, is understood as a familial self, a self related to the whole human family, rather than an individualist self, as found frequently in Western thinking (Dhand, 2002, p366). The human person is understood as part of a web of family relationships.

Equality and difference

The human person is complex in Hinduism. A person's identity is affected by hierarchy, class, **caste** and sex. A moral person might be a man or woman, a simple worker, scholar, student or householder. An act in one situation may be right for one person but wrong for another person (Dhand, 2002, p352). Things are further complicated by the rich diversity which exists within Hinduism. There are many sources of the Hindu traditions and they rarely give moral principles (Dhand, 2002, p360).

The different castes that exist within traditional forms of Hinduism imply an inequality which seems incompatible with contemporary Western ideas of equality. David Smith writes in the Hinduism section of *Religions in the Modern World* that the caste system is not a publicly admitted form of hierarchy but remains very influential, with people saying it is comfortable to marry and socialise within their caste. A movement for the removal of caste privileges led by Indian scholar B. R. Ambedkar (1891–1956) ended with him and his 4 million 'untouchable' followers converting to Buddhism (Smith, 2002, p32). Smith writes

> ### Key terms
>
> **Brahman or Paramatman:** the universal absolute being or supreme soul.
>
> **Caste:** a hereditary social class among Hindus; stratified according to ritual purity.

that the former outcastes, the lowest caste, have given themselves the name *dalit*, meaning downtrodden, and they number 200 million. The suggestion that reincarnation offers the possibility of a return in a higher caste and that different castes perform different roles in society, remains a challenging and objectionable idea by modern standards.

Gender equality is also a contentious issue within Hinduism. On the one hand many women play an active and vigorous role in public life, while accepting arranged marriages as the norm. Women play a leading role in domestic religious life, tending the family shrine. Grandmothers teach children religious stories and rituals. Nevertheless, in religion and politics men retain leadership roles. There are great concerns about the practice of killing newborn girls in rural India because of the cost of dowries and the preference for boys to secure the family inheritance. There remains controversy over the practice of sati, the death by suicide of a wife at her husband's funeral by immolation. It is illegal in India but the practice continues (Smith, 2002, p32). These practices may be cultural in source, rather than religious, but the two seem to intermingle.

■ Buddhist perspectives

Human nature and the human condition

In Buddhism there is not the emphasis on the person having an individual value that is found in Western religious traditions. Harvey writes that there is no permanent 'I' or 'self'. The more attached we are to the self, the more we seek gratification or satisfaction and push aside others. So all selfish action towards others is rooted in a self-centredness.

The idea of 'not-self' does not mean that each of our personal histories or characters are denied but that they are linked by factors which are universal or common to all. Peter Harvey writes that the suffering we share in is the suffering that all share in. Each person is formed by combinations of universal factors.

For most lay-people the way to liberation is understood in terms of the five precepts: to abstain from killing (non-injury), stealing, misconduct of the senses, false speech and drinking intoxicating substances. The first precept (non-injury) directly concerns the importance of living beings:

> Laying aside violence in respect of all beings, both those which are still and those which move ... he should not kill a living creature, nor cause to kill, nor approve of others killing.

*quoted in **Harvey**, 2000, p69*

All sentient beings are in the cycle of birth and rebirth and so the non-injury precept applies to all such beings. This precept has a powerful impact on many ethical issues related to the taking of life.

'The Noble Eightfold Path' – an important guide to Buddhist ethics – is a profoundly ethical path to enlightenment. Within it, the eight elements include 'right resolve', 'right action' and 'right livelihood', all of which relate to moral virtue or, more specifically, virtuous living (Buddhist ethics is often described as 'virtue ethics', rather than either deontological or teleological). By following the Noble Eightfold Path a person can become a noble person. A noble person is one who has been changed permanently by spiritual insights and may be reborn into a lower and ultimately higher heaven. Each stage is progress towards the final goal of enlightenment. Following the ethics of the Noble Eightfold

Activities

1. How is human life valued in Hindu thinking?

2. To what extent are Hindu ideas of equality compatible with the caste system and the treatment of women?

3. Is it possible to distinguish cultural practices from religion?

Path is principally about reaching the final goal (Harvey, 2000, p41). This progress towards perfection involves purity of mind and of view, and the abandonment of attachment. Holy life is lived for the final goal.

Free will and fatalism

Human lives are special because they have the possibility of reaching enlightenment. This is because of their ability to make free choices and their capacity of understanding (Harvey, 2000, p150). This is central to the law of karma because the intentions and actions that we choose have a causal link to the next life: what we do in this life affects how we exist in the next. Human beings can make moral and spiritual progress – they are special, and they are free to choose how to act. They have responsibility for their actions (and consequences flow from their actions because of the law of karma), but also they have the possibility of causing their own moral and spiritual progression towards enlightenment because they are free to act. That freedom means that change is possible for a person. A human being is not locked into evil or good. Change is always possible if a person chooses to go after it.

Equality

There is in Buddhism an idea of equality of all human beings. All humans can seek enlightenment and all bring about good and bad karma by their actions. So treatment of other human beings should be impartial (Harvey, 2000, p37). Buddha rejected the idea that you could be born into a caste. One could only become either an outcaste or a **Brahmin** by actions, not birth. He argued that the human race was one species, not four, and that caste was not divinely ordained (Harvey, 2000, pp110–111).

However, as regards gender equality, Harvey explains that most Buddhist traditions have what he calls a spiritual glass ceiling, which means women cannot become a full **Buddha** but must be reincarnated as a man first. There are examples of women Bodhisattvas – enlightened, or wise, beings – being transformed into men before they become Buddha. Occasionally the Mahayana tradition (one of two main Buddhist traditions, the other being Theravada) accepts female Buddhas. Historically the role of nuns has been to some extent as juniors to male monks. In some traditions nuns would not be included in the philosophy and logic training, something thought to be important for monks. He argues the role of ordained women is stronger today than it was (Harvey, 2000, pp409–410).

In Buddhism, disability may be thought of as a consequence of a past action in a past life. This suggestion is considered outrageous in Western thinking though that is usually because of a misunderstanding of the nature of karma and associating cause and effect with punishment too simplistically. It is important to remember that all the life of all human beings, with the joys and hardships of life, are a consequence of karma. So this does not undermine the idea of equality of all human beings. In Buddhism all people seek escape from the suffering of this life, and all seek ultimate bliss. Human life is not something to remain in (except if you wish to help others reach enlightenment before making that journey yourself).

The value of human life

This differs from the Judaeo-Christian idea that human beings have value in themselves as the image of God. The value of human beings

> ### ■ Key terms
>
> **Brahmin:** a higher caste, holy, man; not the same as Brahman, or supreme soul.
>
> **Buddha:** the title given to the founder of Buddhism, Siddartha Gautama (*c.*563–*c.*483 BC), but also in the sense of **full Buddha**, a person who has achieved enlightenment.

in Buddhism is more instrumental. Human nature offers the chance to reach enlightenment; it is the possibility of reaching that goal which lends value to human nature. Nevertheless, human life is more precious than anything else in the world. Master Hsing Yun (1927–), a renowned Chinese monk, writes:

> Whenever we break any of the Five Precepts of Buddhism, we have violated some other sentient being. Whenever we kill anything, we violate that being at the deepest level possible. Killing, thus, is an action that must be avoided by all Buddhists.

Yun, 1998, p82

Killing senselessly is bad, killing intentionally is worse, and the killing of sentient life is worse still. The *Mahaprajnaparamita Shastra* (*The Great Treatise on the Perfection of Wisdom*, translated into Chinese in 402–05) says:

> If one should decide to kill a sentient being while knowing full well that that being is a sentient being, then one will create karma of the body and defile one's inner moral nature.

quoted in Yun, 1998, p83

In not killing, a Buddhist becomes more sensitive to the needs and feelings of all sentient beings, and expresses an understanding that all life is one. By killing another human one must look with anxiety to rebirth. The *Shurangama Sutra* (one of the main texts of Chinese Buddhism, translated around 705) says:

> Because there is transgression, there is birth. Because there is birth, there is death. Birth and death arise from transgression. When all transgressions have completely ceased, then there is wisdom.

quoted in Yun, 1998, p85

Despite this, moral rules or principles are not approached in quite the same way as Western religious traditions. Harvey writes that:

> Buddhism ... is generally gradualist in approach, so while it has ethical norms which all should follow from a sense of sympathy with fellow beings (such as not killing living beings), others only apply to those who are ready for them ...

Harvey, 2000, p51

Nevertheless Professor Damien Keown argues that on the whole Buddhist ethics is mainly absolutist and objective (Keown, 1996, p32).

■ Sikh perspectives

Human nature and the human condition

In Sikh thinking the goal of human life is closer union with God, to merge one's soul (*Atman*) with God (*Paramatma*). This is done through love, devotion and service. Spirituality is linked with social responsibility. To be a disciple of the **Guru** one must turn towards God, and away from selfishness. W. Owen Cole writes that this is an inner transformation away from lust, covetousness, attachment, wrath and pride, and towards truth, contentment, kindness, karma, charity and ablution (Cole, 2004, p87). This is what it means to be a Sikh. Clearly there are vices which

Activities

1. How do Buddhist perspectives of the value of human life differ from Judaeo-Christian understandings?

2. How significant is that difference?

Key terms

Guru: a spiritual leader or teacher.

human beings can be drawn towards which will lead to harm being done to oneself and others, and there are virtues which if pursued will lead to good being done to others. The physical, material world is a world (among all the worlds, physical and non-physical) in which God is present.

Free will and fatalism

For the human being, what is done in this life has consequences which go beyond this life, 'Forsake evil and practice virtue, so you shall obtain the real thing' (AG 814 in Cole, 2004, p88). Human beings have the freedom to act morally or immorally, but there are consequences in the next life. Virtuous living can lead to union with God and freedom from rebirth. Viceful living can lead to rebirth and can, through the law of karma, bring about negative consequences leading to suffering for the person who has done wrong.

God is involved in human action, the Divine Will (**Hukam**) by which all forms were created. Cole writes that there is the suggestion of predestination in this belief:

> By the Will all life is formed and, by that Will, all life is exalted. The Will determines what is high and what is low; the Will grants all joy and suffering. Some are blessed by the Will, others migrate from birth to birth. All are within the Will, none stands apart. (AG 1)

Predestination is not a judgement of eternal damnation, Cole argues, but simply the consequence of the path chosen (Cole, 2004, p50).

> ### Key terms
>
> **Hukam:** the Divine Will by which all forms were created.

Equality

Human beings should not be divided or discriminated against but treated as one class, which includes everyone, men and women. The caste system is rejected in favour of a single view of human beings, that of the householder (someone, in this usage, who works hard for their living). Human value does not come from caste, but from the possibility of human moral behaviour and the possibility of enlightenment.

> What power has caste? It is righteousness that is tested? High-caste pride is like poison held in the hand, from eating it a man dies. (AG 124)

> Recognise God's light within everyone and do not ask their caste as there is no caste in the next world. (AG 349)

*both in **Cole**, 2004, p89*

Human beings are equal and have worth because of their ability to do good and because of the possibility that human beings can become enlightened. The human body itself must be preserved and protected and so Sikhs abstain from alcohol, meat, drugs and smoking. The temple of the body must be preserved to serve others effectively. The spiritual progress that human beings can make leads to rebirth and reincarnation until union with God is secured.

Guru Gobind Singh (1666–1708) bestowed blessings on disabled people and encouraged them to overcome their disabilities. He also taught a number of his blind disciples the art of music and made them expert at playing instruments. Sikh sacred texts suggest that disability does not preclude human spiritual growth, just as being fully able-bodied is no assistance in spiritual and moral growth. There are people who can see and hear who are also deaf and blind to the truth.

The value of human life

Sikhism teaches, then, that human beings are valuable in terms of the good they can do, and the union with God that is possible for them, and so the body has an instrumental value as a tool for both these goals. Sikhism promotes a non-violent approach to life as other people also have the potential to do good to others and reach union with God, though violence can be justified to protect the vulnerable. Historically Gurus had to fight for religious freedom. Taking of life can be justified to protect human life that is unjustly threatened and to protect religious freedom.

The nature and value of human beings in religion

Fatalism and human freedom

Dignity and freedom seem to be closely related. Human beings have dignity and that is expressed through their free actions. If they are not free to act their dignity is limited, perhaps denied. We cannot be given moral responsibility for our actions if we have no freedom. However, if God is all-knowing, is that freedom meaningful?

Western religious traditions traditionally identify omniscience – all knowingness – as a quality of God. This is found in biblical sources (Psalm 139, Hebrews 4:13) and other important Western philosophers, including medieval Italian philosopher Anselm (1033–1109) and French philosopher Descartes (1596–1650). God knows all the facts. However, if God knows what someone is about to do and what choices they will make throughout their life, in what sense are they truly free? How is their freedom meaningful? Omniscience seems to be incompatible with human free will. This argument was expressed by the early American philosophical theologian Jonathan Edwards (1703–58):

> [I]f there by a full, certain and infallible Foreknowledge of the future existence of the volitions of moral agents, then there is a certain infallible and indissoluble connection between those events and that Foreknowledge; and … therefore … those events are necessary events; being infallibly and indissolubly connected with that, whose existence already is, and so is now necessary, and cannot but have been.

Mavrodes, 2000, p238, quoting Edwards, 1745

Mavrodes explains this in this way: if I am writing this book today, I think I am choosing freely to type these words into my computer, but God, who is omniscient, knew yesterday that I would be writing it today. If the writing was known to be going to happen yesterday then it is not something I can avoid. This argument is logically consistent and leads some to a position of theological determinism (predestination). The belief is that God knows the future choices, but it is not that God causes those choices to be taken, though this still seems to make freedom somewhat less significant. Others claim that God cannot know the future choices of human beings and is not fully omniscient.

The 6th-century Christian philosopher Boethius (480–c.524) and St Thomas Aquinas both argued that God was timeless – existing outside time and with knowledge that is not in any time – and consequently God does not know what *is to happen in the future*, being outside time (Zagzebski, 1997, p293). God exists beyond time and space and perceives the facts of the universe from outside the chronology in which we live. Another way of explaining this is with the suggestion that the knowledge

God has of us is informed by the choices we make. God perceives the decisions we make tomorrow and that informs God's understanding today. Another solution comes from the Spanish theological academic Luis de Molina (1535–1600). He uses the idea of a middle knowledge to explain how God can secure infallible knowledge on contingent future human acts. He argues that God knows what any possible free creature would choose in any possible circumstance. God knows the entire future including all free human acts (Zagzebski, 1997, p293).

Even if God's knowledge of future choices is compatible with free will, what does it say about the dignity of human life, of which freedom is an expression? It makes God seem very different indeed from human beings. The idea that God is omnipotent, omniscient and omnibenevolent (all loving) are also features that make God far different from human beings.

Some Protestant Churches hold the view that God has already decided who will be saved and who will not. This idea, which originates in St Paul's letter to the Romans, is called **predestination**:

> And we know that in all things God works for the good of those who love him, who have been called according to his purpose. For those God foreknew he also predestined to be conformed to the likeness of his Son, that he might be the firstborn among many brothers. And those he predestined, he also called; those he called, he also justified; those he justified, he also glorified.

Romans 8:28–30

St Augustine's writing on the Divine Election suggests predestination: 'The potter has authority over the clay from the same lump to make one vessel for honour and another for contempt' (*Sermon* 26 xii, 13). The Protestant reformer John Calvin (1509–64) described predestination as, 'the eternal decree of God, by which he determined that he wished to make of every man. For he does not create everyone in the same condition, but ordains eternal life for some and eternal damnation for others' (John Calvin, *Institutes*, 1559; quoted in McGrath, 2006, pp381–382).

The idea that God decides who receives salvation and who doesn't at creation suggests that humans don't have free will with regard to their moral or religious behaviour. Salvation is not earned because of something a human being does. This belief has significance in the debate about whether human beings save themselves by their actions or whether they are saved by God's grace alone. As regards the ethical ramifications of such a view, the notion that human beings aren't **autonomous moral agents** raises a number of problems. If you aren't free, how can you be morally responsible for your actions? How can you then be punished for those actions?

The psychologist B. F. Skinner (1904–90) argued that our ideas of dignity and freedom are widely misplaced and that in truth we have neither, as our choices were far more determined than we thought. He thought that he was able to demonstrate through experiments that we act in accordance to the environment in which we live. His thinking is important not only in psychology but also in the education of children. This **behaviourist** thinking suggests that human beings are subject to their social environment, rather than their will. So the knowledge that our actions are perhaps caused by our nature, rather than a true choice, undermines the notion of freedom (Skinner, 1971).

Key terms

Predestination: the belief that one's actions and eventual fate are already determined before one is born.

Autonomous moral agents: the idea that humans are beings capable of free moral decision-making.

Behaviourist: in psychology, behaviourism can be described as the theory that human and animal behaviour can be explained in terms of conditioning, without appeal to thoughts or feelings, and that psychological disorders are best treated by altering behaviour patterns.

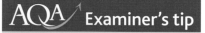

Examiner's tip

Apart from God's omniscience, there are two main constraints on human freedom:

1. Determinism in physics. If nature is causally determined (and for science to work, we generally assume that it is), then maybe brains are too.

2. To be free, the 'I', or self, has to exist in the first place. Many neuroscientists argue that the self is just an illusion produced by the brain's hardware. Perhaps these problems will be overcome at some point, but you cannot just assume that they *aren't* problems.

If indeed human beings do not have freedom, either because their actions are already known by God before they occur, or because they are simply the product of our social environment, then moral responsibility becomes a problem. How can someone be blameworthy or praiseworthy for what they do, if what they do is caused by external factors? Can we really talk about morality at all once freedom has gone? This means that philosophical and theological arguments for moral freedom are important. They raise fundamental questions about human nature, about what it means to be a human being, and what we mean by morality.

Human beings do still seem to surprise each other by their actions, and not always in a bad way. A person can feel as though on occasion they are having to deliberate between courses of actions and are making choices which could easily have gone the other way. You can have a sense of freedom and a sense of responsibility for your actions. Whether that sense reflects the truth is more difficult to be sure of.

Equality among human beings and with non-human life

Within the Eastern religious traditions (Hinduism, Buddhism and Sikhism) there are various responses to the question of equality. In all three religions there are powerful concepts of unity and equality. However, in practice there are difficulties.

In terms of caste, while it remains a central concept in Hinduism (excepting that some Hindus are actively opposed to it), both Buddhism and Sikhism contain strong rejections of the caste system, and Sikhism in particular partly defines itself by this rejection.

Gender equality is a different matter and there remain tensions within both Hinduism and Buddhism. For Buddhism the biggest challenge seems to be a tradition of spiritual ordering, which would mean not accepting that women can reach enlightenment without becoming male first. In Hinduism cultural practices of inequality which seem to undermine women's status seem to be integrated into religion.

Western religious traditions also contain a mixture of powerful concepts of equality before God, while at the same time upholding practices which seem to give more authority to men. The ideas of the status and role of women in Islam seem unrecognised, and, in varying degrees, in both Judaism and Christianity, authority figures are dominated by a patriarchal idea of religious leader. However, there is also a picture of quite substantial change in the last few decades, with more Christian denominations ordaining women, and both conservative and reform Jews rethinking their approaches to the role of women. There seems to be some significant movement across the Western religious traditions in responses to a modern idea of equality.

All religions profess a concern for the sick and those who are typically socially excluded, so by extension this can include disabled people. In some religions there is the development of a theology of the disabled which challenges older and arguably outdated conceptions of the place of 'the disabled' in society.

It is difficult to separate religion from the cultural context within which it exists. There is clearly an interplay between religious ideas influencing social practices, and vice versa, when it comes to the issue of equality.

Are human lives more important than animal life?

Religion seems always to place human life above other animal life forms. In Hinduism, Buddhism and Sikhism it is human beings who

Activities

1. Consider the view that humans are not as free as they think. What evidence for this can you think of?

2. What consequences would the lack of freedom have for moral responsibility?

can reach nirvana, enlightenment or God. In Judaism, Christianity and Islam, human beings are the only earthly beings who have such a special relationship with God. Animal life, on the other hand, is not without value (see Chapters 10 and 11) but never does an animal have the same status or greater than a human being.

Animals aside, within the human family there are some subtle differences in attitudes towards the value of human life. Few religions seem to have escaped the patriarchal cultures within which they have developed and some could be accused of having ideas which, by modern moral standards, need to change. Indeed, in all religions there seem to be considerable pressures and movements to further make real the ideals of equality found within each tradition.

Chapter summary

- Religions have a view of humanity and what role or purpose it has.
- Humans are distinct from other living creatures because they either have a divine destiny, or they offer a chance to reach eternal bliss.

Jewish perspectives

- God created humans in his image but this image and likeness may be in terms of a divine quality or a similar behaviour.
- Maimonides argued that God and human beings were alike as they were thinking creatures with the ability to distinguish between good and evil.
- They have freedom to act in a morally good or bad way – fatalism is rejected.
- Human desire to satisfy personal needs is not bad in itself but can lead to wrong actions.
- God has male and female qualities, and men and women have different but equal roles.
- In recent decades both reform and conservative Judaism have changed their views on the role of women in the synagogue and there is some debate in orthodox Judaism.
- These rational, moral and creative features of human beings, this image of God which they reflect, mean they have a dignity or value which makes human life special – to be loved as oneself.

Christian perspectives

- The Bible teaches that people should love God, and love your neighbour as yourself.
- Human beings have a special nature and value in all creation:
  - a natural nature in terms of rational thought and moral decision-making powers
  - a supernatural nature in terms of their ultimate purpose and destiny to be with God.
- St Augustine says the dignity of the human comes from its thinking intellect and moral will.
- In Genesis, Adam and Eve exercise free will in choosing to eat the forbidden fruit.
- Human beings who live their lives following Christ become Christ-like, or sons of God.

- The value of human beings is a gift given out of love which then reaches out from human beings to other human beings, leading humans to kingly status. In the figure of Christ dignity leads to service.

- Humans can choose to do ill, rather than good, and have a need to be saved and redeemed by God.

- Some Protestant traditions hold that the dignity that human beings had is largely lost due to sin.

- In Christianity, all are one in Christ Jesus, although other texts raise problems for the idea of equality. Christian Churches respond differently to the possibility of women being involved in ministry.

- Christian texts express mixed ideas about the place of disabled people but seem to appreciate diversity.

- From this flows much of Christian thinking about how important human lives are. The killing of life destroys the being that God has both made good and in God's image.

- God made humankind as a sacred animal, and so humans have dignity – human beings are made in the 'image and likeness of God'.

- Humans are distinct from animals as they may have a personal relationship with God.

- They have the capacity of self-sacrifice for another, an ultimate act of goodness.

Muslim perspectives

- All human beings have dignity from the moment of birth by virtue of their human nature as children of Adam.

- Human beings are God's beloved children.

- Human dignity is the basic unity in the creation of mankind, and represents equality in the eyes of the Creator.

- Man is created in God's image and so has speech and moral freedom.

- Muslim women are entitled to education at all levels, entitled to engage in any business and may have control over their own earnings.

- Some argue that faithfulness to Islam has been misunderstood as meaning faithfulness to what was traditionally done in the culture or society, leading to discrimination towards women.

- Human beings have freedom of conscience and yet God is all powerful, all knowing and intends for God's will to be done, indicating an element of fatalism.

- Human beings, then, have infinite value in Islam and should not be harmed. If a single life is saved the whole of humanity is saved.

- The taking of life is not always completely prohibited, such as in self-defence, but even then only in proportion to that which is necessary.

Hindu perspectives

- Sentient beings have a divine or immortal soul within sentient life (the Atman) born and reborn in the cycle of rebirth.

- Human life is important in the cycle as a step towards union with God.

- Human beings are able to choose whether to do good or evil and have responsibility for those decisions.

- Human beings have special value or worth because they are an instrument by which the soul can be liberated from the body and the cycle of rebirth.

- The human body can lead to wrong or harm being done as it can be made impure or abused by over-eating, drinking and sensual behaviour.

- From human birth there is the possibility of gaining absolute freedom from the world and the merging of the individual immortal soul.

- A person's identity is affected by hierarchy, class, caste and gender.

- The self, then, is understood as a familial self, a self related to the whole human family, rather than an individualist self, as found frequently in Western thinking.

- Human beings, then, have free will to act and the possibility, through the pursuit of purity and virtuous behaviour, of reaching towards Brahman, the universal soul.

- The caste system undermines the idea of equality and there have been movements against it.

- Women have important roles in domestic religious life, but in public life men have leadership roles, and practices such as sati and the killing of baby girls (in preference for boys) remain in rural areas.

Buddhist perspectives

- There is no permanent 'I' or 'self' – the suffering we share in is the suffering that all share in.

- Human lives are special because they have the possibility of reaching enlightenment.

- By following the Noble Eightfold Path a person can become a noble person.

- The way to liberation is understood in terms of the five precepts, the first of which is to abstain from killing (non-injury).

- A noble person is one who has been changed permanently by spiritual insights and may be reborn into a lower and ultimately higher heaven.

- Humans have the ability to make free choices and have a capacity of understanding.

- They have responsibility for their actions (and consequences flow from their actions because of the law of karma).

- Change is always possible if a person chooses to go after it.

- All humans can seek enlightenment but most Buddhist traditions have a spiritual glass ceiling for women.

- Disability may be thought of as a consequence of a past action in a past life.

- The value of human beings is more instrumental as human nature offers the chance to reach enlightenment.

- Killing is an action that must be avoided by all Buddhists.

- In not killing, a Buddhist becomes more sensitive to the needs and feelings of all sentient beings, and expresses an understanding that all life is one.

Sikh perspectives

- The goal of human life is closer union with God, to merge one's soul (*Atman*) with God (*Paramatma*) which is found through love, devotion and service.

- There should be an inner transformation away from lust, covetousness, attachment, wrath and pride, and towards truth, contentment, kindness, karma, charity and ablution.

- Virtuous living can lead to union with God and freedom from rebirth.
- Viceful living can lead to rebirth and can, through the law of karma, bring about negative consequences leading to suffering for the person who has done wrong.
- God is involved in human action as the Divine Will (Hukam) suggesting predestination.
- Human beings should not be divided or discriminated against but treated as one class, which includes everyone, men and women.
- Human beings are equal and have worth because of their ability to do good and because of the possibility that human beings become enlightened.
- The human body itself must be preserved and protected.
- Sikhism promotes a non-violent approach to life as other people also have the potential to do good to others and reach union with God.
- Violence can be justified to protect the vulnerable and religious freedom.

Questions about the nature and value of human beings
Fatalism and human freedom

- Dignity and freedom are closely related.
- Western religious traditions see omniscience as a quality of God.
- If God knows what I am about to do and what choices I make throughout my life, in what sense am I truly free?
- I think I am choosing freely to act but an omniscient God knew before what I would do.
- If God cannot know the future choices of human beings he is not fully omniscient.
- God may be timeless, with knowledge of all that is from a perspective beyond time, so human freedom is real.
- Perhaps God knows what any possible free creature would choose in any possible circumstance so freedom is real.
- Some Protestant Churches hold the view that God has already decided who will be saved and who will not (predestination).
- This implies humans do not have free will with regard to their moral or religious behaviour.
- B. F. Skinner argued that our ideas of dignity and freedom were widely misplaced and that our choices were determined by environmental factors.
- Is our sense of freedom reliable?

Equality among human beings and with non-human life

- Hinduism, Buddhism and Sikhism have powerful concepts of unity and equality but caste challenges this idea in Hinduism and Buddhism, while Sikhism directly rejects this.
- Gender equality is a problem for Buddhism which suggests that women must first be reincarnated as men before reaching enlightenment.
- Islam, Judaism and Christianity all seem to have difficulties implementing the idea of equality to the role of women in religious authority.

- It is unclear whether cultural patriarchal tendencies are influencing religion (or vice versa).

Are human lives more important than animal life?

- Religion places human life above other animal life forms, but for different reasons.

- Within the human family there are some subtle differences towards the value of human life.

- Patriarchal culture influences religious ideas, and some of those ideas, by modern moral standards, need to change.

Further reading

Singer's argument for the equality of animals is very helpful for examining in depth the question of whether humans are special:

Singer, P., *Practical Ethics*, Cambridge University Press, 1993, pp55–82

Chapter 3 in Glover's book is a great exploration of the sanctity of life:

Glover, J., *Causing Death and Saving Lives*, Penguin, 1990, pp39–57

More generally a consideration of religion and ethics in this book is helpful:

Pojman, L., *Ethics, Discovering Right and Wrong*, US Military Academy, 2002, pp194–210

For those looking at Buddhist ethics, this is an indispensable guide:

Harvey, P., *An Introduction to Buddhist Ethics*, Cambridge University Press, 2000

while for Christianity this is useful:

Hoose, B., *Christian Ethics*, Cassell, 1998, pp95–109

and for Judaism:

Sherwin, B. L., *Jewish Ethics for the Twenty-First Century*, Syracuse University Press, 2001, pp1–13

This is another favourite book, and in particular two sections of this excellent book are useful for this topic: 'Christian ethics and ethnicity' for issues to do with race and 'The status of women' for a detailed discussion about Christian responses to women and equality.

Crook, R., *Introduction to Christian Ethics*, Prentice Hall, 2002, pp172–189 and pp190–207

This book has two relevant sections in particular that are useful for exploring Sikh attitudes to the nature and value of human life, 'The human condition in Sikhism' and 'Ethical teachings'.

Cole, O., *Understanding Sikhism*, Dunedin Academic Press, 2004, pp54–59 and pp87–104

In this chapter you have:

- considered different religious teachings on the nature and value of human life, including in particular: human nature and the human condition, free will and fatalism, equality and the value of human life

- evaluated some of these perspectives in terms of their ethical implications.

8 Abortion

By the end of this chapter you will:

■ be familiar with the technical language associated with abortion

■ have considered different arguments associated with the value of potential and real life

■ have considered the ethical implications of conflicts of interest between the mother and the child and the doctrine of double effect

■ have considered different religious and philosophical arguments about abortion

■ have examined a number of issues arising from abortion.

Key terms

Abortion: the deliberate termination (ending) of a pregnancy, usually before the foetus is 24 weeks old.

Women's rights: freedoms and liberties guaranteed to women in law.

Key questions

1 What does it mean to claim that life is sacred?
2 If a pregnant woman is killed, and her unborn child also, how many murders have there been, and why?
3 Is a foetus a person or a potential person, and how does your answer affect the rights it should have if at all?
4 When a mother's interests conflict with a foetus's interests, whose interests should be prioritised?
5 Should abortion be available on demand, only in special circumstances, or under no circumstances? To what extent should the legal situation mirror the moral principles?

Introduction

Abortion means the deliberate ending of life after the fertilisation of the human ovum and before birth. Today, abortion is common for a number of reasons: sex is seen as being more for pleasure than procreation, women have a greater social and legal status, low child mortality has reduced the need for so many children, and foetal abnormalities can be detected. Abortion is commonplace in many countries, with tens of millions of abortions taking place each year. According to Department of Health data in 2006 there were over 193,700 abortions in England and Wales, the vast majority of which were conducted under 13 weeks' gestation. The proportion of women having abortions in England and Wales is increasing.

Although it is legal in many countries, its morality is disputed. Religious organisations such as the Roman Catholic Church campaign against the availability of abortion, while **women's rights** groups campaign for greater access.

Important aspects of the ethical dimensions in the abortion debate include the question of the status of the human being at different stages from conception to birth, the issue of conflict between the interests of the baby and the mother, and the question of the impact of public policy, such as the legal prohibition, on society at large.

The value of potential and real life

> To my mind life begins at the moment of conception … Conception is the magic moment.

> *John Grigg in the* Guardian, *29 October 1973, from Glover, 1977, p119*

> What could ever be a sufficient reason for excusing in any way the direct murder of the innocent (directam innocentis necem)?

> *Pope Pius XI quoted in Childress and Macquarrie, 1986, p163*

I do not believe a fertilized ovum is a human life in the commonsense meaning of the term: I believe human life begins at birth. Or more technically, when a foetus is sufficiently developed to be capable of living if removed from the mother's womb. That human life begins at the moment of conception is a religious tenet that makes no claim to scientific truth.

Dee Wells in the Guardian, *29 October 1973, from Glover, 1977, p119*

The status of human life between conception and birth is central to the abortion debate. While some form of life is clearly present at conception, whether that form of life should get the full protection of the law is disputed. Not all human tissue is a *person*, a full human being. Living cells such as human cancer cells are not persons. A baby born with no brain may be a human being, but arguably it isn't a human person. A human person develops attributes throughout its life.

- When should full human rights status be conferred?
- When should human life be afforded the status of a human being, a member of the human species?
- Should status increase incrementally as the **embryo** and **foetus** becomes more like a born human being, or should it be bound to a certain point such as the point of conception, the presence of the **primitive streak**, **viability** or birth?

Conception is the point at which the unique selection of genetic information is present and, if allowed to continue and successful in development, will go on to be a unique human being (notwithstanding the precariousness of the pregnancy process). In 1869, Pope Pius IX declared that a foetus is a human person from the moment of conception. This has become the basis for Roman Catholic Christian teaching on abortion that to kill a foetus is to murder a human person.

Critics of this position argue that the fertilised egg is too different from anything that we normally recognise as a person to be called the same thing. In her article 'A defence of abortion' (1971), Judith Jarvis Thompson accepts that there is continuous development in foetal growth, but suggests that there is a point at which it is not a human being. There is a continuous growth from acorn to oak tree, but an acorn is not an oak tree; just as a **fertilised ovum** – a newly implanted clump of cells – is not a person. In his 1977 book *Causing Death and Saving Lives* Jonathan Glover writes that to call a foetus at the point of conception a person stretches the term beyond normal boundaries (p123).

Others have identified the presence of the primitive streak, on the fourteenth day after fertilisation, as the point at which a unique human being can be said to exist, albeit in potential form. The primitive streak provides the structure around which embryonic structures organise and align themselves. Up until that point it is not clear whether one individual or more than one individual will form, and at this point it becomes clear which cells will go on to form the placenta and which go on to form the human embryo. Thompson's and Glover's observations could still be made about the foetus at this stage.

Consciousness may be suggested as a definition of **personhood**. Consciousness cannot be applied to all living tissue, as it implies sensory experiences, the ability to feel pleasure and pain. However, consciousness would include many animals, and most would argue that animals are not persons in the same sense as humans are. The presence of rationality, and our ability to develop complex language and make complex tools, are

AQA Examiner's tip

Do not get anecdotal with abortion questions and just tell stories. Focus on:

1. The concept of personhood/ when a person becomes a person.

2. The question of rights and duties. At what stage does a foetus have a right to life)? Can right to goods (such as an uninterrupted career, or economic stability) outweigh any right to life in the foetus? What are the duties of parents (and others) towards a foetus? Can any being have rights without duties?

3. Religion-specific principles such as the sanctity of life principle).

Key terms

Embryo: an unborn human baby (especially in the first eight weeks), after implantation but before the development of organs.

Foetus: an unborn human baby after eight weeks.

Primitive streak: the faint streak which is the earliest trace of the embryo in the fertilised ovum of a higher vertebrate, often regarded as day 14.

Viability: in the context of abortion, the point at which the developing foetus/child becomes capable of living outside the womb. A viable ovum/embryo is one that has the potential to develop into an adult organism.

Fertilised ovum: a female reproductive cell which has been fertilised by a male reproductive cell (sperm).

Consciousness: a state of being awake, aware of, or sensitive to one's surroundings.

Personhood: the ethical quality or human condition which denotes a morally significant or valuable individual being.

distinctive features of personhood. However, studies of chimpanzees and dolphins show that many higher animals use complex communication and can make tools with which to manipulate their environments. Perhaps self-consciousness or self-awareness defines a human person. This includes a sense of our own past and future. However, very young babies are not self-aware in this sense, and yet very few people would argue that killing a baby is not the same as killing a human. It could be argued that the foetus is a potential person, but this does not necessarily imply that full legal status should be awarded on the basis of what it has the potential to be. A potential victory is not the same as a victory. A potential person is not equal to a person.

Others have argued that viability is the point at which human personhood should be recognised. Viability means when the foetus can survive a birth and exist independent of the mother. This used to be referred to as quickening, when the mother first felt the foetus move although now first-movement feeling and viability are not connected. There are two objections to viability. First, the age which the foetus can survive outside the womb is reducing as medical technology progresses. In other words, the moral judgement is made on the basis of technological ability, rather than anything inherent to the foetus. Second, there are many people who are dependent on continual medical assistance, such as dialysis, in order to survive. We consider them to be persons despite their medical conditions. Also, even healthy born human babies would not survive without adult aid.

Mary Anne Warren (1991, p313) argues that, 'birth, rather than some earlier point, marks the beginning of true moral status'. She argues that if a foetus is a person, then sperm and ovum are persons. Birth provides a clear boundary. However, Glover rejects this argument, because of the similarity between later foetuses and premature babies. Birth marks a clear stage in the process of coming into the world, and presents a stage of recognition by others that the baby is an individual. However, it seems more reasonable to base the moral value of a human being on something inherent about the human being rather than the recognition of others.

Activities

1 When is human life a person with a right to life? (Consider the strengths of the arguments you have read for each of these positions and your own views before coming to a conclusion.)

   a At the point of conception?

   b Once the primitive streak is present (and you know how many individuals there will be and which cells will form the placenta and which will form the embryo)?

   c When the embryo has consciousness or brain activity?

   d When the foetus is viable (can live outside the womb independent of the mother)?

   e At the point of birth?

2 A person is a being that deserves protection under the law equal to that of a born human. Examine this list and decide which should be given the status as persons and which should not:

A baby boy; a foetus; a baby born with no head; a chimpanzee or great ape; ET, the extra-terrestrial; a deranged psychopath who is unable to tell good from bad; someone in a permanent vegetative state (PVS) kept alive by a life-support machine; someone with severe brain damage; someone who has severe Alzheimer's disease; conjoined twins, who share all major organs except the brain; sperm; a dolphin.

   a Which caused the most disagreement, and why do you think this was?

   b Does the ability to think make a difference?

   c Does the ability to make moral decisions make a difference?

   d How might it be argued that some animals are moral persons?

The definition of personhood is unresolved, as is agreement over the point at which a potential human being becomes a full human being. Peter Vardy and Paul Grosch (1994, p155) note many attempts at drawing a dividing line at a particular point in the foetus's development – to indicate that before this point the foetus is tissue with potential and after this point a person – but there is no easy way of drawing the line with certainty. In his 1985 report *Is the Human Embryo a Person?* John Gallagher asks us to recognise that change is gradual. If an embryo is *x* at one time and James at another time, then there will be a time when it is part *x* and part James. While personhood does not provide a clear solution to the abortion debate, the moral status of the foetus is crucial. In an introductory book on Christian ethics – in a section called 'The human person' (1998) – Joseph Selling has argued that if a being qualifies as a person, then it has a direct moral standing with rights, and others have a duty towards it. Whether that duty extends to full human status remains in dispute.

■ The life of the mother versus the life of the child

A pregnancy, and a growing foetus, have an enormous impact on the mother. Not only does it cause physiological and emotional changes, it also places the mother's body under enormous pressure and has significant health risks attached. In the past, when healthcare was less developed, childbirth was a principal cause of the woman's death and it remains a high-risk process for women in poorer, less-developed parts of the world. Even in richer countries there are still real dangers both during pregnancy and during childbirth.

There is a complex question about the conflicting interests between mother and child. At one end of the spectrum are the severe danger of death examples – an **ectopic pregnancy** will kill both the mother and the child if left uninterrupted. There are also increased chances of pregnancy aggravating existing health problems – mothers with heart complaints or high blood pressure are under increased risk of serious problems. If mothers become unwell, decisions about taking medicines are complicated by the possible harmful effects those medicines may have on the unborn foetus – one must be weighed against the other. These seem to suggest a rather unpalatable reality, that what may be good for a mother can sometimes harm a baby, and vice versa. Interests can conflict, leaving a moral problem centred on the question of mother and baby equality.

> ■ Key terms
>
> **Ectopic pregnancy:** a pregnancy in which the foetus develops outside the uterus.

In 'A defence of abortion', Thompson presents one consequence of this puzzle, where she sees abortion as an issue of self-defence, and justifies it in some cases. The foetus threatens the mother, in terms of increased risk, and so abortion is a defensive measure against unacceptable dangers. Thompson uses the example of a cardiac condition which, should the pregnancy be allowed to continue, would place the mother in real danger. How should a decision be made about the two rights to life, that of the mother and the baby? Who should decide which life should be preserved over and above the other? While we might kill in defence, it is unclear whether we should kill an innocent in self-defence. Perhaps the foetus has the right of self-defence against the mother? Thompson argues that it cannot be seriously suggested that a person must be stopped from saving their own life for the life of another. It cannot be suggested that they must sit by and wait for death. We can think of examples where someone is reasonably prevented from risking their life for a child, such as entering a burning building to save a child stranded inside. Once the

Key terms

Double effect: this is a doctrine devised to deal with moral conflicts in natural law theory. It says that it is always wrong to do a bad act intentionally in order to bring about good consequences, but it is sometimes permissible to do a good act while at the same time knowing that it will bring about bad consequences. In rough terms, this is sometimes translated as, 'Provided your intention is to follow the rule, you can "benefit" from any unintended consequences.'

fire is too bad, the decision is made not to risk further life, even though the desire of the parent to risk all and try is instinctive and laudable. To prevent someone from escaping such a fire out of a duty to another seems unreasonable and unnatural.

One position which takes account of the threat to the mother's life is that which argues for a **double effect** way of thinking. It may be that a medical procedure is necessary to protect the life of the mother which inadvertently and indirectly leads to the termination of the pregnancy. In this way of thinking the action is not deliberately to kill but deliberately to save life. The death of an innocent is an unfortunate side-effect.

Pregnancy does increase certain risks, but it does not mean death is likely for the mother, except on rare occassions. What is difficult is deciding what risk is reasonable for mothers to have to take before permission for an abortion can be given. Linked to this is the question of who has the authority to decide if not the mother herself. Your view of a reasonable risk may differ from someone else's. Risk may also be influenced by other factors – such as the risk to other children in the family who may lose their mother. How are these to be accounted for?

Ethical issues in legislation about abortion

In Britain, abortion is not legally available at the request of the woman. After a woman has decided that she wants to end her pregnancy, she has to persuade two doctors to agree to her decision on the basis of restrictive legal criteria.

This requirement is not only paternalistic, but more damagingly, it allows the approximately one in ten doctors who are opposed to all abortion the opportunity to delay, obstruct or even veto women's decisions.

Abortion Rights: The national pro-choice campaign

Some have argued that there are other compelling reasons to permit abortion in all, or almost all, cases, not just when there is certain risk to the mother. The feminist position begins from the historical experience of female suppression and a patriarchal society, and the role of religion in that history. Women were subordinated within the family and had their freedom limited by the constraints of motherhood and the unreliability of contraception. Women's roles have primarily been defined in terms of motherhood, and it was only towards the latter end of the 20th century that women in large numbers began to have equal legal rights and equal opportunity of employment.

Mary Anne Warren (1991, 1997) puts forward a case for granting women the right to abort unwanted pregnancies, because if the state was to prohibit abortion undesirable consequences would follow, such as dangerous illegal 'backstreet' abortions. The absence in the past of safe legal access to abortion and contraception has meant that women in history have paid a terrible price. They have been forced to bear many children at short intervals, become debilitated and died young – a situation that aggravates poverty and places stress on families and whole societies. If the morality of an action is determined by its consequences, then women deserve access to abortion. Without it, they have a limited possibility of education and employment, and no reproductive autonomy. For Warren abortion is essential for the health and well-being of individuals, families and society.

Warren maintains that abortion must be permissible to guarantee women's human rights of life, **liberty** and **self-determination**. The World Health Organisation (WHO) says that unsafe abortions kill 200,000 women every year. To be forced to bear a child is to be forced to undergo a risky process that may lead to the possibility of giving up work and education, and consequent hardship. Self-determination includes freedom from the infliction of bodily harm. Prohibition of abortion infringes on these rights. Warren argues that in most cases killing is wrong, but to prohibit abortion on demand would deny a woman's basic human rights. If the foetus is given equal rights then, in principle, a court could force a woman to go through with a dangerous birth rather than abort, because her life would be considered to be no more valuable than that of the foetus.

This kind of ethical observation takes account of the political and social climate in which moral decisions are made. It suggests that we simply cannot make idealistic ethical judgments and then enforce them in laws without looking at social and political consequences that may follow. This presents an interesting difficulty for idealistic religious and philosophical ethical points of view which aspire to a more perfect world. What we would like to be the case may not in fact turn out that way, because of factors beyond our control.

Key terms

Liberty: freedom.

Self-determination: the process by which a person controls and directs their life.

Activities

1. From the discussions considered so far, which is of greater significance in determining your view over the ethics of abortion – the debates about when a human being is a human being, the clash of rights (child vs. mother), or the question of public policy (what might happen if abortion is permitted or forbidden by law)?

2. You're on a sinking ship and there is one lifejacket left. You get the jacket and put it on, but another passenger arrives without one. If you keep it you will live, while the other passenger will die. Should you keep it or give it away, and why? What are the ethical issues at stake in this situation, and how do they relate to abortion?

Key terms

Hippocratic oath: an oath stating the duties and proper conduct of doctors.

Life is sacred: has a special, holy value, beyond a material, exchangeable price.

Pastorally: pastoral care is typically guidance, in the way of counselling, given by a religious figure.

■ Religious and philosophical teachings on abortion

Ancient views of abortion differed, just as they do now. Aristotle favoured abortion to control the size of a family, but the **Hippocratic oath** prohibited it. No biblical text specifically prohibits abortion, although a number are cited as providing a framework for prohibiting abortion (in the Hebrew scriptures see Genesis 4:1; Job 31:15; Isaiah 44:24, 48:1, 5; Jeremiah 1:5; and in the New Testament see Matthew 1:18; Luke 1:40, 42).

To say that life is sacred implies reverence and respect. It's commonly assumed that killing is wrong, although there are justifications such as self-defence that allow it. The act of killing ends the life, the autonomy of the person and any possible future contributions that life could have made. It leaves friends and family bereaved. However, none of these in themself justifies a total prohibition of killing humans. There may be people who will not make positive contributions to life, such as compulsive serial killers, and there may be people who have no close friends or relatives who would mourn their passing. Capital punishment and killing in war have been justified to prevent undesirable consequences such as the deaths of innocents, and acceptance of these is at odds with an attitude against abortion based on an idea of the sanctity of life.

Religious perspectives on abortion

Religious arguments against abortion stress the limits of human authority over the taking of life and tend to be disapproving of abortion. God is the life-creator and giver, and humans must not destroy what God has given. In most religious traditions, there is something inherently good about life, and about creating more life. **Life is sacred**, protected by divine authority, with a specific destiny.

Most religious traditions view life as sacred but differences emerge in applying that principle to specific ethical issues. Within religions, specific traditions vary in degrees from being completely opposed in all circumstances with virtually no exceptions, opposed in principle but **pastorally** sensitive in practice, supportive of abortion in some specified cases, and finally those who are supportive of leaving the decision entirely to the mother.

Conservative religious traditions have a deontological or absolutist approach to ethics and find statements in sacred texts or other religious teachings to support a complete prohibition on abortion. Other traditions take a more proportional approach and are willing to set aside convictions in certain situations. Some traditions give more authority to the individual in making moral decisions, seeing the role of religious leaders in matters of morality as advisory, but not binding on every believer. So it is not only the extent to which a religion is deontological or teleological, proportional or situational that matters, but also the extent to which it gives individual autonomy and conscience a major place in the decision-making process of believers.

There are some distinctions between what religious teaching authorities (sacred texts, religious leaders, etc.) teach and what believers actually do. In some cases the official position is expected to be adopted by all believers, while in others this is meant as a recommendation, rather than a mandate. Evaluations of religious views of abortion should show sensitivity both to the diversity of views within religions and difference between those authorities' teachings and believers' actual practice.

Activities

1 How much moral weight should be given to the 'act' in considering abortion and how much to the consequences?

2 Should religions direct the moral behaviour of believers or simply provide advice and leave them to make up their own minds on issues such as abortion?

Jewish perspectives

Though there are prohibitions on the taking of human life, the Halacha – or Jewish Law – suggests that a foetus is not to be treated as a full human being. The killing of a human being cannot result in monetary compensation – human life is too important, but in Exodus 21:22–23 assault which causes miscarriage is identified as resulting in monetary compensation. From an ethical point of view killing the mother would be a murder because the mother is a human person, but killing the foetus is not murder because the foetus is not a human person. Lenn E. Goodman has argued that the issue of abortion seems to have been beyond the moral horizon of the Torah's original audience, possibly because the memory of genocide and infanticide was recent and every birth precious (Goodman, 1998).

Jewish commentators have argued that before birth it is permissible to take the life of the foetus in order to save its mother. In the Mishna – a written recording of the oral Torah – abortion is permitted if the foetus or pregnancy threatens the life of the mother:

> If a woman has (life-threatening) difficulty in childbirth, one dismembers the embryo within her, limb by limb, because her life takes precedence over its life. However, once its head (or its 'greater part') has emerged, it may not be touched, for we do not set aside one life for another.

Ohalot 7:6

The great Jewish scholar Maimonides wrote that if the foetus endangers the mother it can be removed.

Traditionally, in Orthodox Judaism it is only in situations where the life of the mother is threatened that abortion is permissible, although in practice a threat to the life of the mother is interpreted quite widely. Other branches of Judaism permit abortion when there is a risk of physical and psychological harm. For instance, Reform Judaism also permits abortion in cases of rape, or the risk of severe disability of the child, or if it will place the parents in a very difficult situation:

> The Reform perspective on abortion can be described as follows: Abortion is an extremely difficult choice faced by a woman. In all circumstances, it should be her decision whether or not to terminate a pregnancy, backed up by those whom she trusts (physician, therapist, partner, etc.). This decision should not be taken lightly (abortion should never be used for birth control purposes) and can have life-long ramifications. However, any decision should be left up to the woman within whose body the fetus is growing.

Rabbi Jonathan Biatch

One of the reasons for such a range of views in Judaism is that Jewish legal code is not a set of policies but a collection of debates about possible policies (found especially in the Talmud).

Key terms

Ensoulment: the process in Christian belief, by which a body is endowed with a soul.

Excommunication: the act of banishing a member of a Church from the communion of believers and the privileges of the Church; cutting a person off from a religious society.

Link

For more on exterior and interior acts in natural law thinking, see p65.

Activity

What ethical language would you use to characterise each of the different Church perspectives on abortion? Write four sentences for each of the Roman Catholic Church, the Church of England and the Episcopal Church in the USA, using these words as you think appropriate: absolutist, autonomy, conscience, deontological, moral law, proportional, relativistic, situational, teleological.

Christian perspectives

Historically Christianity has viewed abortion as sinful. It's prohibited in Christian writings such as the *Didache ton Apostolon* (a 1st century Christian guide to living; see Staniforth, 1968) and those of Clement of Alexander (c.150–211/6) and Tertullian (c.160–235). Christian writers disputed the point at which the soul infused with the body (**ensoulment**) and also whether early abortions were as morally grave as later ones, but essentially it was viewed as murder.

Christian teaching on abortion varies across the different Churches. In principle the taking of innocent life is a grave sin. The Roman Catholic Church maintains that it is intrinsically evil and condemns it absolutely. Abortion goes against natural law and the Word of God, and there are no exceptions or scenarios that make it right. The foetus deserves the same status as a born human being. Those involved in procuring abortion leave themselves open to **excommunication**. This is restated in Pope John Paul II's *Encyclical Letter on Abortion, Euthanasia, and the Death Penalty in Today's World*:

> The Church has always taught and continues to teach that the result of human procreation, from the first moment of its existence, must be guaranteed that unconditional respect which is morally due to the human being in his or her totality and unity as body and spirit: 'The human being is to be respected and treated as a person from the moment of conception; and therefore from that same moment his rights as a person must be recognized, among which in the first place is the inviolable right of every innocent human being to life …'

Pope John Paul II, 1995, paragraph 60

Orthodox Churches agree, as do evangelical Churches, which oppose abortion on the basis that God alone is the author of life. David Smith (1997) identifies four principles that broadly summarise the Christian absolute rejection of abortion: God alone is Lord of life and death, humans have no right to take life, human life begins at *conception* and so abortion at any stage is the murder of an innocent.

The Church of England has not ruled as emphatically as the Catholic Church and leaves individual Anglicans to make their own decision. The General Synod, the Church's governing body, has expressed opposition to abortion, on the basis of both the right to life argument and the argument that it contravenes moral law, and they are concerned about the growing numbers of abortions. Nevertheless, the Church recognises that there can be limited conditions under which it may be morally preferable, such as when a pregnancy threatens the life of the mother.

In an ectopic pregnancy, the fallopian tube is usually removed and the embryo dies, thus saving the mother. A Christian response to the problems of an ectopic pregnancy makes use of the double effect rule. The doctors intend to save the mother, rather than killing the foetus, so the action is morally permissible. The idea behind double effect, which was inspired by St Thomas Aquinas, is that the intention is not to kill and the action is either good or morally indifferent. There must be a proportionate need, such as saving a life, to perform an action which has a second evil effect. That evil effect must be equally immediate to the good effect so that there is no question that what is in fact going on is doing evil for a good reason.

Double effect can be illustrated as this:

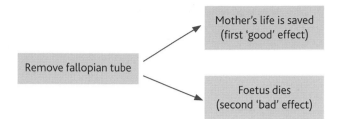

Roman Catholic thinking has accepted double effect as a justifiable ethical doctrine for such cases to preserve the life of the mother. However, Peter Vardy and Paul Grosch (1994, p134) have identified a problem with the application of double effect thinking in this particular example. In the event of an ectopic pregnancy new laser technology will enable women to have a safer operation which involves the foetus being 'lasered' rather than the fallopian tube removed. The result for the mother is much better, but it is difficult to suggest that the death of the foetus in this case is a secondary feature of saving her life. All that is really different is the intention of the doctor.

In other words it is represented as follows:

This does not fulfil the traditional understanding of the double effect doctrine and presents a problem for ethical thinking based on the double effect doctrine.

Other Churches have left open the ethical route by which saving the mother's life can be prioritised over the unborn. A report presented to the Thirty-eighth General Assembly of the Orthodox Presbyterian Church, 24–29 May in 1971 concluded:

> … that the Christian should regard the unborn child as a human person made in the image of God. Such a regard for the unborn child will involve rejection of abortion, except possibly in order to save the life of the mother.

Frame, 1988, p121

Liberal Protestant Christians oppose abortion in principle, and advocate the preservation of life, but allow for abortion in certain situations. These variously include abortion prior to the formation of the nervous system and brain, situations where the mother's life is threatened, in the case of rape or incest, and when the mother's mental or physical health is endangered. The **Episcopal Church** in the USA takes a pro-choice stand supporting a woman's right to choose and opposing government action that limits a woman's right to choose.

■ Key terms

Episcopal Church: the name given to the Anglican (Church of England) Church in Scotland and the USA.

Activities

1. Identify four different factors that can play a role in Muslim moral decision-making with regards to abortion.

2. What role does the value of the mother play in Muslim approaches to abortion?

3. How does this compare with Judaism and Christianity?

Key terms

Ayatollah: high-ranking religious leader among Shiite Muslims, especially in Iran.

Muslim perspectives

In general terms, abortion of a formed foetus is forbidden by God in Islam and is also a crime against a human being. Muslim scholars argue that the right to end life is God's not ours. Respect for life is a central Islamic value, based on the idea that life is sacred (Qur'an 5:32).

It is often suggested that 120 days is the point at which the foetus becomes fully human and should no longer be aborted as a rule, coinciding with the mother feeling the first movement of the child. After four months (120 days) of gestation it is believed that the human 'spirit' (ruh) enters the body which then is referred to as 'another creation' (23:14). However, modern science challenges the use of the mother's feeling of movement to indicate a significant stage in foetal development:

> Then [God] made [man] of an extract, of water held in light estimation. Then He made him complete and breathed into him of His spirit.

32:8–9

Traditionally, then, abortion was thought to be impossible by Muslim scholars although threats to the mother's health have been seen as a reason for therapeutic abortion. Differences emerge over the specifics of when an abortion is permissible with Shiite scholars forbidding it after implantation of the fertilised ovum and Sunni scholars holding various opinions on the matter. There is general agreement that after four months abortion is not permitted. In a 2006 *Journal of Medical Ethics* article Hedayat, Shooshtarizadeh and Raza note that:

> All scholars, from the four Sunni and the Shiite schools of thought, agree that after the fourth month of gestation an abortion cannot be performed unless it is to save the mother's life.

Hedayat, Shooshtarizadeh and Raza, 2006, pp652–657

The mother as a source of life is extremely important and so in these cases abortion is the lesser of two evils. The mother may well have responsibilities and has a distinct role in the family which should be protected.

The therapeutic abortion law passed by the Iranian Parliament in 2003 allows therapeutic abortion before 16 weeks in circumstances which include medical conditions related to both foetal and the mother's health (Hedayat, Shooshtarizadeh and Raza, 2006, pp652–657).

Beyond foetal and maternal health difficulties other justifications for abortion have received different responses. In principle offspring should not be killed because the family fear poverty if there is another child to feed. Recent Iranian ayatollahs have restated this prohibition, although there is a growing sensitivity of the difficulty families in poverty have in caring long-term for severely disabled children (Hedayat, Shooshtarizadeh and Raza, 2006, pp652–657).

> But Islam is also a religion of compassion, and if there are serious problems, God sometimes doesn't require his creatures to practice his law. So under some conditions – such as parents' poverty or overpopulation – then abortion is allowed.

Grand Ayatollah Yusuf Saanei, quoted in the Los Angeles Times, *29 December 2000*

In other exceptional cases, such as rape or incest, some scholars have ruled that all life should be protected, while others make exceptions.

During the Kosovo War in the 1990s Ikrima Sabri, chief **mufti** of the Palestinian Authority, ruled that women raped by Serbian soldiers could take abortifacient (abortion-causing) medicine.

Disagreement over rape has emerged over the decision of Muhammad Sayed Tantawi, the Grand Sheikh of Al Azhar in June 2004 to approve a draft law permitting abortion when a pregnancy has resulted from rape, even later than four months after conception. Other Muslim scholars reject this. The mufti of Egypt, Ali Gomaa, argues Tantawi's decision violates the Qur'an which 'forbids killing innocent souls'. Ali Gomaa argues: 'It is haram [forbidden] to abort the fetus after life is breathed into it, in other words after 120 days.'

Islam holds what could be described as a conservative position on the matter of abortion but scientific and medical progress and understanding seems to be leading to new discussions on how abortion laws may be applied. Important here is the position of Iran where religious leaders have had, since the revolution, a leading position of responsibility in passing judgments on these matters.

Key terms

Mufti: a Muslim legal expert who is empowered to give rulings on religious matters.

Hindu perspectives

Hindu ethical thinking on the taking of life is based on the principle of ahimsa (non-violence) and traditionally Hindu sacred texts interpret this deontologically where it is compared to the killing of a priest, or is said to be worse than murdering your parents.

Because of the doctrine of reincarnation, the cycle of birth, death and rebirth, foetuses are thought to be full human persons from a very early stage in development; the soul is reincarnated into the body at conception. Aborting a foetus deprives it of all the opportunities that life may have offered, and all the good karma it may have achieved. The soul's progress is hindered. Nevertheless, the soul will return to the cycle of life and will be reborn so it does not have the totality of abortion in Christianity, Islam or Judaism.

Hindus today commonly hold that abortion is wrong except when the mother's life is threatened and this is reinforced by a common sense of duty to produce children. The production of offspring is often regarded as a 'public duty', rather than an 'individual expression of personal choice' (Lipner, 1989, pp41–69). However, more utilitarian understandings of ahimsa are also common among Hindus today. Ahimsa is sometimes interpreted as that which does the least harm to all of those involved, rather than exclusively the human foetus. Under these terms abortion can be seen as acceptable in situations other than simply when the mother's life is threatened.

Another practice thought to be widespread in India is abortion for the sex selection of boys over girls:

> The root of the problem is ancient and economic. Male children are favored since they carry the family name and frequently get the family inheritance. Girls are viewed as liabilities, who will cost their parents a dowry when they marry and move into their husband's homes [sic] …

Cover Story: 'Sex Selection in India', Religion and Ethics News Weekly, *1 June 2001*

However, traditional Hindu teaching condemns sex-selective abortion as part of the general prohibition of abortion,

> [F]rom earliest times … abortion (viz., deliberately caused miscarriage as opposed to involuntary miscarriage) at any stage of pregnancy has

been morally condemned as violating the personal integrity of the unborn, save when it was a question of preserving the mother's life. No other consideration, social or otherwise, seems to have been allowed to override this viewpoint.

Lipner, 1989, p60

Buddhist perspectives

Buddhists have different views of abortion. Traditionally Buddhism sees abortion as breaking the first precept which forbids the killing or injuring of living beings and it is suggested in early Buddhist scriptures that a human being begins at conception:

> The Buddhist religion places great importance on the principle of ahimsa, or non-harming, and therefore has grave reservations about any scientific technique or procedure that involves the destruction of life, whether human or animal ... Buddhism teaches that individual human life begins at conception. By virtue of its distinctive belief in rebirth, moreover, it regards the new conceptus as the bearer of the karmic identity of a recently deceased individual, and therefore as entitled to the same moral respect as an adult human being.

Damien Keown, quoted in McLaren, 2001, p130

As with Hinduism, abortion is thought to cut off the possibility of rebirth at conception of life, preventing the possibility of the being reaching enlightenment. Human consciousness is not something that is thought to develop gradually; without the soul, the body could not be in the womb. From conception, life exists:

> When in his mother's womb, the first mind-moment has arisen, the first consciousness appeared, his birth (to be reckoned as) from that time.

Pitaka, 1966, Vin 1.93

Early texts make reference to the descent of the embryo, which Damien Keown interprets as taking place at fertilisation, a point of origin from which everything else flows (Keown, 1995, pp78–79).

It causes bad karma proportionate to the age of the foetus at the time of the abortion. Buddhist monks assisting with an abortion can be thrown out of the Sangha:

> Whatever monk deprives a human being of life, even down to destroying an embryo, he becomes not a (true) renouncer, not a son of the Sakiyans.

Pitaka, 1966, Vin 1.97

Buddhist monks are forbidden to cause abortion. It destroys life with all its potential for moral and spiritual development. Even if being aborted is a result of a being's past bad karma, and despite the opportunity of rebirth that the being will have, neither is an excuse for an adult to kill an unborn, according to Peter Harvey (Harvey, 2000, p315).

Although causing an abortion is generally condemned, Buddhist principles support abortion as a necessary evil in situations where there is a real or possible threat to the life of the mother, and in some Buddhist countries this is the only legal exception for abortion to be allowed. On the matter of abortion because of rape, Buddhist texts say nothing,

Activity

What different ethical principles are found in Buddhist perspectives on abortion?

but some, such as Philip Lesco and Shoyo Taniguchi, have argued that taking a life adds to the violence and harm done (Lesco, 1987, p216 and Taniguchi, 1987, p78). Both are also critical of abortion for a foetus that will have disabilities, such as Down's syndrome or spina bifida. Peter Harvey (Harvey, 2000, p325) notes that Buddhism sees suffering as part of any life. However, different views have been expressed elsewhere. The **Dalai Lama** has expressed a more situational approach:

> Of course, abortion, from a Buddhist viewpoint, is an act of killing and is negative, generally speaking. But it depends on the circumstances. If the unborn child will be retarded or if the birth will create serious problems for the parent, these are cases where there can be an exception. I think abortion should be approved or disapproved according to each circumstance.

> *Dalai Lama*, New York Times, *28 November , 1993*

When abortion is to be considered, preference is for an early abortion, rather than a later one. In Theravada Buddhist countries the moral stigma increases with the size of the foetus. This follows from the view that sanctity of the being increases with its size and development, just as relatively speaking it is less serious to destroy a mosquito, than it is a dog (Ling, 1969, p58).

James J. Hughes and Damien Keown (1995) observe that Buddhist perspectives on abortion vary according to whether the ethic is absolutist, utilitarian or virtue-based. Absolutist Buddhists argue that bad karma is incurred from any act of murder irrespective of the situation. Utilitarian Buddhists argue that murder could be a compassionate response, for instance to a danger to the mother's health, and would have positive karmic consequences. Virtue-oriented Buddhists would argue that the attitude and motivations of the pregnant woman and her collaborators would determine the ethics of an abortion.

W. A. LaFleur (1990) explores Japanese Buddhist tolerance for, and ritualisation of, abortion. Abortion is a 'sorrowful necessity', and Buddhist temples sell rituals and statues to represent parents' apologies to the aborted, and their wishes for a more propitious rebirth. LaFleur argues that the Japanese have reached these accommodations consensually, with little debate, and without discussion of the rights of women or the unborn (LaFleur, 1990, 1992).

Sikh perspectives

In Sikhism, it is believed that life begins at conception. Following from this principle, once conception has taken place, to destroy the life would interfere in God's creative work and commit a sin. That said the Sikh code of conduct does not deal specifically with abortion and abortion is not uncommon among Sikhs. According to Coward, abortion is allowed only in certain circumstances such as in the case of a rape or to save the mother's life (Coward, 1993, pp454–456).

Nevertheless the pressure to bear sons means that in the Punjab sex-selective abortions take place among Sikhs (Coward and Sidhu, 2000, p1170). This is strictly forbidden by the Guru's teachings and directives have been issued by Sri Akaal Takht Sahib, the Sikh Supreme Authority, to prevent parents from checking the gender of the foetus before birth in an attempt to ensure the rights of the child and those of the mother (Sikhism101.com).

Key terms

Dalai Lama: the spiritual head of Tibetan Buddhism.

AQA Examiner's tip

Another exam black spot is the insufficient attention paid to religious pluralism. Within any one religious tradition, there are often big differences of approach, and candidates often gloss over these by inclusive phrases about what all Muslims, Hindus, Sikhs, etc., believe. Don't say things like, 'Abortion is killing, and killing is wrong'. The Jewish/Christian commandment does not say, 'Do not kill': the word used is 'murder', and to label abortion as 'murder' begs the question.

Other perspectives

In his essay 'An argument that abortion is wrong' (1997), Don Marquis makes a case for what he calls the 'Future like Ours' (FLO) account of the wrongness of killing. Instead of getting bogged down in questions to do with the embryo and the time of abortion or the clash of rights, he focuses on the issue of the premature death: the deprivation of possible futures, possible contributions and possible projects that may be fulfilled by that life. The loss of a future conscious life is the loss of the future goods of consciousness. I may not now desire these goods, and indeed I may desire things today that in future years I no longer desire. However, another person may in fact be correct in seeing a valuable future for my life that I do not see, such as happens in cases where people try to prevent the suicidal from taking their own lives.

Marquis bases his argument on the claim that the premature deprivation of life is a misfortune and a serious one at that. Killing is one of the worst of all crimes because it takes away all value of that person's future. There seems to be something particularly wrong about killing the young for this reason. Killing can only be justified in very extreme circumstances, such as self-defence, and killing the young must have even more of a requirement of extremity of consideration attached.

Issues arising from abortion

Does the definition of human life stop abortion being murder?

Abortion defines a specific act which ends human life. Religious or philosophical views which consider innocent human life to have the highest value and significance in any moral consideration are always likely to conclude that abortion is a moral crime. This is especially the case in moral thinking which is profoundly absolutist and deontological. In other words in moral viewpoints which are principally concerned with actions and see moral norms (rules) as having universal binding authority.

Nevertheless there is a question about how we regard life at different stages before birth. It is uncommon, for instance, for miscarried unborn children to be treated in the same way as born children who die, even by religions, and as a significant proportion of all pregnancies are not successful it has never been a rare occurrence. Both may be mourned but in different ways and there is little social recognition of the loss of an aborted child. This may reflect a social attitude to the unborn as they are simply not recognised to the same degree as born humans – they do not have the same legal status and are not registered as a death. This may also reflect subtle differences between an embryo, a foetus and a born human being. Here the arguments explored in the first part of this chapter on the value of potential and real life become important.

We ordinarily use the phrase murder to describe the killing of human beings, rather than other sentient life forms so the decision about when to grant a human life full status as a human being is important. It is also the case that in other instances of murder the situation is taken into account and does change the judgment of courts and also the punishment given out, typically in cases of self-defence. It is difficult to separate the moral question about the life of the unborn, from the moral question of the mother's situation.

In answering the question is abortion murder irrespective of the age of the unborn baby, these questions should be considered: What do you mean by murder? What do you mean by human life? You should consider what factors are involved in deciding how we answer each of these questions.

Can abortion ever be said to be good?

Religious teachings frequently describe abortion as intrinsically evil in any situation and irrespective of the consequences. The sanctity of a human life is often given a value greater than all other factors when making a moral decision. It is one of those issues which in religious teaching seems to carry the equivalent to a trump card which counters every other condition.

It is difficult to consider the killing of a life as being good in any situation. If we think in absolute deontological terms then the act of killing seems evil. In some situations we make exceptions, such as self-defence where lethal force may be necessary, or in the case of war. We can ask then whether abortion can be considered as one of these exceptions where it might actually be right (rather than good, perhaps). However, abortion involves the death of an innocent, making it difficult to compare with other cases.

How we answer the question of whether abortion can ever be thought of as good, right or justified, changes if we give moral value to the situation and the consequences, and in particular how those affect the mother for whom both abortion and childbirth present medical risks and social consequences. If we give consideration to the possible implications of overburdening an impoverished family with a child that cannot be fed (perhaps a case in poorer rather than richer countries) or the perceived psychological harm done through allowing incest or rape to lead to a human life, then we might take a different moral view from the absolutist deontological view that abortion is always evil. This might also be the case if we accept arguments that reproductive rights are basic human rights without which women are prejudiced in society.

Perhaps the phrase 'necessary evil' is one which better captures the possibility of accepting abortion, rather than a good, though for many religious perspectives, a necessarily evil is (or should be) an impossibility.

Do humans have a right to life?

The language of rights dominates the arguments about abortion. The right to life of the unborn versus the right of choice (or reproductive rights) for women. Rights language can be used in different ways. Human rights are said to be universal rights and freedoms recognised by states and in international agreements, and they are frequently based on the dignity of the human person. The right to life then is the most fundamental of these rights and on this right all other rights rest. However, in most cases these human rights are defined as applicable to born human beings. The idea that others in society, be they the community at large or government or international body, grant us moral recognition might not seem acceptable – surely we should not depend on others to give us moral recognition? However, human rights exist against a backdrop where communities and governments failed to give moral recognition to human beings during the mass killings of the Second World War. Human rights also reflect a practical reality that the only freedom someone really has is that which those around human rights grant.

People also use the language of rights to express the basic value and importance they place on life, perhaps for religious, philosophical or humanistic reasons. This approach is sometimes referred to as 'natural rights' and is sometimes linked to natural moral law. This perhaps captures what people really feel about rights – that they proceed from the nature of who we are, not from any political recognition. They may be thought to proceed from what God thinks of us, from what our status is in God's view, rather than ours. This then reflects back to the question of what human nature is and what we mean by human beings.

Human beings may have a right to life, but can that right be challenged, ever limited or even withdrawn? This does happen on occasion where criminals are concerned, or in times of war. The rights question for abortion is whether that should also be the case for the unborn.

Activities

1 What moral principles imply that abortion is wrong in any situation?

2 Consider the scenarios in the list below, and suggest what ethical principles in each example challenge your answers to 1:

   a A woman aborts a child caused by rape.

   b A woman aborts a child because the pregnancy is inconvenient for a film in which she's starring.

   c A woman aborts her child because it's the product of incest.

   d A woman aborts her child because she can't afford another child in her family.

   e A woman aborts her child because it's so disabled that it will die at birth.

   f A woman aborts a child because it has such severe learning difficulties, with no ability to communicate with or sense the world around it, or to think in a normal human way.

   g A woman aborts a child because the pregnancy is ectopic and both will die unless abortion takes place.

   h A woman aborts a child because she has a serious heart condition and may die in childbirth.

3 How might you go about deciding acceptable levels of risks for others to undergo medical procedures?

Extracts from key texts

Mrs Jill Knight, MP, 1966

House of Commons debate (in Glover, 1977, p120)

Babies are not like bad teeth to be jerked out just because they cause suffering. An unborn baby is a baby nevertheless. Would the sponsors of the Bill think it right to kill a baby they can see? Of course they would not. Why then do they think it right to kill one they cannot see? ... I have come to believe that those who support abortion on demand do so because in all sincerity they cannot accept that an unborn baby is a human being. Yet surely it is. Its heart beats, it moves, it sleeps, it eats. Uninterfered with, it has a potential life ahead of it of seventy years or more; it may be a happy one, or a sad life; it may be a genius, or it may be just plain average; but surely as a healthy, living baby it has a right not to be killed simply because it may be inconvenient for a year or so to its mother.

Judith Jarvis Thompson, The Violinist Example

In 'A Defence of Abortion' (quoted in Cahn and Markie, 1998, p738)

I propose, then, that we grant that the fetus is a person from the moment of conception. How does the argument go from here? Something like this, I take it. Every person has a right to life. So the fetus has a right to life. No doubt the mother has a right to decide what shall happen in and to her body; everyone would grant that. But surely a person's right to life is stronger and more stringent than the mother's right to decide what happens in and to her body, and so outweighs it. So the fetus may not be killed; an abortion may not be performed.

It sounds plausible. But now let me ask you to imagine this. You wake up in the morning and find yourself back to back in bed with an unconscious violinist. A famous unconscious violinist. He has been found to have a fatal kidney ailment, and the Society of Music Lovers has canvassed all the available medical records and found that you alone have the right blood type to help. They have therefore kidnapped you, and last night the violinist's circulatory system was plugged into yours, so that your kidneys can be used to extract poisons from his blood as well as your own. The director of the hospital now tells you, 'Look, we're sorry the Society of Music Lovers did this to you – we would never have permitted it if we had known. But still, they did it, and the violinist now is plugged into you. To unplug you would be to kill him. But never mind, it's only for nine months. By then he will have recovered from his ailment, and can safely be unplugged from you.' Is it morally incumbent on you to accede to this situation? No doubt it would be very nice of you if you did, a great kindness. But do you have to accede to it? What if it were not nine months, but nine years? Or longer still? What if the director of the hospital says, 'Tough luck, I agree, but you've now got to stay in bed, with the violinist plugged into you, for the rest of your life. Because remember this. All persons have a right to life, and violinists are persons. Granted you have a right to decide what happens in and to your body, but a person's right to life outweighs your right to decide what happens in and to your body. So you cannot ever be unplugged from him.' I imagine you would regard this as outrageous, which suggests that something really is wrong with that plausible sounding argument I mentioned a moment ago.

Chapter summary

- Abortion is common – it's legal in many countries, with tens of millions of abortions taking place each year.
- Religious organisations such as the Roman Catholic Church campaign against abortion, while women's rights groups campaign for greater access.

When is a human being a human being?

- While some form of life is clearly present at conception, whether that form of life should get the full protection of the law is disputed.
- Should status increase incrementally as the foetus becomes more like a born human being, or should it be bound to the point of conception, the presence of the primitive streak, at viability, or the point of birth?

- Opponents of abortion argue that to kill a foetus is to murder a human person – the foetus contains the necessary genetic material.
- Others argue that the fertilised egg is too different from anything that we normally recognise as a person to be called the same thing.
- Personhood may be recognised when the primitive streak appears as that indicates the number of individuals present.
- Personhood may be given when the foetus is viable, when it can survive a birth – although people who are dependent on continual medical assistance are considered to be persons despite their medical conditions.
- Some argue that birth is the moment when we should give full rights, though in biological terms there is little difference between a baby at birth and a baby in the womb days earlier.
- Personhood may be defined by consciousness, rationality, self-awareness, and our ability to develop complex language and make complex tools.
- Is a foetus a person or a potential person?
- The definition of personhood is unresolved, as is agreement over the point at which a potential human being becomes a full human being.

The life of the mother versus the life of the child

- Pregnancy places great stress on the mother and can harm her or endanger her life.
- The interests of the mother can conflict with the interests of the child.
- There is a historical experience of female suppression and a patriarchal society, defining women's roles in terms of motherhood.
- Judith Jarvis Thompson sees abortion as an issue of self-defence – although, arguably, the foetus has the right of self-defence against the mother.
- The double effect principle argues that actions to save the mother's life but which also lead to abortion are moral.

Ethical issues in legislation about abortion

- Mary Anne Warren argues that women should have the right to abort unwanted pregnancies, because if the state was to prohibit abortion undesirable consequences would follow.
- Illegal abortions would claim lives – and basic women's rights would be lost, as control over the reproductive system and process is essential if women are to experience basic rights to life, liberty and self-determination.

Religious and philosophical teachings on abortion

- In most religious traditions life is sacred and God-given.
- Conservative religious traditions tend to be more deontological and more focused on narrow readings of sacred scripture.
- Liberal religious traditions tend to be more sensitive to the situation and mother's predicament, and give more attention to the consequences of any decision. They interpret scripture less strictly.
- Religious teaching sometimes diverges from what religious people actually do.

Jewish perspectives

- Ancient Hebrew texts are unclear about the issue of abortion.
- It is permissible to abort to save the mother's life.
- Reform Judaism also permits abortion in the case of rape and other kinds of harm.

Christian perspectives

- Abortion intentionally destroys a foetus in the womb, and biblical texts provide a framework for prohibiting abortion.
- Christianity holds all human life to be sacred – deserving of reverence and respect.
- The act of killing ends the life, the autonomy of the person and any possible future contributions that life could have made.
- Religious organisations argue that humans do not have authority over the taking of life as God is the life-creator and giver.
- Christianity rejects the taking of innocent life and so abortion is considered a grave sin, intrinsically evil, and condemned absolutely by the Roman Catholic Church, as it goes against natural law and the Word of God.
- God alone is Lord of life and death, and humans have no right to take life.
- Human life begins at conception and so abortion at any stage is the murder of an innocent.
- Liberal Protestant Christians oppose abortion in principle, and advocate the preservation of life, but allow for abortion in certain situations (where the mother's life is threatened, in the case of rape or incest, and when the mother's mental or physical health is endangered).
- The double effect principle may be applied to allow for an abortion to save the life of a mother when otherwise neither the mother nor the foetus would live (for example, an ectopic pregnancy).
- Some more liberal Churches support a woman's right to an abortion.

Muslim perspectives

- Abortion is forbidden in general terms, especially after 120 days.
- Exceptions are granted when the pregnancy poses a threat to the mother's life, as mothers are held in high esteem as the bringers of life into the world.
- There is a growing sensitivity to the demands placed on impoverished families by severely deformed foetuses being allowed to be born with terrible disabilities.
- Other exceptions have been allowed in certain rape cases, though these are less widely accepted.

Hindu perspectives

- Based on the principle of ahimsa (non-violence).
- The doctrine of rebirth leads to a presumption that the being is complete from conception.
- Abortion hinders the progress of the soul.
- Sometimes non-violence includes harm done to the family and others if birth is allowed to take place, not just harm done to the foetus.

- Traditionally, abortion for sex-selection is prohibited in Hinduism but it is widespread in India.

Buddhist perspectives

- Based on the principle of ahimsa (non-violence).
- The doctrine of rebirth leads to a presumption that the being is complete from conception, expressed in early Buddhist texts.
- Abortion hinders the moral and spiritual progress of the soul towards enlightenment.
- Monks are prohibited from helping with abortions.
- Some Buddhist countries only allow abortions when the mother's life is threatened, while others allow it more or less on demand.
- The Dalai Lama takes a more situationist, less dogmatic, position to those in very difficult circumstances.
- An early abortion is preferred over a late abortion.
- In Japan there is a degree of ritualised acceptance of abortion.

Sikh perspectives

- In principle abortion is sinful as it interferes with God's intention of new life.
- It is allowed in certain circumstances including danger to the mother's health, and rape.
- Though prohibited by Sikh leaders, abortion for sex-selection is widespread in India.

Other perspectives

- Don Marquis argues for the wrongness of killing (abortion) as robbing the unborn of a life like ours with all it might bring: future consciousness , development, etc.
- The premature deprivation of life, especially in the young, is a serious misfortune.

Issues arising from abortion

- Religious views which give primacy to human life and are influenced by deontological and absolutist thinking are likely to consider abortion to be murder.
- Society treats the unborn differently from the born (in law, and social and religious rituals).
- Arguments about the nature of the unborn human influence broader judgements on whether abortion is murder.
- Situational and consequentialist thinking values other aspects of the dilemma when making a moral decision, including the mother's situation.
- Religious teaching tends to argue abortion is always bad but some perspectives think it is sometimes a necessary evil when the mother's situation is taken into account.
- Human rights, as laws or principles upheld by states or international organisations, tend to be applied only to born human beings and reflect the reality that freedoms must be observed by others to be secure.

- Natural rights express views about the moral significance of human life based on the nature of the human being, not a socially agreed law, and is often influenced by religious teaching about human life or natural law theory.

- Rights are not maintained indiscriminately – they may be withdrawn from criminals and set aside for individuals for the good of the community (in the case of war).

Further reading

Quite different perspectives on this issue are available from:

Glover, J., *Causing Death and Saving Lives*, Penguin, 1977, pp119–149

and the controversial:

Singer, P., *Practical Ethics*, Cambridge University Press, 1993, pp135–174

For a detailed study of Buddhist approaches see:

Harvey, P., *An Introduction to Buddhist Ethics*, Cambridge University Press, 2000, pp311–352

and for Christian approaches see:

Hoose, B., *Christian Ethics*, Cassell, 1998, pp95–109

This is a very useful exploration of Muslim approaches to the issue:

Brockopp, J., *Islamic Ethics of Life: abortion, war and euthanasia*, University of South Carolina Press, 2002, pp25–96

And my favourite anthology:

Singer, P., *Ethics*, in the Oxford Readers series, Oxford University Press, 1994

In this chapter you have:

- examined the technical language associated with abortion
- considered different arguments associated with the value of potential and real life
- considered the ethical implications of conflicts of interest between the mother and the child and the doctrine of double effect
- considered different religious and philosophical arguments about abortion
- examined a number of issues arising from abortion.

9 Euthanasia

By the end of this chapter you will:

- have considered the distinct ethical issues of active, passive, voluntary and involuntary euthanasia, and the moral questions arising out of those ideas

- examined religious arguments for and against different kinds of euthanasia and their relative strengths and weaknesses.

Key terms

Euthanasia: inducing a painless death, by agreement and with compassion, to ease suffering. From the Greek meaning 'Good Death'.

Active euthanasia: carrying out some action to help someone to die.

Passive euthanasia: not carrying out actions which would prolong life.

Key questions

1 Is there any moral justification for taking your own life?
2 Is it wrong to assist in killing those who don't want to live?
3 Is there a difference between withdrawing life-sustaining treatment and delivering a lethal injection?
4 Should comatose patients who have no hope of recovery be kept alive for as long as technology permits?
5 Is human dignity better defined or sustained by having freedom to choose to end life or not having that freedom?

What is euthanasia?

The Greek philosopher Hippocrates (c.460–c.370 BC) wrote: 'I will not prescribe a deadly drug to please someone, nor give advice that may cause his death.' Some doctors maintain this view, arguing that killing a patient does not fit with what a doctor should do. A doctor should heal, prevent diseases and assist people in living a healthy life. On the other hand, the English philosopher Francis Bacon (1561–1626) wrote that physicians are 'not only to restore the health, but to mitigate pain and dolours; and not only when such mitigation may conduce to recovery, but when it may serve to make a fair and easy passage' ('New Atlantis', 1627, in Vickers, 1996). Some doctors today feel that the need to preserve the patient's quality of life extends to a duty to help that patient to end his or her life in the way that he or she sees fit.

In thinking about what sort of death a person should have, one can say that a peaceful death is one in which pain and suffering are minimised, where the patient is never neglected and whose needs are always taken account of. However, in all countries, the peaceful death is not thought in legal terms to include euthanasia.

In the UK **active** (or direct) **euthanasia** (involving specific actions such as lethal injections intended to bring about death) is illegal. **Passive** euthanasia (patients are allowed to die by withdrawing treatment and/or nourishment) is common and generally considered to be legal though there are objections on grounds of religion.

It should be noted that indirect euthanasia (often the provision of pain relief, which has a side-effect of hastening death) is both widely practised and generally considered legal as long as killing was not the intention. This is not usually controversial.

R. H. Crook notes that medical science presents us with the ability to keep some human bodies alive almost indefinitely while at the same time it leaves us unable to prevent the suffering of many people approaching death (Crook, 2002, p164). This raises questions of whether someone should be allowed to bring death on at a time of their choosing, and whether it is right to switch off the support systems keeping a body alive when there is no hope of recovery.

Consider someone who has led a full and active life, but is now suffering from an incurable disease that slowly limits that person's ability to move, communicate with others and think as he or she has normally done. Should a person be allowed to take his or her own life while he or she still has some ability to control his or her own destiny? Closely associated with this question is whether it is right for a doctor to assist with that process. Advocates of **voluntary euthanasia** point out that while such people remain *able* to kill themselves, they have a quality of life that they do not want to end. What they want is for someone to help them to end their lives – or directly bring them to an end – once they have *lost* the ability to do so alone, and their quality of life is no longer desirable. Today, euthanasia is a criminal offence in virtually all countries, and it is strongly opposed by most governments and religious organisations. In Holland, about a thousand assisted deaths take place each year, and organisations such as the Voluntary Euthanasia Society (VES) campaign for a similar practice to be available in the UK. It is worth noting that the VES, along with most other pro-euthanasia groups, would never support ending someone's life against that person's will.

Associated with this dilemma is the question of **involuntary euthanasia**. If a patient does not or cannot express his or her opinion because he or she is unconscious – typically when a person is comatose, with no likelihood of regaining consciousness, or with such serious brain damage that consciousness could never be possible – does there come a time when the ventilator should be switched off, medical treatment withdrawn, or food and water withdrawn? Should a person be able to write a **living will** so that, in the event that severe injury is endured, which removes the capability of basic mental functions, medical treatment is not used to prolong this state? How about a 'do not resuscitate' (DNR) order which instructs medical staff not to try to restart the heart and breathing of an elderly patient in considerable discomfort? Should doctors or some other authority be able to decide when it is right to switch off life-support and/or withdraw artificial feeding?

In addition to these questions about voluntary and involuntary euthanasia, there are active and passive dimensions to the ethical debate. If someone is terminally ill they may ask you not to intervene medically to help them and allow them to die sooner (passive voluntary euthanasia) or you may wish to do so after they have lost consciousness and basic brain functions (passive involuntary euthanasia). The person may ask you to give them medicines which will bring about their death (active voluntary euthanasia) or you may wish to do so once they have lost consciousness and basic brain functions (active involuntary euthanasia). This chapter explores voluntary and involuntary euthanasia, considering both passive and active varieties and both philosophical and religious thinking about these ethical issues.

Arguments for voluntary euthanasia

Should a person have the right to choose the manner and time of his or her own death, and should that person be given assistance in that process? The ethical arena of voluntary euthanasia is divided between those who tend to feel that it is right and merciful for us to have the freedom to decide the time and nature of our deaths, and those who claim that such autonomy would have harmful side-effects on society, or that it goes against religious beliefs. Allowing for the possibility that in many cases pain relief can help people who are terminally ill, there may be situations where people are in terrible pain or have such a profound sense of indignity because of their mental deterioration that they wish while they still have the chance to express a choice, to bring about death

more quickly. There are several arguments in favour of legal voluntary euthanasia.

Voluntary euthanasia is not murder

In his article 'Why physicians should aid the dying' (1997), Gregory E. Pence argues that killing humans who don't want to live is not wrong. It isn't wrong to help the dying to die, because they are actually dying.

Voluntary euthanasia is merciful

Voluntary euthanasia shows mercy for those suffering with intolerable pain from an incurable disease. The English humanist Thomas More (1478–1535) argued in his famous 1516 book *Utopia* that when a patient suffers 'a torturing and lingering pain, so that there is no hope, either of recovery or ease, [they may] choose rather to die, since they cannot live but in much misery' (More, 2004, Chapter 8). Voluntary euthanasia is a merciful opportunity to end needless suffering – one which we offer to animals and should offer to humans as well.

Voluntary euthanasia gives people autonomy

In his book *On Liberty* (1859), John Stuart Mill argued that in matters that do not concern others, individuals should have full autonomy: 'The only part of the conduct of any one, for which [a citizen] is amenable to society, is that which concerns others. In the part which merely concerns himself, his independence is, of right, absolute. Over himself, over his body and mind, the individual is sovereign.' We expect to have control over our bodies in matters of life, and it should be the same in matters of death. The VES (www.dignityindying.org.uk) argues that every human being deserves respect and has the right to choose his or her own destiny, including how he or she lives and dies. Controversial American doctor Jack Kevorkian has said: 'In my view the highest principle in medical ethics – in any kind of ethics – is personal autonomy, self-determination. What counts is what the patient wants and judges to be a benefit or a value in his or her own life. That's primary' (quoted in Gula, 1988, p279). Advocates of voluntary euthanasia argue that it should be an option for a competent adult, who is able and willing to make such a decision. They argue that it should be on offer as one option among many, along with the kind of **palliative care** offered by hospitals and hospices.

Key terms

Palliative care: the care of patients with a terminal illness, not with the intent of trying to cure them, but to relieve their symptoms.

Euthanasia goes on already

In 1994, the *British Medical Journal* published a survey that showed that some doctors already help patients to die. Doctors can legally give pain-relieving treatment in doses that will bring about people's deaths more quickly, and, in certain circumstances, such as in the case of the brain dead or comatose, they may also withdraw or withhold treatment even though a person will die if they do. They cannot directly help someone to die at that person's request. The VES holds that it would be more honest and much safer if voluntary euthanasia was legal and regulated. They argue that there is no ethical difference between withdrawing treatment and delivering a lethal injection.

Voluntary euthanasia maintains quality of life

Human beings should be able to maintain their dignity up until the ends of their lives. This is not simply a matter of pain, but of self-respect. If someone's standard of living is such that they no longer want to live, then they should be able to end their life and, if necessary, be assisted in doing so. What is more, the quality of life worth living is one that only they can define. Having control over their life is a way of enhancing their human dignity.

Arguments against voluntary euthanasia

There are a number of difficulties with legalised voluntary euthanasia.

Motives

When a person asks for death, can we be sure that the person isn't crying out in despair, rather than making a definitive decision? In desperate moments, someone may feel that they want their life to end – that the pain is too great and life too agonising – but perhaps those moments will pass and they will be glad that no one acted on their pleas. Can doctors be sure that they know and understand all the facts? Is it possible that they may fear a future which will not be realised? Any euthanasia process would have to be able to establish, beyond any doubt, the true intentions of the patient who is requesting euthanasia and that the patient is fully aware of the situation. The risk of misinformation or a failure to comprehend the situation leaves the patient vulnerable to a decision that he or she might not truly want to make.

Mistakes

Can we be sure that mistakes will not occur? Suppose that someone chooses death because they have been diagnosed with a fatal, incurable and painful illness. Then, after the person has died, it becomes apparent the diagnosis was incorrect (Hooker, 1997). There would have to be certainty about the diagnosis, but can there always be medical certainty about what the condition will entail and how long it will take to develop? There is an area of doubt here that could lead to terrible mistakes. Refusing to allow voluntary euthanasia safeguards us against this.

Abuse of the system

Would elderly relatives who think they are burdens to their families ask for voluntary euthanasia out of a sense of duty to the family? Jonathan Glover (1977) notes that people who feel they are burdens on their families sometimes commit suicide. On the other hand, could they be pressured into asking for assisted death by scheming relatives? The conviction of Harold Shipman for multiple murders – where he, as a general practitioner, murdered dozens of elderly patients over a period of many years – highlights the power of doctors, especially over the elderly. A voluntary euthanasia system could allow such people even more scope for murder, by manipulating patients and documentation.

Impact on the community

What cultural effect might voluntary euthanasia have on society? Might it lead to other forms of euthanasia being supported – ultimately concluding with the kinds of involuntary euthanasia carried out by the Nazis on the sick, the elderly and the disabled? Glover rejects this argument as unconvincing, and Helga Kuhse has observed that this has not happened in the Netherlands (Kuhse, 1991, p302). It is more likely that it might damage the care of patients who are dying.

While opposing voluntary euthanasia, people have developed caring and sensitive provision for the terminally ill within the hospice movement, but legalisation would affect the culture in which that approach to care has been developed. If voluntary euthanasia were made legal, would people become concerned about visiting hospitals, fearful of what might happen? Perhaps they would be put off by a perceived risk of an unwanted assisted death. Ultimately, voluntary euthanasia, in its physician-assisted form, is not simply an individual matter. It affects others and society as a whole – the doctor who assists, the nurses who are caring for the patient, the hospital in which it takes place and the wider community. The argument of an individual's right to die must be set against the interests of the community in which individuals exist. Acceptance of the practice of killing in hospitals could reduce the respect for life that civilisations uphold now more than ever in terms of human rights.

Activities

1. Consider these arguments against voluntary euthanasia. Which are more convincing and why? Think of additional evidence or ideas which you can add to them to build a better argument.

2. In carrying out voluntary euthanasia, what dangers would you have to avoid?

3. Outline step-by-step procedures to ensure that a patient's request for euthanasia is truly meant and of his or her own accord (not manipulated by others).

4. Now consider if you think these procedures are reliable enough to permit voluntary euthanasia.

5. What are the possible negative consequences of legalised voluntary euthanasia?

   a What impact do you think voluntary euthanasia would have on the community? Consider attitudes to the dying, hospitals and doctors.

   b Some assert that an argument about the quality of life could lead to dangerous assumptions about the disabled. Explain the possible danger here if voluntary euthanasia was to be legalised.

▪ Involuntary euthanasia

Voluntary euthanasia refers to situations where a person is able to make wishes known, perhaps at the time or possibly by an advance directive. However, there are other cases where a patient cannot let their wishes be known, such as in instances where they are in a comatose state from which recovery is very unlikely or impossible, or in the case of babies who at the start of life have severe, permanent and possibly deteriorating health difficulties causing great suffering. In these instances the withdrawal of treatment (passive) or the application of certain medicines (active) may bring about involuntary euthanasia. Involuntary euthanasia means that it is compulsory and without the consent of the patient because they cannot give such consent.

The principle of withdrawing treatment that has no further benefit, or simply extends a painful deterioration is relatively uncontroversial. However, the question of withdrawing food and water is controversial. Tony Bland was a victim of the 1989 Hillsborough disaster in which many football fans were crushed to death. He survived but was left in a coma from which doctors believed he would never recover – a 'persistent vegetative state' (PVS). In this state the body can breathe and main organs function properly. In Bland's case he could open his eyes but did not respond to anything around him. He could not feed but could digest food so needed to have food and water provided through a feeding tube. There was no cure for Tony's condition but he was not dying. The question, which eventually ended up in court, was whether or not it was right to remove artificial feeding, so leading to the death of the patient. The court allowed Bland to die through starvation and dehydration, which seems a painful and cruel way if he was able to sense such pain, though this was presumed not to be the case. The 2005 Mental Capacity Act for England and Wales enshrines in law the view that assisted food and fluids (given through a feeding tube, for instance) is a medical treatment that could be withdrawn. This seems to take a step towards active involuntary euthanasia or even non-voluntary euthanasia. The ethical challenge here is that there are instances where doctors are convinced that a person will never wake up from a coma, or indeed has no capacity for higher life function, and yet can be sustained indefinitely. Does it show more or less respect for the value of the human person to withdraw life-sustaining measures?

Another area of controversy surrounds the care of severely disabled babies. As medical advances improve, it is possible to keep alive more and more severely physically disabled babies. Some argue that allowing a disabled baby to live is to disable a family. In November 2006 the Royal College of Obstetricians and Gynaecologists urged health professionals to consider euthanasia for seriously disabled newborn babies (*Scotland on Sunday* 5 November 2006) to spare the emotional burden of families bringing up the very sickest of children. Others are concerned that the precedent of actively killing a baby or withdrawing treatment to bring about death much sooner cultivates a culture in which all disabled people are considered to be of less value.

AQA Examiner's tip

Involuntary euthanasia can be divided into two categories: cases where the patient is not in a position to choose (non-voluntary euthanasia) and cases where the patient's choice is ignored (involuntary euthanasia).

For this specification, both categories are classified as involuntary, as in most medical dilemmas patient responsibility reverts to a living spouse or relative and therefore the patients wishes can be explored, though clearly this raises further ethical questions. The distinction between these two sub categories is disputed.

AQA Examiner's tip

The death of Tony Bland is an example of 'passive euthanasia', or 'letting die', which is often held up as morally better than active euthanasia. Is it better? James Rachels argues that if you (passively) 'let someone die' by watching them drown, then your action is morally as bad as actively drowning that person. Rachels is on pp285–90 of *Ethics: Theory and Practice*, M. Velasquez and C. Rostankowski, Prentice Hall, 1985. Rachels gives other examples where 'passive' euthanasia can be morally worse than active euthanasia.

■ Activities

1 Do you think there is a danger that in starting to choose who to medicate and who to feed, and who not to, we begin to place human beings in different categories of dignity?

2 In the UK patients who are in sound mind and maturity can refuse medical treatment, even if it leads to their death. Consider the following patients suffering in terrible pain and terminally ill but unable to express their wish to have medicine withdrawn or to ask for a lethal injection: a patient suffering from senile dementia, a severe mental disability or with severe brain damage. How should these patients be best cared for towards the end of their lives and why?

3 Who should decide where to draw the line between a life worth living and life not worth living? A judge, a doctor, a spouse, partner or other member of the family, someone else?

4 Why might some argue that the focus should be on better palliative care rather than euthanasia?

■ Activity

■ A dying soldier on the battlefield pleads for his fellow soldiers to shoot him and put him out of his misery.

■ A soldier on the battlefield comes across a fellow soldier writhing in agony from a horrific, fatal injury.

How can these two situations help us clarify the moral question of euthanasia?

■ Religious perspectives on euthanasia

There are similarities between the religious approaches to euthanasia and those to abortion. Many religious perspectives work from interpretation of sources (sacred texts) and applying them to the ethical issue at stake. In the case of euthanasia many religions have encountered the issue before so current believers are also able to draw on those perspectives. While several religions take positions on euthanasia which are broadly held throughout that religious tradition, when exploring different kinds of euthanasia, differences emerge. There is diversity both within and between religious traditions. In some cases quite distinct values emerge, such as the idea of the intrinsic value of life and the instrumental value of life found between Western and Eastern religious traditions. There are also changes under way in contemporary religious thinking with believers placing more significance in their own freedom and judgement, rather than relying on traditional sources of moral authority. It is also clear that in some cases the ethical position taken does not distinguish between whether euthanasia is active or passive, voluntary or involuntary, while in other cases it does.

Jewish perspectives

> The value of human life is infinite and beyond measure, so that any part of life – even if only an hour or a second – is of precisely the same worth as seventy years of it, just as any fraction of infinity, being indivisible, remains infinite.

Immanuel Jakobovits, former UK Chief Rabbi

In Jewish thinking the view of death is informed by the view of life. Byron L. Sherwin (2001) argues that life should be viewed and lived in such a way that death is a catastrophe.

Dr Rachamim Melamed-Cohen, quoted in the online magazine *Jewsweek*, March, 2002 says:

> The message of Judaism is that one must struggle until the last breath of life. Until the last moment, one has to live and rejoice and give thanks to the Creator …

There are accounts where an inevitable death has not been hastened on the principle of not doing harm to oneself. The Talmud gives an account of Rabbi Chanina ben Teradion, who was being burned alive by the

Romans. He was urged to hasten his end and suffering by opening his mouth to inhale the flames but he refused saying, 'It is better that He who gave [me my soul] should take it rather than I should cause injury to myself.'

Preserving life is an ultimate goal of Judaism. Deuteronomy 30:19 says 'Choose life' but at the same time Ecclesiastes 3:2 says 'There is a time to die'. Rabbi Joshua Heschel (1907–72) captures the attitude which draws on both of these ideas when he writes,

> Life's ultimate meaning remains obscure unless it is reflected upon in the face of death ... [Judaism's] central concern is not how to escape death but rather how to sanctify life.

*Quoted in **Sherwin**, 2001, p38*

This is background from which an approach to euthanasia comes, rather than the question of rights which tend to dominate secular Western approaches. Jewish law presumes that the human body ultimately belongs to God (Sherwin, 2001, p39) so it is not simply to be treated as a possession of the person. The Talmud forbids the killing of another person unless it is self-defence, in a justifiable war or to protect another from deadly harm. However, there is a concept of martyrdom, as the ultimate expression of sacrificing all for God and in these cases it can be seen as a privilege. Martyrdom is an exemption from the usual prohibition of suicide. While active voluntary euthanasia is prohibited this is not the case for passive voluntary euthanasia which may be allowed. The artificial prolonging of life can be withdrawn.

Jewish law considers active euthanasia to be murder. If a dying person is moved and this brings about a quicker death then murder has been committed irrespective of the wishes of the person (whether it is voluntary or involuntary). Maimonides writes:

> One who is in a dying condition is regarded as a living person in all respects ... He who touches him [thereby accelerating his death] is guilty of shedding blood.

Mishneh Torah – LM, chapter 4, section 5

Jewish codes restate this and specifically address the doctor and the family and friends of the patient, even if the person is in agony (Sherwin 2001, pp43–44). All others are stewards of God's property, including their dying friend or family member and they cannot act as agents for the dying person to bring about their death sooner. It is God who gives the soul to a person and God who takes it away, and the quality of the person's life does not matter and is of no concern. The former UK Chief Rabbi Immanuel Jakobovits (1921–99), writes:

> It is clear, then, even when the patient is already known to be on his deathbed and close to the end, any form of active euthanasia is strictly prohibited. In fact it is condemned as plain murder ... At the same time, Jewish law sanctions, and perhaps even demands, the withdrawal of any factor ... which may artificially delay his demise in the final phase.

Jakobovits, 1959, pp123–124

It would appear then that passive euthanasia may be permitted in certain circumstances, of both a voluntary and an involuntary nature. If a person is so badly wounded that they are bleeding to an inevitable death, removing the bandages of the wounds will accelerate the bleeding and bring a quicker death. This may be done at the dying person's wish or indeed if they can no longer speak. However, this could not extend to all life-supporting facilities, such as essential medicines without which a person would die, or die sooner. Dying should not be artificially prolonged. In the Sefer Hasidim (Book of the Pious) it says:

> One may not [artificially] prolong the act of dying. If for example, someone is dying and nearby a woodcutter insists on chopping wood, thereby disturbing the dying person so that he cannot die, we remove the woodcutter from the vicinity of the dying person. Also, one must not place salt in the mouth of a dying person in order to prevent death from overtaking him.

Sefer Hasidim, 1924, no. 315, 100, quoted in Sherwin, 2001, p46

However, Sherwin argues that the situation is less clear when we come to treatment that has already been initiated (Sherwin, 2001, p46). Using the example where the salt can be removed from a person so that they die sooner some argue that this simply refers to initiating the treatment. Once it has been initiated any treatment cannot be withdrawn.

Others hold that this justifies the withdrawal of other treatment keeping the person alive and also that heroic attempts to prolong life when death is inevitable is inadvisable. This might include switching off a ventilator since such a device is preventing the natural end – the 'time to die' (Ecclesiastes 3:2). In this way of thinking a dying patient should not be kept alive artificially by treatment which cannot cure but merely and temporarily prolongs life. This then could be seen to apply to situations of involuntary euthanasia.

This view could also support DNR orders, used when people have given an early indication that they do not wish for doctors to try to resuscitate them after their heart has stopped. Sherwin writes that this could be considered just as presumptive as bringing about death more quickly.

It would appear then in Jewish thinking that the division between voluntary and involuntary euthanasia is not a key distinction. More important is the distinction between active and passive euthanasia.

Christian perspectives

Roger Crook captures the Christian perspective on euthanasia by posing the question in terms of how we care for the dying. What do we do for the person who is comatose with no hope of recovery? How do we care for the terminally ill person whose remaining days are increasingly, agonisingly painful? (Crook, 2002, p162). The human being is not simply a biological entity but a person, in the image of God and Christ. Death marks the end of personhood in this life.

Biblical teachings prohibit killing; the Sixth Commandment states 'You shall not kill' (Exodus 20:13) both in terms of murder and involuntary manslaughter. Life should not be violated. There is also a powerful message of the importance and role of healing from Jesus's ministry to the sick providing an emphasis on care for the sick, not to mention his concern for the weakest in society. While the prohibition of killing seems to be a moral absolute of Christianity there are exceptions for warfare and self-defence. There are also examples in the Bible where the sacrifice of life is considered virtuous: 'Greater love has no man than this: That a man lay down his life for his friends' (John 15:13). The Bible does not prohibit all taking of life in all circumstances, although Christians have traditionally considered taking one's own life to be wrong. These different messages provide a backdrop against which the different contemporary Christian perspectives on euthanasia can be seen. This section considers Roman Catholic, liberal Protestant and conservative Protestant perspectives to illustrate the range of views.

Roman Catholic perspectives

At the Second Vatican Ecumenical Council, the Roman Catholic Church condemned crimes against life 'such as any type of murder, genocide, abortion, euthanasia, or willful suicide' (*Pastoral Constitution, Gaudium et Spes*, no. 27). Life is sacred and a gift from God, 'which they are called upon to preserve and make fruitful' (*Declaration on Euthanasia*, 1980). To take a life opposes God's love for that person, and rejects the duty of a person to live life according to God's plan. In the same declaration, the Roman Catholic Church made it clear that it was wrong to ask someone for an assisted death, and that an individual cannot consent to such a death: 'For it is a question of the violation of the divine law, an offence against the dignity of the human person, a crime against life, and an attack on humanity.' The kind of autonomy that John Stuart Mill argues for is rejected by the Roman Catholic Church. We simply don't have that freedom, because we are made by God for the purpose of loving God. God has created us for a purpose, and it is our duty to live and pursue that purpose.

A distinct argument is made about suffering and its role in Christian theology. Jesus died in pain on the cross, and human suffering at the end of life connects us to the suffering that Jesus felt. This does not mean that Christians should refuse to take painkillers or should actively seek pain, but it does grant suffering the possibility of having a positive effect on the individual. It provides the chance that he or she may grow closer to God. In an article on euthanasia (in Childress and Macquarrie, 1986), Thomas Wood writes that while suffering can seem meaningless, is terrible and is never sought, it is not the worst evil – it can be an occasion for spiritual growth and it can have moral effects on those in attendance. It can have meaning in the context of a life lived in faith.

Burdensome excessive treatment, however, should be avoided. Similar positions are held by other Churches. For instance, the Orthodox Church and the Evangelical Lutheran Church in America (ELCA), agree with the Roman Catholic Church that physician-assisted suicide is prohibited. They also all accept the principle of withdrawal of unduly burdensome treatment in cases where it would not lead to any improvement in the patient's underlying condition and could not prevent death. In such circumstances it may be morally responsible to withhold or withdraw treatment and allow death to occur.

Protestant perspectives

Nevertheless there is some diversity among Christian perspectives, especially among Protestants. R. T. Goldberg takes the views of Joseph Fletcher and Arthur Dyck as representing two ends within the broad spectrum of Protestant thought, while accepting they do not represent every view (Goldberg, 1987, pp21–39).

Liberal Protestant

The Protestant Joseph Fletcher is an active advocate of the patient's 'right to die' on the basis that Christian faith emphasises love for one's fellow human being, and that death is not the end for Christians. Acts of kindness may embrace euthanasia, for instance when a human being is dying in agony, as a response to human need. Fletcher's (1975) argument for euthanasia is essentially based around four points:

1 The quality of life is to be valued over biological life.

2 Death is a friend to someone with a debilitating illness.

3 All medical interventions place human will against nature and extraordinary means.

4 Special equipment and unnecessary surgery are not morally required for a person who is terminally ill.

People are prepared to 'face death and accept death as preferable to continuous suffering for the patient and the family' (Fletcher, 1969). There is no distinction between our response to a suffering animal or human. There is no difference between passive and active euthanasia (withdrawing treatment or using treatment to bring death to a close) as the result is the same. He extends his view of active euthanasia to very severely disabled children.

Conservative Protestant

A quite different Protestant perspective is represented by Arthur Dyck (1975). Dyck thinks an act of kindness can result in withdrawing treatment but not doing something actively to bring about death. Permitting some acts of active euthanasia, such as in the case of severely disabled children, seems to be creating a class of human beings who are treated as less valued. He argues that a mentally retarded child is not dying, is not in pain, and cannot choose to die. 'Since killing is generally wrong it should be kept to as narrow a range of exceptions as possible' (Dyck, 1975, p119). While mercy is a moral obligation, killing is never a mercy. The term mercy killing is a contradiction and when we use the term to justify the killing of the disabled or the mentally incompetent, we fail to care for the most needy in the community, which is a fundamental moral duty. Dyck's view is in keeping with traditional Christian thought, and most Christian theologians, which holds that active, direct help in the taking of human life is prohibited.

Whereas voluntary euthanasia, self-willed by a rational, legally competent person, has been permitted by some theologians, active euthanasia in which the person plays no role, has been condemned by the majority of Christian thinkers. The ethical approaches to the problem taken by Christians sometimes reflect a move from general principles to specific applications (the sanctity of life to the prohibition of euthanasia) and also at times the concern about the sinful nature of human beings and their unreliability at making good decisions through the use of 'right reason' (Veatchi, 1981).

Muslim perspectives

In 1981 the First International Conference on Islamic Medicine endorsed the Islamic Code of Medical Ethics (Islamic Organization of Medical Sciences, 1981, p65), which states the following:

> Mercy killing, like suicide, finds no support except in the atheistic way of thinking that believes that our life on this earth is followed by void. The claim of killing for painful hopeless illness is also refuted, for there is no human pain that cannot be largely conquered by medication or by suitable neurosurgery …

Classic Muslim sources say very little about euthanasia explicitly but there are references to suicide which provide a starting point for thinking about Muslim perspectives of voluntary euthanasia. The Qur'an states:

Activity

Consider three different religious perspectives and identify the ethical principles underlying their approach to euthanasia.

Take not life which Allah made sacred otherwise than in the course of justice.

Qur'an 6:151 and 17:33

do not cast yourself into perdition by your own hand.

2:195

do not kill yourselves, surely God is merciful to you.

4:29

Muhammad Sayyid Tantawi (1928–), a major Sunni authority, adds to these references the Prophet's opposition to suicide and concludes that:

Islamic law … orders physicians to be concerned for the sick, and, at the end, to take pains to care for them, and for both patient and doctor to leave the result up to God – may He be praised and exalted – and for the physician not to answer the plea for the patient to end his life.

*Quoted in **Brockopp**, 2003, p178*

In other words Tantawi moves from the scriptural prohibition of suicide to a ban on voluntary euthanasia (ignoring the pleas of a patient for doctor-assisted suicide) but he goes on to argue that in the case of involuntary euthanasia, when a doctor has a patient who has a beating heart but no brain life, accepting God's will can involve disconnecting the life-support machine.

Human dignity does not reside in the individual person's freedom to choose death, to exercise a right to die, but rather in the relationship with God. The value of life comes from God. Brockopp sees this attitude in the Qur'an:

Perish humankind! How unthankful they are?
Of what did He create them?
Of a sperm-drop
He created them, and determined them,
Then the way eased for them,
Then makes them to die, and buries them,
Then, when He wills, He raises them.
No indeed! Humanity has not accomplished His bidding.

Qur'an 80:16–23

God's involvement in human life begins at conception and lasts through life, death and to resurrection. God is actively involved in a human life, an active principle in the world. The moment of death is of little importance compared to the afterlife and attitude near death should be one of resignation or acceptance. God gives life and only God can take life and, indeed, one verse suggests that he determines the lifespan of the person (Qur'an 6.2). This emphasises not only God's authority in questions of life but also the need to respect life.

Brockopp argues that there are distinctions between euthanasia as killing and euthanasia as letting someone die (Brockopp, 2003, p179), between the intention of easing pain and the intention to observe God's wishes, and the actions of suicide or homicide and natural death. In each case, the first is unacceptable and the second is acceptable. In each case there is either an acceptance of God's will or an attempt to interrupt or get in the way of God's will.

However, there is some diversity in some of these interpretations. For instance it is not clear that 'do not kill yourselves' (4:29) is the correct translation and others argue 'do not kill each other' is a better translation, even though it is useful to understand as including a prohibition of suicide (Brockopp, 2003, p183). Classical scholars do not require a blood money payment in response for suicide, as there is for homicide, but differ over whether the imam should pray at the funeral. Perhaps as only God can know for certain whether a person truly intends to seek death, it is difficult to be absolutely sure about cases of suicide.

Brockopp also observes a considerable amount of interest in martyrdom which he argues shows a distinction between ethical principles and practice. There are Prophetic hadiths which give insight. The soldier fighting a jihad, who accidentally slays himself when fighting in battle, was not seeking martyrdom or suicide and is looked favourably upon by the Prophet, while another soldier who is fatally wounded falls on his own sword so is not looked on favourably. Intention here is crucial.

Much of this addresses voluntary euthanasia, including assisted suicide, but what of involuntary euthanasia? It has already been noted that some argue that if the brain is dead God's will has already been accomplished but other scholars oppose this, suggesting that the failure of the brain stem is not valid proof of death because of the possibility that a person may come back to life (see Krawietz, 2003, pp200–201). It is possible that the soul may return to a body. And Egypt, for example, still uses the heartbeat as the indicator of life or death. Another argument against involuntary euthanasia is that life remains holy and should be respected and protected. This argument makes reference to the example of a brain-dead woman giving birth, or the continued growing of fingernails and hair (see Krawietz, 2003, p201). A further argument is that there is no line between life and death but, in fact, there is a process from one to the other and only God can truly know the exact hour of death, the exact time at which the soul departs. This theology of the time of the departure of the soul makes involuntary euthanasia, such as switching off life-support machines or withdrawing feeding, very difficult if not impossible to resolve.

Hindu perspectives

Key terms

Self-willed death: the decision to accept death in the hope of enlightenment.

In classic Indian thought, the concept of the **self-willed death** influences Hindu perspectives on euthanasia. It is informed by four values:

- a respect for life
- an understanding that human life is necessary for enlightenment but can prevent it
- an ascetic idea of the value of accepting death when it comes and rejoicing in that
- an idea of the heroism of accepting defeat honourably.

Life has a special place, though not quite a sanctity in the sense found in Western religious traditions. In ancient Indian texts (the Rig Veda) long life (Rg III.3.7), good health (Rg I.89.4) and prosperity are rewards from the gods. Deities are called upon and prayed to, to protect the body and keep it from disease for a full life, thought of as a hundred years. Life is affirmed.

In addition to this sense of respect for long life, is the idea that life is an instrument to something beyond life, that the body is also an expression of bondage and suffering from which we want to escape. Coward, Lipner and Young argue that the rupture of the soul from the body and all matter is viewed as a positive thing in the **Upanishads** (Coward, Lipner and Young, 1989, p85) because of the bliss of liberation which transcends the human condition. Of course the human condition is needed to reach enlightenment, but the body is also something that holds you back from enlightenment.

An extension of this value within **Jainism** is the idea that the wise one should know when the time for death has come and should rejoice in its arrival, even refusing food to bring it to fulfilment. It should be accepted. This is *sallekhana*, voluntary death through fasting. The elimination of the body is done to bring about the elimination of suffering near the end of the natural life span. This is an interesting paradox, that within a religion an idea both of non-violence and also self-willed death can exist.

It is thought that there is some connection between the idea of the virtuous self-willed death and the heroic death in battle, the struggle against the opposition. In ancient times in India soldiers defeated in battle might commit suicide to avoid shame, and wives of killed husbands might also take their own lives. Coward, Lipner and Young argue that in this culture the idea that self-willed death would lead a person to Heaven can be traced (Coward, Lipner and Young, 1989, pp82–83).

There is a sense then in which there can be 'freedom to leave' the suffering of an incurable disease or debilitating old age. This can be seen as a heroic and religious decision, a choice to seek to move on beyond this life. A self-willed death can be seen as a legitimate response to debilitating old age and incurable disease. This is quite a different ethic than that found in Western religious traditions and in ancient Greece or Rome. Once someone had declared they wanted a self-willed death, of their own accord, they could be assisted by others. Other people could not choose to mercy kill them – an autonomous decision is necessary.

Nevertheless it is clear that there are tensions between these values. A particular tension is that between the sacramental view of life, where life is sacred in and of itself and the instrumental view of life where life has fundamental value but not intrinsic value. In the first view life must be preserved because of that which it is. In the second view life is valued as a tool for a greater good.

The idea of self-willed death gives a Hindu perspective on voluntary euthanasia, something actively chosen by the individual for religious grounds. The Brahmic lawgivers view it as a legitimate way of dealing with extreme old age and severe ill health, distinct from suicide. Voluntary euthanasia can be **dharmic**, righteous and religious. The **Bhagavad-Gita** disapproves of mindless starving of the body (17.6), and places importance on the state of mind of the person at the hour of death (8.5, 8.6). Meditation on God will lead to salvation, but thoughts of a different kind lead to rebirth.

However, there are different views on this matter. Some commentators on the Bhagavad-Gita argue that people should live out their lives to the full and this relates to the theory of the four stages of life all of which need to be passed through to complete all goals. There is criticism which emerged in the 10th century where commentators argued that there should be no mourning for those who sought death by starvation, immolation or poison. However, Coward, Lipner and Young argue that it is clear that while there was this opposition, including opposition to sati, the self-immolation by widows, the practice continued (Coward, Lipner and Young, 1989, pp110–11).

Key terms

Upanishads: philosophical teachings that form the later part of the Vedas.

Jainism: founded in India in the 6th century BC as a reaction against orthodox Brahmanism. The religion teaches salvation by perfection through successive lives, and non-injury to living creatures.

Dharma: has different shades of meaning, but can be taken in this context as the 'right way of living' or 'proper conduct'.

Bhagavad-Gita: the sacred 'Song of God', composed c.200 BC; a holy text revered by followers of Hinduism.

Under British rule, suicide and euthanasia were deemed illegal and the distinction between the two has blurred. In modern times there is a concern to distinguish between self-willed death through starvation, and suicide, which has been complicated by the availability of new medical technologies. Some may find it too difficult to fast to death. In these cases perhaps the withdrawal of treatment is legitimate, extending the idea of self-willed death, but this conflicts with Western views on the legitimacy of voluntary euthanasia or doctor-assisted death. If the freedom to die has no medical or legal limits there is a danger that it may be exploited to extend far beyond the religious ideas behind self-willed death.

This section has largely looked at voluntary euthanasia, but with the possibilities of extending the idea of self-willed death to included doctor-assisted euthanasia, we can ask the question of whether that perspective could be extended to involuntary euthanasia in situations where patients are in an irreversible coma. Here the tradition of self-willed death does not seem to offer many resources for establishing a Hindu perspective if there is no individual determination to seek death. A living will might offer some scope for this if a person's intention has been laid down in appropriately religious terms, and the tradition of releasing a person from the bondage of their body might also present an argument for the justification of removal of life-support or feeding. Against this rests the non-harm rule and the need to respect life. Would a doctor involved in such a process bring bad karma on him or herself? There are sources for justifying such actions but there are also sources for opposing it.

Buddhist perspectives

Peter Harvey writes that for Buddhists, death is the most important life crisis, as it is the link to the next life. The state of mind that a person has at the point of death has an impact on the next life. Buddhism, as a result, is especially interested in advocating good deaths and supports many of the ideals of the hospice movement. To die in a calm state, undrugged and conscious, free of anxiety, fear or attachment, is preferable and Buddhists may chant around those who are dying or provide pictures of Buddha for them to help their preparation for death.

Damien Keown writes that one who follows the first precept, 'does not kill a living being, does not cause a living being to be killed, does not approve of the killing of a living being' (Keown, 1995, p170). When considering voluntary euthanasia, asking someone to end your life is asking for a living being to be killed. A doctor being asked to kill a patient or follow a living will is aiding a living being to be killed. In principle, then, Buddhism is opposed to euthanasia. Keown argues that the **Vinaya** is a particularly important source for Buddhist ethics as it contains examples and hypothetical cases from which moral viewpoints can be drawn. An important example of this is the monastic rule which prohibits the taking of human life and is a useful place to begin to examine Buddhist perspectives of euthanasia:

> Should any monk intentionally deprive a human being of life or look about so as to be his knife-bringer, or eulogize death, or incite [anyone] to death saying 'My good man, what need have you of this evil, difficult life? Death would be better for you than life,' – or who should deliberately and purposefully in various ways eulogize death or incite [anyone] to death: he is also one who is defeated, he is not in communion.

Vin.iii.72

Key terms

Vinaya: the monastic discipline, or the scriptural collection of its rules and commentaries.

This rule seems specifically to have been written to prevent the taking of life in situations where euthanasia might be considered. Damien Keown writes that there are cases of Buddhist monks caring for patients where the death of the patient was thought desirable because of quality of their life (Keown, 1996, p110). The issue of whether the death of a person is actively sought or passively allowed is immaterial in Buddhism as intention is crucial to moral action. So both active and passive euthanasia are affected by this way of thinking. It is what is intended that determines whether the consequence is bad or good karma, not whether you intervene to do something to hasten death, or stand aside to allow it to happen. The issue of autonomy also seems to be addressed by this rule. It seems that a person's freedom does not extend to the right to seek death. Voluntary euthanasia, a person choosing death, is incompatible with this Buddhist thinking.

Keown also does not think that the Buddhist virtue of compassion would lead to a justification of euthanasia. He describes a case in the Vinaya (Vin.ii.79) where some monks suggest that a dying monk would be better served by having the death brought about sooner, rather than extend the current condition. In making death their aim, the monks were breaking the precept. However, if a terminally ill patient is resigned to or accepting of death, having exhausted all treatments, then this can be seen as different from seeking death. The following account seems to suggest that, in this case, a patient may refuse food. In other words, the life of a terminally ill person need not necessarily be preserved at all costs.

> You should not kill yourself by throwing yourself off a cliff, nor by any other method even down to withdrawal from food. If one who is sick ceases to take food with the intention of dying when medicine and nursing care are at hand, he commits a dukka ta. But in the case of a patient who has suffered a long time with a serious illness the nursing monks may become weary and turn away in despair thinking 'when will we ever cure him of this illness?' Here it is legitimate to decline food and medical care if the patient sees that the monks are worn out and his life cannot be prolonged even with intensive care.

VA.ii.467

This does not extend to putting someone out of their misery, or mercy killing. Two examples from the Vinaya suggest this. In one instance a monk kills someone with a single blow to bring to an end a slow torturous execution, and in another instance an elderly, severely injured man is made a drink which kills him. In both cases the monks in question were found guilty of breaching the precept. In mercy killing, the act of killing is still doing something to the 'doctor'. A desire to end the suffering is mixed with an aversion to the act of ending life and, of course, there is no guarantee that killing the patient will end the suffering as the next life may contain more suffering.

This does not prevent giving pain relief to the terminally ill which may as an unintended consequence hasten death. If death is not the intention then this does not break the precept, even if foresight suggests this may be the case. If the medicine is given to alleviate pain even though it may also hasten death, the rule has not been broken, though this is not the case in situations where a patient's family are pressurising a patient. Treatment may also become an excessive burden for the patient in circumstances where the patient is in the advanced stages of a disease.

Keown (1996) argues that these texts should not be put aside lightly, though whether they should be followed in modern contexts is another question. In other words, while it is possible to draw moral conclusions from examples in ancient texts, this may not be the only Buddhist way of making moral decisions. Nevertheless, as a general rule it would appear that Buddhism suggests that nature should be allowed to take its course. Keown notes that there seems to be little interest from Buddhists in campaigning for euthanasia to be made legal so it seems that euthanasia, from a Buddhist perspective, is unethical.

Peter Harvey writes that Buddhist counselling for those approaching death is to help acceptance and allow the patient to let go of life, to relinquish attachment (Harvey, 2000, p302). Jacqui James notes:

> Learning how to die properly is all about learning how to let go, learning how to watch the natural ebb and flow of all things, learning that life is a process of continual birth and death. When you see this cyclical movement clearly then there is no more fear of death. When you have learnt that not only have you learnt how to die but you have also learnt how to live.

*Quoted in **Harvey**, 2000, p302*

Harvey writes that there are some Buddhists who are concerned that if someone refuses life-sustaining treatment, they are not allowing bad karma to run its course, and could allow it to continue into the next life. Karmically caused suffering is better faced in this life. In fact, allowing for more life may lead a person to have more virtuous thoughts at the point of death and if there is a possibility of such thoughts it is better to allow the person to live on than to bring death more quickly. Equally, if that treatment reduced the possibility of such thoughts then it is better not to have it.

What about cases of involuntary euthanasia? What about people who might not be persons any more because they are in a coma from which they will never return? In these situations the possibility of a good death seems impossible. If the patient is not conscious, or is unable to gain consciousness, ideas about preparing for a good mental state before passing into rebirth are inappropriate.

Patients in comas lead to quite different views among Buddhists. In cases where the patient does not have severe brain damage, they might be able to breathe and digest food but are they a person? Buddhists value all living creatures, including those which are not human, so consciousness is not necessarily a condition of moral significance. Some might say that a person in a coma is incapable of conscious volition, of moral action, and therefore a life not worth living. Others would argue that meditation reaches states of non-normal consciousness and that there are qualities in the mind of a coma patient, even if they are dormant. Even if there is no evidence of mental activity some Buddhists believe in the possibility of formless rebirths, where there is a consciousness without a body.

However, if the patient is brain-dead then they could be regarded as already dead and if this is the case disconnecting the life-support machine could not be considered killing them. Cases such as that of Tony Bland (see p123) would not be insurmountable. The decision could be made to disconnect the life-support machine.

So it would appear that Buddhists would object to many cases of voluntary euthanasia though they might approve of withdrawing excessive or burdensome treatment if that helped the patient to prepare for death. Whether it is active or passive makes no difference because in Buddhist ethical thinking it is the intention that matters. In cases of involuntary euthanasia, if the brain is dead then the person is dead but in other cases it is less clear whether withdrawing treatment could be justified.

Sikh perspectives

Sikh ethics come from a number of sources including the teachings of the Guru Granth Sahib, the Sikh Code of Conduct (the Rehat Maryada), the examples set by the gurus, and the living experience of the Sikh community. There are a number of principles from which Sikh perspectives may be deduced. First is the belief that life is a gift from God, to be highly respected and not curtailed. Such matters are the will of God. The gurus opposed and rejected suicide as it prevents God's plan and this can be extended to include voluntary euthanasia. Not unlike other religions Sikhism sees suffering as part of God's intention. It is, in fact, part of karma, to be accepted rather than avoided.

Nevertheless, there is a responsibility to treat life responsibly. This could include not prolonging life unnecessarily, through excessive or burdensome treatment, or indeed leaving a person who is brain-dead on life-support, and artificial feeding indefinitely should not be encouraged.

Beyond this is a basic need to care for others, especially those who are less fortunate; those seeking euthanasia need to be cared for and supported to see that other options are more desirable.

In broad terms, then, assisted suicide and euthanasia are not encouraged but nor is maintaining a terminal patient on artificial life-support for a prolonged period in a vegetative state. That said, there is no prescriptive doctrinal view on euthanasia.

Activities

1. How would you respond to a member of the Jewish faith who argued that the question of euthanasia is not so much about the rights of people but the covenant between us and God?

2. Some people argue that the religious view of suffering expressed by the Roman Catholic Church is outdated and insensitive. Why might they make this claim?

3. Explain the religious principle that rejects the view that we should have control over the nature and timing of the ends of our lives.

4. What objections might Catholics have to Fletcher's view that euthanasia can be a loving thing to do based on Christian principles, and how might he respond?

5. On what basis might some Hindus argue in favour of euthanasia and why might other Hindus object?

6. How would you respond to a Buddhist who argues that every moment of life is worth living for the possibility of better thoughts at the moment of death leading to enlightenment?

7. Examine the religious view that because life is sacred, euthanasia should not be permitted.

■ Evaluating euthanasia

While euthanasia is prohibited in the UK, there are practices close to it that take place within the framework of the law. Some philosophers, such as Peter Singer, argue that there is no moral difference between the withdrawal of treatment (which is currently legal in the UK) and the active killing of a patient by a lethal injection. Consider someone standing by a canal, watching a boy drowning. The bystander fails to throw the ring to the boy and the boy drowns. This is morally reprehensible, but the bystander has not actually drowned the boy. In some countries, to pass a road accident where no one is attending the casualties is a criminal offence, but it is not the same as murder.

The religious arguments against euthanasia carry the weight of theological and teaching traditions. Some have challenged those traditions. Catholic theologian Hans Kung (1928–) has stated: 'as a Christian and a theologian I am convinced that the all-merciful God, who has given men and women freedom and responsibility for their lives, has also left to dying people the responsibility for making a conscientious decision about the manner and time of their deaths' (www.dignityindying. org.uk). This goes against the Judaeo-Christian prohibition of killing. However, there have always been exceptions, such as killing in just wars and in self-defence. If a believer were to oppose all killing, taking a pacifist line with regard to personal and national moral behaviour, then euthanasia would be untenable. A believer who endorses killing in war or in self-defence might be able to find a starting-point for a theological case for euthanasia. The Roman Catholic Church doesn't go for this, but approves the ending of treatment in situations in which death is inevitable and the treatment is precarious and burdensome (*Declaration on Euthanasia*, 1980). The Church argues this is not euthanasia and is not evil.

Many arguments in the euthanasia debate relate to consequences about which we cannot be certain. It seems unlikely that a country following the Netherlands' lead could ever slide into the kind of non-voluntary euthanasia that took place in Nazi Germany. There was an ideological system that underpinned that development. More likely dangers are to be found in the systems that might regulate the practice. Could they ever be foolproof? The protection of the system from error or deliberate misuse raises real concerns – and more so in the light of concerns already being raised about the power of doctors.

We cannot predict the impact that euthanasia might have on people's perceptions of hospitals, or how it might affect an elderly person's perception of whether he or she is a burden. The Netherlands can be used as a test case for detecting any **slippery slope** or negative impact that it may be having, but even within Europe cultures differ widely, and whether such a model could operate in a different society is open to question. Because of this, it is not clear that a society which endorsed legalised voluntary euthanasia would ultimately be better than one where it existed only as an illegal practice.

These potential social dangers stand against the severe restrictions on individual autonomy that result from prohibiting voluntary euthanasia. If you decide that the risks to the community are too great, then you must reject the claims of those who want to avoid deaths that, in their eyes, are too painful and humiliating to accept. While the palliative care provided by organisations such as the hospice movement is undoubtedly a benefit to society, as it cultivates respect and sensitivity towards the terminally

■ **Key terms**

Slippery slope: the idea that once one seemingly insignificant ethical restriction is lifted, much more serious ones are likely to follow; the thin edge of the wedge.

ill, and is a benefit to the individuals who receive the care, this will never satisfy those who claim that only the terminally ill can know that their lives are not worth living.

Activities

1. How might pre-existing religious teaching on the taking of life be used to support voluntary euthanasia?

2. Can you suggest reasons why people might say that voluntary euthanasia is not just about the rights of the patient who wants to die?

3. What evidence can you draw on to support each of these claims: a) the autonomy of the individual is paramount; b) the sanctity of and respect for human life is paramount. In what ways do these claims converge and in what ways do they diverge?

4. A doctor withdraws treatment from a patient in a permanent vegetative state and then waits as the patient dies. Another doctor delivers a lethal injection to a patient in an identical state and the patient dies almost immediately. Are there any moral differences between what the two doctors have done? Which is better? Justify your view.

5. What are the religious and ethical arguments in favour of and against euthanasia?

6. Traditionally religious believers trusted sacred scripture and religious teaching authorities for giving guidance on moral conduct but in modern times many believers value their own freedom and judgement over those traditional sources. How might this affect views of euthanasia in the future?

Extracts from key texts

The Church of England, 2004

A letter sent to the House of Lords on behalf of the Archbishop of Canterbury and the Cardinal Archbishop of Westminster, with the Joint Submission of the Church of England House of Bishops and the Catholic Bishops' Conference of England and Wales, to the House of Lords Select Committee on the Assisted Dying for the Terminally Ill Bill, 2nd September 2004.

> Dear Lord Mackay,
>
> Select Committee on the Assisted Dying for the Terminally Ill Bill
>
> We are writing to send your Committee a joint submission from the Church of England House of Bishops and the Catholic Bishops' Conference of England and Wales.
>
> We believe very strongly that respect for human life at all its stages is the foundation of a civilised society, and that the long term consequences of any change in the law to allow euthanasia in limited circumstances would be immensely grave. This is a view shared not just within our Churches, but very widely among those of all faiths and none who share a moral outlook founded on respect for human life and the protection of vulnerable people.
>
> As you know, having considered the evidence and the arguments against legalising euthanasia in great depth, the House of Lords Committee on Medical Ethics in 1994 firmly rejected any change in the law to allow euthanasia. They concluded:

'The right to refuse medical treatment is far removed from the right to request assistance in dying. We spent a long time considering the very strongly held and sincerely expressed views of those witnesses who advocated voluntary euthanasia … Ultimately, however, we do not believe that these arguments are sufficient reason to weaken society's prohibition of intentional killing. That prohibition is the cornerstone of law and of social relationships. It protects each one of us impartially, embodying the belief that all are equal. We do not wish that protection to be diminished and we therefore recommend no change in the law to permit euthanasia. We acknowledge that there are individual cases in which euthanasia may be seen by some to be appropriate. But individual cases cannot reasonably establish the foundation of a policy which would have such serious and widespread repercussions. [HMSO, London, 1994, paras 236–7].

We hope and pray that your Committee will reaffirm and endorse that conclusion, given that the strength of the arguments against euthanasia are undiminished, and the empirical evidence of the damaging effects of legalising euthanasia in the Netherlands is even stronger now.

In our submission we have sought briefly to set out what seem to us the key fundamental principles and then we make some specific points on this particular Bill. We hope your Committee will find it helpful.

With every good wish

Yours sincerely,

Archbishop of Canterbury

Cardinal Archbishop of Westminster

■ Chapter summary

What is voluntary euthanasia?

- 'I will not prescribe a deadly drug to please someone, nor give advice that may cause his death.' (Hippocrates)

- Physicians are 'not only to restore the health, but to mitigate pain and dolours; and not only when such mitigation may conduce to recovery, but when it may serve to make a fair and easy passage'. (Francis Bacon)

- Euthanasia is a criminal offence in virtually all countries, and it is strongly opposed by most governments and religious organisations.

- Should we have the ability to control our own destinies, by being offered assistance to take our own lives when we judge that the quality of our lives has deteriorated to the point at which they are no longer worth living?

- In the Netherlands, about a thousand assisted deaths take place each year.

- Voluntary or assisted euthanasia is when a person asks to be helped to die.

- Involuntary euthanasia is when a person cannot express their wishes and it is questionable whether it is appropriate to sustain their life.

- Euthanasia may be passive in that treatment may be withdrawn and a person allowed to die, or active, for instance in the case of the administering of a lethal injection.

Arguments for voluntary euthanasia:

- Voluntary euthanasia is not murder, as killing humans who do not want to live is not wrong.

- It shows mercy to those suffering with intolerable pain from an incurable disease.

- It gives people autonomy – the right to choose their destiny, including how they live and die.

- Voluntary euthanasia should be an option for a competent adult who is able and willing to make such a decision.

- Euthanasia goes on already, in an uncontrolled and therefore unsafe way.

- It allows human beings to live dignified lives – the ends of their lives should be dignified.

Arguments against euthanasia:

- Motives may be questionable – we may ask in moments of despair, or out of misplaced fears of the future.

- Mistakes could be made through faulty diagnosis.

- The system might be subject to abuse in the case of elderly relatives.

- Euthanasia might have a negative impact on the community by reducing the importance of care of patients who are dying, or by preventing people from going to hospital for fear of the possible consequences.

- Acceptance of the practice of killing in hospitals could reduce the respect for life that civilisations uphold.

Involuntary euthanasia

- Typically discussed in relation to patients who are comatose or in cases of severely terminally ill newborn babies.

- Withdrawing burdensome medical treatment is not controversial but withdrawing food and water is more controversial, as in the case of Tony Bland who was starved to death.

- Some argue severely disabled babies are a burden on families and society and should be allowed to die.

Jewish perspectives on euthanasia

- Human life is of value beyond measure and its ending is catastrophic, so every last breath must be fought for.

- Preserving life is an ultimate goal of Judaism, and the body belongs to God.

- The Talmud forbids killing so active euthanasia is forbidden.

- Artificial treatment which prolongs life can be withdrawn.

Christian perspectives on euthanasia

- The human person is the image of God.

- Bible teachings prohibit killing and promote healing although there are some exceptions in terms of self-sacrifice for others.

- Catholic teaching opposes all euthanasia as it interferes with God's plan – the Gospel is a gospel of life – killing is an offence against the dignity of the human person and sometimes suffering in life is there for a purpose.

- However, excessive burdensome treatment is unnecessary.

- Some liberal Protestants argue that euthanasia can be an act of love as the quality matters as much as quantity, death is not the end and can be a friend to those suffering terribly.

- Other more conservative Protestants argue that while withdrawing treatment could be an act of kindness when death is inevitable and life is intolerable, it should only take place in exceptional cases and cannot include actively taking life.

Muslim perspectives on euthanasia

- Mercy killing is prohibited and the Prophet was opposed to suicide.

- The end of brain life is the point of death so disconnecting life-support is acceptable.

- Human dignity resides in the relationship with God as God is involved in human life throughout.

- Self-sacrifice in jihad is possible but not if the intention is to die.

- There are differing views on involuntary euthanasia as some argue the body has sanctity and others feel the line between death and life is difficult to draw in cases of comas.

Hindu perspectives on euthanasia

- There is a concept of self-willed death based on respect for life, an understanding that human life is necessary for enlightenment, that death should be accepted when it comes and that there is heroism in such acceptance.

- Long life is advocated but the body is something we want to escape from to eliminate suffering.

- On the other hand some argue that life should be lived out to the full.

Buddhist perspectives on euthanasia

- Death is the link to the next life so a good death is important for that transition.

- What we think of at death matters as it influences rebirth.

- Monastic rules prohibit euthanasia, even to end suffering more quickly, though this does not extend to pain relief, even if it hastens death.

- Some argue that karma must be allowed to run its course so death must not be hastened.

- Some argue that even in comatose people it is possible that consciousness remains in some form.

Sikh perspectives on euthanasia

- Life is a gift from God and God decides when it should end.

- Prolonging life in a burdensome way when death is inevitable and close is unnecessary.

- Assisted suicide and euthanasia are not encouraged but nor is maintaining a terminal patient on artificial life-support for a prolonged period in a vegetative state.

Evaluating euthanasia

- Some argue that there is no moral difference between the withdrawal of treatment and the active killing of a patient by lethal injection.

- The theological traditions that underpin the religious arguments have been challenged, as there are exceptions for the no-killing rule in the case of self-defence and war.

- The consequences of legalised euthanasia are uncertain.

- There would be flaws in the systems that might regulate the practice. Could they ever be foolproof?

- We cannot predict the impact that voluntary euthanasia might have on people's perceptions of hospitals, or how it might affect an elderly person's perception of whether he or she is a burden.

- The potential social dangers stand against the restrictions of individual autonomy that result from prohibiting voluntary euthanasia.

Further reading

Again, very divergent views on this subject can be found among my favourite authors such as:

Glover, J., *Causing Death and Saving Lives*, Penguin, 1990, pp119–149

Pojman, L., *Ethics, Discovering Right and Wrong*, US Military Academy, 2002, pp1–23

Singer, P., *Practical Ethics*, Cambridge University Press, 1993, pp175–217

Brockopp, J., *Islamic Ethics of Life: abortion, war and euthanasia*, University of South Carolina Press, 2003, pp173–213

Harvey, P., *An Introduction to Buddhist Ethics*, Cambridge University Press, 2000, pp286–310

Sherwin, B. L., *Jewish Ethics for the Twenty-First Century*, Syracuse University Press, 2001, pp35–61

Hoose, B., *Christian Ethics*, Cassell, 1998, pp95–109

And my favourite anthology:

Singer, P., *Ethics*, in the Oxford Readers series, Oxford University Press, 1994

In this chapter you have:

- considered the distinct ethical ideas of active, passive, voluntary and involuntary euthanasia and the moral questions arising out of those ideas

- examined religious arguments for and against different kinds of euthanasia and their relative strengths and weaknesses.

10 Religion and the created or uncreated world

By the end of this chapter you will:

■ have explored religious perspectives on the created or uncreated world: including the nature of creation, intention behind creation, God's role in sustaining the world, human status in creation and duties to creation, the status of the non-human world

■ have considered some ethical implications of these beliefs and issues arising from them.

Key questions

1 Is the universe created by a supreme being and is there a divine plan?
2 What do religions say about how humans should treat the world around them and the other life-forms in the world?
3 Does the universe have a moral status – is it good, bad or neither?
4 Do human beings have a purpose in the universe?

Introduction

Religions do not, for the most part, put forward a single **cosmology** but they attempt to try to give an account of the nature and origin of the universe, or creation. This chapter explores the important features of the religious contributions in the matter of religion and the created world. In many religious traditions there are subtle, and sometimes substantial, differences, but to represent each of these differences is beyond the scope of this text. To provide some depth in covering religious perspectives, important and interesting contributions from religious traditions are included. Each tradition is explored in separate sections because cosmologies vary considerably (Bowker, 1997, p238) though similarities can be found in some areas.

Jewish perspectives on the created world

The Creation and sustaining of the world

Jewish scriptures have several cosmologies. The Bible begins, in Genesis 1:1, with the phrase 'In the beginning' and in Proverbs 8, 22 states that Wisdom is called, 'the beginning'. In joining this with Genesis 1:1 it can be argued that the Wisdom of God created everything. Psalm 104 contains the phrase: 'How manifold are thy works O Lord In wisdom hast thou made them all: The earth is full of thy possessions.' This Psalm is full of praise for the wonder, beauty and wisdom of the Divine Creation. Rabbi David Rosen writes: 'Indeed, fundamental to Biblical teaching is the affirmation that our world is created by God and thus belongs to Him' (Rosen, p1). The created world is beautiful and wonderful, reflecting the greatness of the creator.

The second creation account (or second part of the creation account) focuses on Adam and Eve. It also suggests that God is the origin of everything. It is divine will that creates everything and it was created out of nothing. This is not a single act, but creation is an ongoing act. The **liturgy** in the Jewish prayer books states that God renews the work of creation every day. It is ongoing (Bowker, 1997, p239).

God sustains the world and also it is made and sustained according to God's plan, His Wisdom. It is not an accident but is created with a purpose.

The status and duties of humankind and the non-human world

Because of the special place of human beings in creation, and their special powers, they have special duties, a specific responsibility and purpose in relation to creation. Rosen writes: 'The human person is placed in the world in the Garden of Eden "to work and preserve it"' (Genesis 2:15). Jewish tradition describes this task as a 'Divinely mandated "partnership" with God in His creation' (Rosen, p1). The duty of human beings is to work creation, preserve it, develop it and protect it, all within the framework of obedience to God's law.

D. B. Fink notes that in the first chapter of Genesis human beings are not made until the sixth day, 'after light and darkness, water and dry land, plants and animal life'. Human beings are the final act of the Creator God. Does this mean human beings are the pinnacle of creation? If so then God made the world for the enjoyment of humanity. Alternatively perhaps human beings were made as an afterthought after the main business of creation and are not quite as important in the divine plan of things as we might like to think. The place of human beings in the world seems very different according to whichever interpretation you take.

Human beings have great power over the created world but, at the same time, the living things of the created world are good intrinsically. Maimonides writes: 'All the other beings have been created for their own sakes, and not for the sake of something else' (quoted in Fink, 1998) and this includes human beings.

Genesis, however, also makes reference to human beings having **dominion** over the created world, which seems as though God is giving humanity the right to exploit nature to the full.

> And God said, 'Let us make man in our image, after our likeness; and let them have dominion over the fish of the sea, and over the fowl of the air, and over the cattle and over all the earth, and over every creeping thing that creeps upon the earth.'
>
> *Genesis 1:26*

However, Fink argues this interpretation is not the case. He notes that 900 years ago, Rashi, a distinguished commentator on the Torah …

> … noted that the Hebrew word for 'take dominion' (v'yirdu) comes from the same root as 'to descend' (yarad). Thus, he declares: 'When humanity is worthy, we have dominion over the animal kingdom; when we are not, we descend below the level of animals and the animals rule over us.'
>
> *Fink, 1998*

Any superiority is only given when responsibility is upheld. Responsibility is precisely what is not shown when aspects of the created world are exploited to extinction.

Through an understanding of both creation stories (that of Genesis 1 and Genesis 2) other important ideas come to inform the relationship between humanity and creation. The concept of **stewardship** is found in the story of the Garden of Eden. God places human beings in the garden with instructions to work it and care for it. The idea of dominion in Genesis 1 is understood as stewardship through Genesis 2. The German-Jewish scholar Benno Jacob (1862–1945) sees God's commandment in

Key terms

Dominion: this refers to the view that the scriptures give humans power over animals and the environment, as opposed to theories of stewardship.

Stewardship: the religious doctrine that humans are responsible to God for animals and for the rest of the environment/created world, since the mode of the creation of humans singles them out as the species that rules the earth on God's behalf. Stewardship in theory should lead to the preservation of both the human and the non-human world, although in practice the diversity of interpretation of what appears to be a simple idea leads also to environmental destruction.

Psalms to watch over the garden as suggesting that the land is God's property and not ours: 'The earth is the Lord's' (Fink, 1998). Human beings are stewards of the divine trust of creation.

Having given human beings the role of steward and dominion, the day of rest, Shabbat, seems to be a recognition that, 'people will frequently choose to misinterpret their stewardship as license to plunder the natural world' (Fink, 1998). Shabbat is there to restrain humans from the tendency to overuse or exploit excessively. Once a week human beings must remember that the value of creation is more than a monetary consideration. This mandate is also found in the consideration to let land lie fallow every seven years. Fink argues that the created world is a gift from God but ultimately it belongs to God and must be kept for the future. He argues that the Koheleth Rabbah, a collection of homilies based on the book of Ecclesiastes should be observed:

> When God created Adam, he showed him all the trees of the Garden of Eden and said to him: See my works, how lovely they are, how fine they are. All I have created, I created for you. Take care not to corrupt and destroy my universe, for if you destroy it, no one will come after you to put it right.

Ecclesiastes Rabbah 7

This beautiful world should be preserved for our descendants. If it is destroyed, no one will be there to repair it.

Christian perspectives on the created world

The Creation and sustaining of the world

The relationship between the created world and God is very important in Christian sources. Creation depends on God, and believers thank God for creation – everything owes its existence to God. It is an ongoing act and God is responsible for the being of creation, its continued existence now, as well as being brought into being (Bowker, 1997, p239).

Crook (2002) writes that there is a great deal of reflection on the relationship between humankind and the natural world in the Bible and much of it draws heavily and indeed mainly from the Hebrew Scriptures (or Old Testament) as covered in the previous section.

Crook emphasises that God is creator, not the same as creation. All the things that exist were brought into being by God, is of his handiwork and he is sustainer over all. God is behind many of the forces of nature but he is not the same as those forces of nature (Crook, p271). Humankind is also part of this natural order, created and brought into being by God from the dust on the ground (Genesis 2:7).

The status and duties of humankind in the created world

Humankind is uniquely important, and in the image and likeness of God. Human beings have a special role in the Garden of Eden, to look after it and from it multiply, fill the earth and subdue it, having dominion over it and every living creature (Genesis 1:28). This is part of humanity's divine purpose in loving each other and loving God. Creation is good; everything God made was good. God's creation is not evil, or bad, but is the work of God, and as such is good.

Human sin, however, can affect the world and disrupts the natural order. In Genesis 2 the human sin of disobedience leads to expulsion from

---

Activities

1 Compare the ideas of dominion and stewardship. What is the ethical difference between these terms? What do they say about religious attitudes and behaviour to the created world?

2 Read the first two chapters of Genesis and make links between the text and religious interpretations. What is your interpretation?

Eden and a more painful existence. Human wrongdoing brings about evil in creation. Human beings and creation, therefore, are in need of redemption. The flood story (Genesis 6–7) points to the need of God to redeem the whole of creation. After the destruction of the flood, God offers a new covenant: 'an everlasting covenant between God and every living creature of the flesh that is upon the earth' (Genesis 9:16).

However, to this account of the relationship between God and creation (found mainly in the Hebrew Scriptures or Old Testament) there is an important **Christological** dimension which adjusts some of these elements in important ways. Christianity associated Christ with God's creation from the beginning (see 1 Corinthians 8:6, Colossians 1:15). Christ is the Lord through which creation comes, the first born of all creatures and it is in Christ that all creatures are created and exist (Bowker, 1997, p239). The view that God and creation are apart becomes less clear in the human person, for God became human and human beings reflect God. This is suggested in the idea that human beings are made in the image and likeness of God, but extended beyond that because, according to the New Testament, Christ exists at the beginning of time.

Crook notes (Crook, 2002, p274) that God is immanent in nature, interacting with all of nature, loving, suffering and struggling with all of creation. All aspects of creation must be respected by humankind not just because it is made by God but because God is engaged in it. Human responsibility for creation is an obligation which comes with their high status. The sense in which human beings have dominion over the earth underlines their responsibility for creation.

Creation is not finished and God's ongoing relationship with creation means he is continually sustaining it, creating it. Human beings, capable of their own acts of creation and destruction therefore are now co-creators of creation, hence the heightened moral responsibility humans have. When human beings sin, nature is damaged or destroyed.

Beyond these reflections there are strong distinctive currents in Christian thinking which reflect a distinctive contribution to broader Christian understandings. All of creation is valuable to God. God did not just create the world but continues to sustain and redeem the world. D. T. Hessel writes:

> God relates directly to and cares for the well-being of otherkind, created to enjoy being in their own right and not only function as companions or helpers of humankind. Christians are recovering an earth-centered **pneumatology** that experiences God's spirit immanent in creation as the power of life-giving breath (ruah), the Wisdom (logos) continually working to transform and renew all life and the love that sustains it. Biblical images portray the Spirit as 'a healing and subversive life-form – as water, light, dove, mother, fire, breath … wind,' and comforter of the suffering.

Hessel, 1998

Christianity had lost interest in the power of the natural world to be revelatory, to show that humanity was living unsustainably, in a polluting manner. Contemporary Christian cosmology tries to rediscover a relationship between human beings and the rest of creation, a communion of subjects that includes all of the created order.

Key terms

Christological: Christology is a field of study within Christian theology which is concerned with the nature of Jesus the Christ. In particular, how the divine and human are related in his person.

Pneumatology: brand of Christian theology concerned with the Holy Ghost and other spiritual concerns.

■ Key terms

Incarnation: the Christian doctrine of the union of God and man in the person of Jesus Christ.

■ **Activity**

Consider the different Christian views of whether God is in creation. How are they different? What are the implications of these different views?

The status of the non-human world

Dermot A. Lane (2000) explores an important perspective on Christianity and creation surveying recent explorations of the cosmic dimension of the **incarnation**, the relationship between Christ and the whole of creation. The incarnation is an especially important doctrine through which to consider the relationship because it is through incarnation that God reveals the dignity and destiny of every human being. However, it is also through the incarnation that a new understanding of the relationship between Christ and the cosmos is possible. This is found particularly in the New Testament in the logos of St John's Gospel and also Paul's writings.

Lane identifies the writing of Tom Berry in particular. Berry presents in 'A new story' a sense of the fundamental unity between galaxies, the earth, life forms and the emergence of human existence. The human person embodies the earth in a new condition of self-awareness and freedom. Berry writes: 'We bear the universe in our beings as the universe bears us in its being' (Berry, 1978, p132). The new story offers a renewed perspective on the Wisdom and Word of God continually present in the entire cosmic process. The earth seems to be more of a living organism within which humanity exists, rather than something apart from humanity. There is an opportunity to rediscover the sacred and sacramental character of the earth and a new sense of unity with the universe, the earth and human existence.

☑ Muslim perspectives on the created world

The creation and sustaining of the world

The Qur'an affirms that God is the creator and has power over all. His word brings about creation (2.117, 6.73). God exists beyond the created universe and beyond time. F. M. Denny writes that in Islam God is the ultimate holder of dominion over the created world (e.g. Sura 2:107, 5:120) and ultimately all things are returned to Him (Sura 24:42).

The status of the non-human world

Creation is a sign of God's existence and his power over all. The diversity and complexity of creation reflects in many ways God's power, wisdom and majesty. God has created and determined all things in the world and the created world glorifies God:

> Have you not seen that God is glorified by all in the heavens and on the earth – such as the birds with wings outspread? Each knows its worship and glorification, and God is aware of what they do.

Sura 24:41

The signs in the world point to Allah.

> Verily in the heavens and the earth, are Signs for those who believe. And in the creation of yourselves and the fact that animals are scattered (throughout the earth), are Signs for those of assured Faith. And the alteration of Night and Day, and the fact that God sends down Sustenance from the sky, and revives therewith the earth after its death, and in the change of the winds, are Signs for those that are wise.

Qur'an, 45:3–5

Consequently they must not be destroyed. The destruction of the signs of God is a destruction of the things that show God's greatness.

The status and duty of humankind in the created world

Human beings bear a responsibility over the creation (Denny, 1998). They are stewards of creation though other living species are also believed to be communities (Sura 6:38).

Human beings then are part of this creation and their purpose within it is the same as all other aspects of creation. They are in the service of God, '**abh**, the human being as the slave or loving servant of God' but they are also the **khalifa**, 'the Regent of God on earth' (Hewer, 2006, p5).

The human being, was declared a regent or a vice-regent before the creation of the first human being:

> Behold, your Lord said to the angels: 'I will create a vice-regent on earth.' They said: 'Will you place therein one who will make mischief therein and shed blood? While we do celebrate Your praises and glorify Your holy (name)?' He said: 'I know what you know not.'

Qur'an, 2:30

God has given human beings all power and authority over creation:

> And He has subjected to you, as from Him, all that is in the heavens and on earth: behold, in that there are Signs indeed for those who reflect.

Qur'an, 45:13

> Do you not see that God has subjected to your (use) all things in the heavens and on earth. And has made His bounties flow to you in exceeding measure, (both) seen and unseen?

Qur'an, 31:20

> He has made subject to you the Night and the Day; the Sun and the Moon; and the Stars are in subjection by His command: verily in this are Signs for people who are wise.

Qur'an, 16:12

However, this requires them to have the high dignity of *khalifa*. Human beings are 'called to tend to the whole of creation, to cherish it and bring it into a state of perfection' (Hewer, 2006, p5). However, human beings are watched by God in this respect and are held to account.

Creation is more than humanity (Sura 40:57) but the position of humanity in creation is privileged, higher than angels. This theology of supremacy of humanity has been heavily criticised by historian Lynn White in an article critical of the Western religious traditions, and there has been much Muslim reflection on religious teachings, discovering or rediscovering theological and moral sources for a different perception of creation in an era of concern for environmental ethics. The earth is mentioned some 453 times in the Qur'an. The earth is good and has a purity about it: 'Do you not observe that God sends down rain from the sky, so that in the morning the earth becomes green?' (Sura 22:63). Denny notes that, 'Clean dust may be used for ablutions before prayer if clean water is not available' (Denny, 1998). He goes on to observe that the Prophet Muhammad said that: 'The earth has been created for me

Abh: the human being as the slave or loving servant of God.

Khalifa: the idea that the human being is vice-regent of God on earth and must act in God's interests.

as a mosque and as a means of purification.' Earth is a sacred place for human service of God.

Hewer writes that human beings are in a relationship with creation, with the natural world, the wildlife, the natural resources and that a concern of the environment is central to that relationship (Hewer, 2006, p6). To pollute, misuse, abuse or destroy God's creation is an abuse of the position as Regent of God on earth. All aspects of creation were made for the service of God so the destruction of some aspects of creation by human beings is unacceptable.

Denny adds a further reflection to this one (Denny, 1998):

> If life on earth is preparation for eternal life in heaven, then the loving care of the natural environment would seem to be appropriate training for the afterlife in the company of God and the angels in an environment that is perfectly balanced, peaceful, and verdant.

Professor Mustafa Abu-Sway argues that protecting the environment is a major aim of the Shari'ah. He says:

> I am not adding to the aims of the Shari'ah; I am only discovering one more … For if the situation of the environment keeps deteriorating, there will ultimately be no life, no property and no religion. The environment encompasses the other aims of the Shari'ah. The destruction of the environment prevents the human being from fulfilling the concept of vice-regency on earth. Indeed, the very existence of humanity is at stake here.

Abu-Sway, 1998

Activity

How should a vice-regent of God behave towards creation? Explain how this idea captures both senior status and duty using examples from human interaction with the created world.

✔ Hindu perspectives on the created world

The continuous transformations of the world

Vedic religion contains an idea that the universe is ordered and there are many different accounts of that creation, some suggesting an agent, a bringer into being of creation, while others suggest an ongoing transformation from a prior state to the current state, continuing – in other words creation is continuous and has no beginning or end but continuing transformations (Bowker, 1997, p240).

For instance there is the tradition of Brahmanda, the idea of a cosmic egg from which all creatures come forth (Rg. 10.121.1; Katha Upanishad 3.10). Alternatively there is the tradition of Hiranyagarbha, the golden embryo and everlasting plan. Visvakarma is seen as creator, the architect of the Gods (Rg. 10.82) and Brahma is seen as the source of the universe, presiding over the universe, both preserving and destroying. The universe may have no origin but simply be an emanation from a ground or source of being.

Key terms

Vedic religion: the ancient religion of the Aryan peoples who entered NW India from Persia (*c.*2000–1200 BC). It was the precursor of Hinduism, and its beliefs and practices are contained in the Vedas.

The status and duty of humankind in the world

Cosmological views of the place of human beings in the natural world are also diverse. Christopher Chapple notes that within Hinduism there are various cosmological views, some of which place human beings in the natural world in an ecologically friendly manner, and others which do not (Chapple, 1998). For instance there are traditions which seem to place human life in a harmonious relationship with the natural world …

… the agrarian and often near-wilderness images of India found in the Vedas, Upanisads, and epic texts present a style of life seemingly in tune with the elements. The Samkhya and Tantra traditions affirm the reality and efficacy of the physical world.

There are also traditions which seem to reject the natural world as having little value …

… the Advaita Vedanta tradition, while adopting the basic principles of Samkhya cosmology, asserts that the highest truth involves a vision of oneness that transcends nature and, in a sense, dismisses the significance of the material world by referring to it as illusion or maya.

Both in **Chapple**, *1998*

Models of Hindu spirituality also reflect these quite different values on the physical natural world. For instance yoga enhances health and sense, and the concern about the destruction of the natural world has led some to reconceive yoga as **Earth yoga**.

Rick Fields writes:

Just as in yoga we relax and stretch muscles constricted by the stresses of civilized life, so would the practitioner of Earth yoga extend his or her practice to include the body of an Earth attacked by the multiple stresses of civilization. From the viewpoint of Earth yoga, the body of the Earth is, like our own, a complex living organism, and like our own, sacred …

The practitioner of Earth yoga seeks to know this body upon and within which we live as we seek to know our own bodies. So the practice of Earth yoga might best begin with that portion of Earth closest to you, your bioregion or watershed …

Yoga teaches us, among other things, to care for our bodies as sacred, inside and out. As we come to know the body of Gaia as intimately as we know our own, we discover places that have been wounded, polluted, poisoned and that need to be restored and healed. This is karma yoga, the yoga of work and action.

Fields, *1998*

However, other practices focus on the renunciation of sense perceptions and the awareness of the impact we have on the environment around us doubting the reliability of what our senses suggest.

Despite the ambiguity there is the doctrine of Dharma and the need to act for the sake of the world. Chapple notes for instance that issues such as the building of dams in the Narmada River Valley requires 'taking into account social ecology or the need to integrate environmental policy with the daily needs of tribal and other marginalized peoples' (Chapple, 1998).

He also suggests: 'Gandhi's advocacy of simple living through the principles of nonviolence (ahimsa) and holding to truthfulness (satyagraha) could give some Hindus pause as they consider the lifestyle changes engendered by contemporary consumerism' (Chapple, 1998).

The idea of simple living could serve to inspire the development of sustainable economies, and, moreover, that the concept of Dharma can be reinterpreted from an earth-friendly perspective.

> ## Key terms
>
> **Earth yoga:** spiritual practice which values the physical natural world, enhances health and senses, and encourages a concern about the destruction of the natural world.

Activity

How might Hindu thinking about the world encourage and discourage concern for it? How could these different ideas be held in harmony? Use a specific example of our human relationship with the non-human world to explore your thinking.

Key terms

Samsara: wandering on.

Buddhist perspectives on the (un)created world

The uncreated world

'Buddhism sees no need for a creator of the world, as it postulates no ultimate beginning to the world, and regards it as sustained by natural laws' (Harvey, 1990, p36). In contrast to Jewish, Christian and Muslim cosmology, Buddhism holds that any such creator would have to be responsible for the suffering that exists in the world. Buddhism holds that life is so full of suffering that it is a thing that must be escaped from. No great all powerful moral being could have had made it because it is so unpleasant.

There are gods in Buddhism but they themselves are subject to rebirth and are incapable of creation. They are higher sentient beings but there is no creator. Gods may delude themselves into thinking they were the creator (Bowker, 1997, p240). There is an idea of a Great Brahma in our own world system. Although he is regarded by some Brahmins as having created the world and is a good being, nevertheless Buddha thought he was mistaken in his view that he had created the world (Harvey, 1990, p36).

Rebirth

The doctrine of the cycle of rebirth (**samsara**) informs Buddhist beliefs about the universe and brings about quite a different perspective from the Judaeo-Christian view.

There is no known beginning to the cycle of rebirths and the world. However far back one goes, there must have been a prior cause for whatever exists at that time. There have been eons of coming and goings of world systems, galaxies, super galaxies and so on. World systems evolve, remain for a while, come to an end and then re-evolve. The cycle of rebirths means that there are innumerable lives over vast stretches of time.

While some religions might see life in the world as having some purpose – there may be the idea that a Creator God has singled out a specific purpose for a human being for them to do this or that – in Buddhism, living in the human world is not a rebirth, is not designed by anyone, is not meant for anything, and has no purpose. The only beings born into the present world are unenlightened beings. The only sensible aim is to avoid the unpleasant realms and ultimately transcend it altogether. The only possible purpose is to get beyond this world.

The nature of the universes

Just as Buddhism differs from Western traditions in that there is no single creator, a further difference is that there is no single world. There are many levels of worlds. Buddhism understands creation to be a series of levels, all of which are subject to reappearance (rebirth in the cycle of samsara) apart from the very highest level, which is a purely mental rebirth. Once at that level one reaches beyond the cycle of rebirth. Below this level are what are known as the realms of pure form where gods dwell in 16 heavens. Below this level there are sense desire levels, which includes this human one. Below this group are the hells which are full of much greater suffering. These lower levels of rebirth are animal levels. All levels contain impermanent motions. None of them have been created. They exist in an eternal process of ongoing change, a process of cycles, which therefore must be escaped from. Only the very highest level offers that final escape from the endless cycle of rebirth.

The lower realms have much suffering and the higher realms have more bliss. One must seek rebirth in the higher realms. The human realm is in the middle and there is enough suffering to motivate the pursuit of the higher realms. There is enough motivation in this world for spiritual development to seem compelling. The human world offers the possibility of escape from the current world, though it also poses the possibility that one might slip back down into a lower world. Buddhists aim for a heavenly or human rebirth because one may reach out for rebirth at a higher level from these levels, possibly even nirvana (Harvey, 1990, p38). Nirvana is beyond both heaven and earth.

Karma, the natural law of the universes

Movement between the worlds is governed by the law of karma (Harvey, 1990, p39). A being is reborn according to the nature and quality of their past actions. We inherit the consequences of our past actions (Harvey, 1990, p39). Actions mould our consciousness; we are what we do. Intentional acts (moral acts) leave some trace on the human psyche which leads to the future results. The law of karma is a natural law which controls our rebirth based on these traces. The more moral our lives have been, the more likely rebirth at the same or higher level. The more immoral our lives have been, the more likely rebirth at a lower level at some point in the future.

Kindness and non-violence are important for all creatures as humans are a part of the same cycle as other beings, though killing human life is worse than killing animal life because it is fortunate to be born a human. Harm or killing of human life then bring bad karma, not because of a Creator God judging the human being, but because of the impact such actions have on the person doing them.

This natural law does not determine the destiny of human beings. Our past lives may have determined our current predicament but they do not determine our current actions which can bring about future change.

This moral dimension is very important in the human world. At this level most good and bad actions take place. Below this level (in the level of animals, ghosts or hell beings) there is little scope for good actions. Above this level the gods have little scope for good or ill but simple enjoy the fruits of their past labours (Harvey, 1990, p41).

> **Activity**
>
> Map out a diagram of Buddhist thinking about the world and how it might encourage and discourage concern for it. Try to make sense of these different aspects of Buddhist thought using a specific example of our human relationship with the non-human world to explore your thinking.

■ Sikh perspectives on the created world

The creation and sustaining of the world

Hukam is the divine order, the fundamental concept, 'one will' (the will of God) which is beyond understanding. It is the agent of creation which determines the physical universe and human existence (Bowker, 1997, p251). Nirmal Singh writes that Sikh cosmology holds that for many eons of time there was just God until, at one point, 'God willed and the creation came into being. In the midst of this creation God installed the earth ... the abode of duty, action' (Singh, 2002). God created the universe:

> God is unseen, inscrutable, inaccessible, omnipotent, and is the bounteous Creator. The entire world is subject to coming and going. The merciful One alone is permanent ... The One alone is eternal. (AG 71)

71

God dwells within the universe not aside it or beyond it:

> Having created the Universe the Creator abides within it. The worth of the One who is in the Universe cannot be told. In whatever direction I look, in that direction I find God. (AG 84)

84

God pervades the whole universe and inhabits every soul and he watches over it (Adi Granth 1039). There is a profound experience of God existing within all things in Sikhism:

> Creating creatures, the One places itself within them. The Creator is detached and limitless. No one knows the mystery of the Creator. What the Creator does surely comes to pass. (AG 937)

937

As well as creating the universe, God sustains life and is permanently active in creation:

> God is the creator, omnipotent and bounteous, who gives sustenance to all beings ... There is no abiding place other than the One. (AG 474)

all in **Cole**, *2004*

The status and duty of humankind in the world

Many different forms of beings arose on earth all part of God's purpose. God gave human beings extra merit. While all living things have a place in God's plan for creation, nevertheless all living things are there also for human beings to be able to fulfil their purpose. More than this, when one perceives God, all other things and beings will be seen as false, or unreal (Cole, 2004, p47). Human beings must also note that, 'God loves His creation the way it is, and looks at it joyfully' (Singh, 2002).

The place of human beings in the world is important in the Sikh perspective on creation. Human beings are especially important, 'The man is a priceless pearl; dwelling on the Name it has been accorded honour' (AG 22). But at the same time man can be unsteady, can get lost; trust should be placed in God not human beings (AG 415).

Human beings can be deluded by greed. In loving gold, silver or material goods the focus can move away from God and on to material pleasures of this world. This way leads to restless instability, a consequence of seeking to serve the self rather than God. Human beings are not intrinsically evil but can become evil when dominated by selfishness. Self-centredness will not lead a person to eternal or ultimate salvation (Cole, 2004, p58).

Human beings need liberation from this condition of self-centredness, from greed, from darkness, and require rebirth into something better. Faith and virtuous living offer the way towards salvation. Virtuous living is understood to be truthful living and that is not as an individual but as a member of a family or community. Becoming God-centred rather than self-centred opens up the possibility that a person may be reborn into union with God.

The world should be a place where good deeds are done, characterised by virtuous living. That is the intention of God. The suffering which takes place then is caused by human beings not being God-focused.

Finally, while creation is made by and sustained by God, it is nevertheless subject to decay, dissolution and death.

Conclusions and issues arising

Religious and ethical views about the human and non-human world

Religion and creation seem to have an ambiguous relationship with each other. Within each religious tradition there are elements which show creation in a positive light and others look on creation more negatively. In the three Western religious traditions (Judaism, Christianity and Islam), God is creator, His creation is good and it should be respected. Humans have a leading position over creation but there are restrictions on how they may use it. God is sometimes thought of as being apart from creation, but in some cases God is understood to be present within creation (for instance in the idea of incarnation and the cosmic Christ). There is also a sense in which creation has been defiled or corrupted by human sin.

Within Hinduism, Buddhism and Sikhism there is a sense in which the physical universe is to be escaped because it is filled with suffering. In Buddhism the universe is uncreated, but in Sikhism it is created. In Hinduism a variety of different perspectives can be found, some seeking to deny the sense world (extreme asceticism), and others seeking to become one with the world (Earth yoga). In Buddhism there is no divine purpose for human beings though there is the possibility of escape through enlightenment. The created world is something to be escaped from.

The relationships between religions and the created world have ambiguities within them and recent theology and thinking on these relationships take account of the issues brought to bear by the environmental challenges of our times. The theological messages which are now heard exist in a context of a concern that perhaps was not there before.

Is God's world perfect and must it be so?

Some religions reject the idea that the world is perfect or made good. Hinduism and Buddhism aim to be free of the life of being and seek release from this world and the cycle of rebirth and the endless suffering it brings. The world is not a very nice place to be and it is best to be left behind by seeking enlightenment. The whole spiritual purpose of life is escaping from this world in the direction of ultimate bliss. That is not to say that human beings are totally unconcerned with the world. They do have a duty to treat all living things with great care if they are ever to escape the cycle of rebirth.

This idea is rather different from the view of the world found in Judaism, Christianity and Islam where the world is good, part of God's intended purpose, there to be a place of worship (in the case of Islam). It has a value as part of God's creative intention. It is special, and whatever the place of human beings in the natural order of things, they have duties and responsibilities to its maintenance. Human beings have a duty to treat the environment as the creation of God. They must not allow it to

> **AQA Examiner's tip**
>
> Student analysis of the various ways in which God can be viewed as being immanent within creation, or transcendent beyond the space-time universe (or both) tends to be hit or miss. A study of ideas such as immanence and transcendence, pantheism and panentheism, and the like, helps to clarify thinking within the different religious traditions about the Key questions referred to at the start of the chapter.

be abused, or fall into a poor state. Part of the purpose of human beings is to attend to God's creation, rather than seek to escape from it.

An extension of both ways of thinking is that if the world becomes a terrible place, this may in fact reflect human activity – the failure to look after it, rather than its natural state. Human action can be for good or for ill and has consequences for our experience of the world. Human sin can be reflected in the deterioration of the world.

The ethical implications of the idea that God sustains creation

Many religious traditions suggest that God sustains the world. In other worlds, God did not simply set it off in some distant past, but is actually involved in maintaining or sustaining it now. This is especially the case in Judaism, Christianity, Islam and Sikhism.

This theological belief has ethical implications. It could imply that God has responsibility for the current state of the world. A perfect situation in the world poses no substantial problems but the world is full of many elements which seem rather less than perfect. The world itself has natural disasters, violent storms, unreliable seasons which can cause immediate or gradual devastation. The failure of crops owing to seasonal irregularities (no rain for instance) can cause famine. Communities or even civilisations can be undermined by such events. Earthquakes and volcanic eruptions can also have such long-term damage as well as cause immediate suffering and the devastation of the surrounding ecosystem. If God sustains the world, why does he allow this to happen?

A different sort of ethical implication is that it suggests that God has an ongoing current interest in the state of the world. His interest is not simply in humanity but the whole of creation. If human beings choose to act in such a way that creation is damaged or undermined, then they are placing themselves in direct opposition to God's current activity. Here the moral challenge is one that is levelled against human beings. Failure to treat God's creation with due respect seems a downright denial of God's very purpose for the world. It is difficult to separate the human treatment of the environment from other sorts of moral behaviour expected within religious traditions, even if do good to your world is not a specific commandment.

Extracts from key texts

> #### From 'The historical roots of our ecological crisis', by Lynn White. Science 155, 1967, pp1203–1207
>
> Especially in its Western form, Christianity is the most anthropocentric religion the world has seen. As early as the 2nd century both Tertullian and Saint Irenaeus of Lyons were insisting that when God shaped Adam he was foreshadowing the image of the incarnate Christ, the Second Adam. Man shares, in great measure, God's transcendence of nature. Christianity, in absolute contrast to ancient paganism and Asia's religions (except, perhaps, Zorastrianism), not only established a dualism of man and nature but also insisted that it is God's will that man exploit nature for his proper ends.
>
> At the level of the common people this worked out in an interesting way. In Antiquity every tree, every spring, every stream, every hill had its own genius loci, its guardian spirit. These spirits were accessible to men, but were very unlike men; centaurs, fauns, and

Activity

Has God created the 'best of all possible worlds'?

mermaids show their ambivalence. Before one cut a tree, mined a mountain, or dammed a brook, it was important to placate the spirit in charge of that particular situation, and to keep it placated. By destroying pagan animism, Christianity made it possible to exploit nature in a mood of indifference to the feelings of natural objects.

It is often said that for animism the Church substituted the cult of saints. True; but the cult of saints is functionally quite different from animism. The saint is not in natural objects; he may have special shrines, but his citizenship is in heaven. Moreover, a saint is entirely a man; he can be approached in human terms. In addition to saints, Christianity of course also had angels and demons inherited from Judaism and perhaps, at one remove, from Zorastrianism. But these were all as mobile as the saints themselves. The spirits in natural objects, which formerly had protected nature from man, evaporated. Man's effective monopoly on spirit in this world was confirmed, and the old inhibitions to the exploitation of nature crumbled …

Possibly we should ponder the greatest radical in Christian history since Christ: Saint Francis of Assisi. The prime miracle of Saint Francis is the fact that he did not end at the stake, as many of his left-wing followers did. He was so clearly heretical that a General of the Franciscan Order, Saint Bonavlentura [sic], a great and perceptive Christian, tried to suppress the early accounts of Franciscanism. The key to an understanding of Francis is his belief in the virtue of humility – not merely for the individual but for man as a species. Francis tried to depose man from his monarchy over creation and set up a democracy of all God's creatures. With him the ant is no longer simply a homily for the lazy, flames a sign of the thrust of the soul toward union with God; now they are Brother Ant and Sister Fire, praising the Creator in their own ways as Brother Man does in his …

The greatest spiritual revolutionary in Western history, Saint Francis, proposed what he thought was an alternative Christian view of nature and man's relation to it; he tried to substitute the idea of the equality of all creatures, including man, for the idea of man's limitless rule of creation. He failed. Both our present science and our present technology are so tinctured with orthodox Christian arrogance toward nature that no solution for our ecologic crisis can be expected from them alone. Since the roots of our trouble are so largely religious, the remedy must also be essentially religious, whether we call it that or not. We must rethink and refeel our nature and destiny. The profoundly religious, but heretical, sense of the primitive Franciscans for the spiritual autonomy of all parts of nature may point a direction. I propose Francis as a patron saint for ecologists.

White, 1967

Chapter summary

Jewish perspectives on the created world

- God's Wisdom created Adam and Eve and the world out of nothing.
- God's Wisdom sustains the world.

- Human beings have special status and duties as stewards of creation.
- Creation is intrinsically good.
- Human beings have dominion over creation, which can be interpreted as exploitation or care.
- Creation is a gift from God which ultimately belongs to God and must be kept for the future.

Christian perspectives on the created world

- God made creation, it depends on and is sustained by Him, and is good.
- God and creation are distinct and humanity is part of creation, but made in the image and likeness of God.
- The whole of creation is in need of redemption.
- Human sin disrupts creation and the expulsion from Eden is an example of this.
- Christological dimension – Christ is also connected to creation, existing at the beginning of time.
- God is immanent in nature and interacting with nature and so nature must be respected.
- All of creation is valuable to God; God's Word and Spirit is in creation.
- Christ, through incarnation (as a human being), is in a relationship with the whole cosmos.
- The human being embodies the whole of creation; humanity is part of the unity of the living creation.

Muslim perspectives on the created world

- God is creator and has power and dominion over all, but human beings bear a special responsibility over creation.
- Humanity is in the service of God, like all other aspects of creation, but is also God's regent over creation which means it has God's power and authority over creation.
- As regents of God, humans are required to cherish dignity and bring it to perfection.
- Creation is a sign to God, so destruction of creation diminishes the signs of God's glory and is evil.
- Creation is more than humanity, but human beings are privileged in creation.
- Earth is sacred because it is a place for worshipping God; humanity is in a relationship with creation and the misuse of creation pollutes the place of worship.
- The destruction of creation prevents human beings from fulfilling their role as regent (or vice-regent) on earth.

Hindu perspectives on the created world

- The universe is ordered, may have been created by a divine agent or may be in a state of ongoing transformation with no end or beginning.
- Some Hindu spiritual traditions place human beings in a harmonious relationship with nature (e.g. Earth yoga) and others seem to deny or renounce nature (e.g. asceticism).

- The doctrine of Dharma requires human beings to act for the whole of the world, not just themselves.

- Ghandi advocated simple living and non-violence which offer a basis for an earth-friendly Hindu perspective.

Buddhist perspectives on the created world

- There is no creator as the world had no beginning and is sustained by natural laws.

- Were there a creator he would be responsible for the suffering of the world.

- Gods are subject to rebirth, like all sentient creatures, and they may delude themselves they are creators.

- There is no beginning or end, just the cycle of rebirth.

- There is no specific divine purpose for humanity although in practical terms the only way to escape endless rebirth into a world of suffering is to transcend it.

- There are many universes and many worlds, some which have more suffering (e.g. the animal world and hells) and some which are happier places (the heavens).

- The human world has enough suffering to motivate humans to leave it and seek rebirth at a higher level or enlightenment.

- The law of karma determines the nature of our rebirth and links to our actions for good or ill.

- Most good and bad actions are located in the human world.

Sikh perspectives on the created world

- There is a divine order, a fundamental will of God which is the agent of creation and determines the universe.

- God dwells in the universe, not apart from it; God inhabits every soul.

- God sustains and is active in creation.

- All living things have a place in creation, and creation is good, but humans have extra merit.

- Human beings can become deluded by greed and material wealth, making them self-centred not God-centred.

- Being God-centred offers a person the possibility of being reborn into union with God.

- Being self-centred leads to suffering in the world.

Further reading

This provides a detailed exploration of this issue:

Harvey, P., *An Introduction to Buddhist Ethics*, Cambridge University Press, 2000, pp150–186

as does Keown in a really excellent and readable book:

Keown, D., *Buddhist Ethics: a very short introduction*, Oxford University Press, 1996, pp39–52

Very good treatments for Christian views are found in this book in the 'Ecology and moral responsibility section':

Crook, R., *Introduction to Christian Ethics*, Prentice Hall, 2002, pp266–282

In this chapter you have:

- explored religious perspectives on the created or uncreated world: including the nature of creation, intention behind creation, God's role in sustaining the world, human status in creation and duties to creation, and the status of the non-human world

- considered some ethical implications of these beliefs and issues arising from them.

11   Environmental ethics

Key questions

1 Does the environmental system have value in itself that must be respected?

2 Is it more convincing to argue that we should take care of the environment for its own sake or for our sake?

3 Do religious believers have a moral obligation to look after the environment, and if so, for what reason?

What is environmental ethics?

Environmental ethics is concerned with our attitudes towards and impact on the biological and geological dimensions of the planet, in terms of how that impact affects humanity, whether it enhances or diminishes the well-being and diversity of other forms of life on earth, and whether humanity maintains or disturbs the balance between the planet's different life-forms and geological systems. While many ethical issues value only the human person, environmental ethics widens the circle of moral significance to include the non-human natural world. In addition religious believers have a particular view of their duty and responsibility towards creation. Environmental ethics is concerned both at international and intergovernmental level, and also at a local level, in the way people live their lives.

Threats to the environment

The vast majority of all scientists specialising in this field agree that the scientific evidence is now overwhelming that climate change presents very serious global risks and demands an urgent global response. This was evident in the report made by the Intergovernmental Panel on Climate Change, established to provide decision-makers throughout the world with objective information. In its report (*Synthesis Report of the IPCC Fourth Assessment Report*, 16 November 2007) it stated:

> Warming of the climate system is unequivocal, as is now evident from observation of increases in global average air and ocean temperatures, widespread melting of snow and ice, and rising global average sea level ... many natural systems are being affected by regional climate change ...

pp1–2

The report states categorically that greenhouse gases have 'increased markedly as a result of human activities since 1750 and now far exceed pre-industrial values determined from ice cores spanning many thousands of years' (pp4–5) and that it is very likely that the increase in temperatures in the 20th century is a result of the increase in greenhouse gases (p6). Current projections indicate this is likely to continue and that there are likely to be serious consequences for agriculture, forestry, ecosystems, water resources, human health, industry settlement and society. Crop yields will be reduced, deaths among the elderly and the sick will increase because of hotter days, those without appropriate

housing will have a reduction in the quality of life, and there will be water shortages, more flooding, and more wildfires (p12).

The key features of environmental risks are as follows:

■ The different delicate and interconnected systems that nurture and sustain life, providing clean air, water and soil, are breaking down through pollution and abuse. Deforestation and emissions of 'greenhouse gases' affect the atmosphere and threaten to disrupt or damage life on earth.

■ The world's finite natural resources are being depleted at an unsustainable rate because of our way of life and the increasing population. The reduction of non-renewable natural resources threatens international stability as well as the local inhabitants who depend on them.

■ It is likely that environmental damage will disproportionately affect the poor, who tend to live in vulnerable areas. What is more, 80 per cent of the world's resources are controlled by the richest 20 per cent of the world's population, while 20 per cent of humanity lacks clean water, adequate food, shelter and clothing. The rich take a greater proportion of what the environment has to offer than the poor. The industrialised world is more protected from the effects of climate change because of its wealth and geographical position.

■ Industrialisation and technological and scientific development, often for commercial gain, have led to the destruction of grasslands and forests, the over-exploitation of oceans, and the extinction of species, reducing biodiversity.

The environment is in need of protection, preservation and conservation if shortages are to be addressed, disruption to human society reduced, endangered species given a lifeline and distinct and particular life-forms and systems retained.

In his book *An Introduction to Christian Ethics* (2002), Roger H. Crook observes that technological advancement and scientific investigation had been seen as positive human activity, perhaps paving the way towards a better society, but that there is now a view that this activity is threatening humanity's long-term survival (Crook, 2002, p267). The term 'environmental ethics' covers a wide range of concerns, such as the preservation of endangered species, the conservation of natural habitats, the effects of over-fishing or deforestation, the depletion of the ozone layer, and the effects of pollution on human health and the natural world.

Conservation, preservation and protection

It could be argued that the only concern for any environmental ethic is the feeding and protection of people and that all other moral considerations come second to that. There are clear religious requirements to place the needs of humans above all other moral considerations. However, there are ethical arguments for other considerations. Holmes Rolston III makes a qualified case for placing nature above people (Rolston and Light, 2003, pp451–458). He argues that there are situations where it is reasonable to consider other factors above feeding people. He suggests that if all efforts were directed at feeding starving people and nothing else then civilisation would halt. Writing would not have been invented, or music written, or aeroplanes designed and the discovery of electricity might not have happened. We regularly choose to enjoy the features of civilisation over saving lives.

However inequitable it may appear, wealth is distributed unevenly and it seems unlikely the wealth of the richest countries will ever be distributed among the poor (the seven richest countries consume 75 per cent of the world's resources). In fact many of these seemingly inconsequential aspects of civilisation benefit people, for instance in the development of healthcare and the ability of human beings to bring people out of poverty through development. More unpalatable is the fact that societies are prepared to make moral decisions which do sacrifice human beings, such as raising the speed limit on motorways which has been shown to lead to more deaths in road traffic accidents. Zimbabwe has a shoot-to-kill policy for black rhinoceros poachers because the rhino population has declined by 97 per cent in 20 years. This policy places the life of a rhino above a human's, though it is being done to stop the extinction of an entire species.

Concern for animals

Some argue that animals have rights because they have some intrinsic value. At one time, animals were considered to be a resource for us to use and enjoy as we pleased. There is now growing concern about the suffering that we cause to animals. We use animals to carry burdens and we use them in sporting events. We keep them in zoos and rear them for their products. We also experiment on them for research. Around the world, billions of animals die every year because of these activities.

There is an ethical idea that we should not only avoid the mistreatment of animals but also that we should seek to improve the quality of life of animals. Tom Regan argues that this idea of **animal welfare** includes conserving habitats for those animals which might otherwise be threatened by development (Regan, 2003, pp66–67). Support for animal welfare involves both a concern for individual animals as well as animals (including humans) in general. The broader moral concern means that in some cases animals are treated in ways which are not ideal. For example, they may be held in captivity for breeding purposes and also their numbers may be controlled so that other species are not driven to extinction.

In his article 'The case for animal rights' (1985), Tom Regan argues for the total abolition of the use of animals in science, the total dissolution of commercial animal agriculture and the total elimination of commercial

Activity

Given that you and your children are far more likely to suffer the consequences of climate change than your teachers, evaluate how seriously your school takes environmental ethics. What policies do they have in place and are they practised? Research ways of making your school more sustainable and draft a plan of action to present to your school council, headteacher and board of governors.

AQA Examiner's tip

The intrinsic or instrumental value of animals and the rest of the environment is a difficult area of environmental ethics because of the lack of agreed criteria for defining that value. Both Aquinas and Kant held that mistreatment of animals is wrong because it coarsens the human spirit, not because of any intrinsic value in animals. It is a good idea to decide what your own 'baseline' is in such matters by studying the various instrumentalist and intrinsicalist approaches discussed in the textbook.

Key terms

Animal welfare: ethical concern for the care of domestic, farmed or wild animals.

and sport hunting and trapping. He argues that it is not simply the pain that we put animals through but the whole system that is wrong. It is wrong to view animals as our resource, here for us – to be eaten, surgically manipulated, or exploited for sport or money. A mentally normal mammal is subject of a life, and this life has inherent value and requires treatment as an individual. All beings who have inherent value have it equally. A difficulty with Regan's position is that it gives us no guidelines for action where values conflict (Gruen, 1991, p343). Consider the following situation:

> [I]magine five survivors are on a lifeboat. Because of limits of size, the boat can only support four. All weigh approximately the same and would take approximately the same amount of space. Four of the five are normal adult human beings. The fifth is a dog. One must be thrown overboard or else all will perish. Whom should it be?

Regan, 1985, p285

In the end, Regan argues that we should kill the dog, as the death of a human is a greater loss than the death of the dog, but this seems inconsistent with his general view.

Peter Singer's book *Animal Liberation* (1995) offered a new system of ethics for our treatment of animals. He argues that by treating animals differently we are guilty of being speciesist:

> If a being suffers, there can be no moral justification for refusing to take the suffering into consideration. No matter what the nature of the being, the principle of equality requires that suffering be counted equally with the like suffering – in so far as rough comparisons can be made – of any other being.

Singer, 1995

The point that animals are different from humans should not mean that we treat them differently. Not all humans are of equal worth to society or are equal in what they can do, but they receive equal treatment. If we are prepared to carry out experimentation on a chimpanzee, then it must be for a purpose so grave that we would be prepared to use a human being with learning difficulties (Singer, 1995, p75, pp77–78). If we're unwilling in principle ever to use a human being with learning difficulties in such experimentation, then we should not carry out experimentation on animals with a similar mental capability. To discriminate against animals in this way is speciesist.

We allow procedures on animals which give them pain. Animals feel pain and they respond to painful experiences just as we respond, by screaming or withdrawing from the source of the pain, in the same way as humans do. We kill animals for food, in sport or in experimentation, and yet we would never do so to humans. The 'sanctity of life' argument is arbitrarily reserved for humans alone.

> Why is it that we lock up chimpanzees in appalling primate research centres, and use them in experiments that range from the uncomfortable to the agonising and lethal, and yet we would never think of doing the same to a retarded human being at a much lower mental level? The only possible answer is that the chimpanzee, no matter how bright, is not human, while the retarded human, no matter how dull, is ... This is speciesism, pure and simple, and it is just as indefensible as the most blatant racism. There is no ethical basis for

elevating membership of one particular species into a morally crucial characteristic. From an ethical point of view, we all stand on an equal footing – whether we stand on two feet, or four, or none at all.

Singer, 1985

Singer argues that the principle of equality that we apply for men and women and people of different races should also operate with animals. This does not mean that we think that animals are equal to humans, but that our treatment of all humans and animals should be equal. Singer is a modern utilitarian in many respects and he builds his case on Jeremy Bentham's 'each to count for one and none for more than one' idea. He does not think that animals should necessarily be treated in the same way as humans, but that they should receive equal preference. Singer is a preference utilitarian.

Singer's approach is a mainstay of the animal liberation movement, but it is radical. It would require a commitment to vegetarianism, and would place considerable limitations on science. Inevitably human experimentation would become more prevalent, as only humans can give informed consent. For many, the extreme conclusions of preference utilitarianism are unpalatable.

Critics of animal rights

In his book *The Case for Animal Experimentation* (1986), Michael A. Fox argued that animals are not members of the moral community and that we have no moral obligation towards them. He defined a moral community as 'a social group composed of interacting autonomous beings where moral concepts and precepts can evolve and be understood. It's also a social group in which the mutual recognition of autonomy and personhood exist' (p50). This recognition cannot exist where animals are concerned and so they are not morally significant creatures.

Fox eventually changed his mind completely – rejecting his earlier belief – but others, such as Carl Cohan, have not. In his 1998 article 'The case for the use of animals in biomedical research', Cohan argues that animals have no rights. Rights can only exist between people, who can make moral claims on each other (p830). This moral capability arises from a number of faculties that animals do not have. These include an inner consciousness of free will, the grasp by reason of moral law, and human membership in a moral community. Humans confront choices that are moral and lay down moral laws: animals do not. They lack free moral judgements and so do not have rights.

The difficulty with attempts at defining the characteristics that make humans morally significant is the fact that human beings sometimes do not display these characteristics. Human babies and toddlers do not display the moral capability that Cohan requires of animals. Nevertheless, we give them moral status and regard them as deserving of special protection. Crimes against young children are considered particularly abhorrent, precisely because they are more vulnerable owing, in part, to their lack of sophistication.

This attitude that animals are simply not worth considering in the moral picture was illustrated in December 1974 when an American public television network brought together the American philosopher Robert Nozick (1938–2002) and three scientists whose work involves animals. Nozick asked 'whether the fact that an experiment will kill hundreds of animals is ever regarded, by scientists, as a reason for not performing it'. One of the scientists answered, 'Not that I know of.' Nozick pressed his question: 'Don't the animals count at all?' Dr A. Perachio, of the Yerkes Center, replied, 'Why should they?', while Dr D. Baltimore, of the Massachusetts Institute of Technology, added that he did not think that experimenting on animals raised a moral issue at all ('The price of knowledge', broadcast in New York on 12 December 1974; quoted from Singer, 1995). At the very least, these scientists displayed a lack of sensitivity. Arguably, they were exhibiting a degree of callous disregard for the animals involved in experimentation, and few scientists would be prepared to make such comments openly today.

Wilderness preservation

There are many arguments for the preservation of wildernesses. Here is a selection taken from a review of the arguments by Michael P. Nelson (Nelson, 2003, pp413–436). At one end of the scale is the argument that wildernesses contain untapped, undiscovered valuable natural resources or scientific treasures, though this is an instrumentalist argument viewing the protection of the wilderness as in the interest of future human exploitation. In other words the argument contradicts any claim that the wilderness should be preserved, rather it will be exploited more thoroughly. Variations of this sort of argument include the preservation of the wilderness for the excellent hunting opportunities it offers (either for sport or religious reasons) or for the potential medicinal value which the undiscovered species might hold within, though presumably once discovered such species could be cultivated in plantations leaving the wildernesses protected.

A different group of arguments is linked around the idea that wildernesses provide much more fundamental services. On the one hand wetlands protect river headways, forests remove carbon dioxide from the atmosphere and while some of these facilities might be repeatable using artificial systems, others could not. For instance some species, such as wild salmon and grizzly bears, can only survive with those wild habitats. An extension of this kind of argument is that the wildernesses are a kind of life-support system for the world, without which the world system would break down. Also they can be said to provide an essential retreat for human beings from the built environment for their psychological, athletic or general all round holistic exercise. Perhaps they offer mental therapy for congested cities, a spectacular arena of aesthetic beauty, perhaps for the inspiration of civilisation or even a sense of the transcendent, a celebration of creation.

Perhaps the wilderness should be preserved for the diversity of the life-forms within. They hold the world's accumulated evolutionary and ecological wisdom, a kind of bio-diverse genetic pool of knowledge. They present a learning ground for human exploration and understanding, and offer an explanation for the ways in which human beings and human communities, in all their rich diversity, have developed. They might offer valuable cures for as yet untreatable diseases and are a treasure chest of possibilities for future generations which, once lost, will never be replaced.

Lastly wildernesses could be protected simply because of what they are, rather than what they might offer humanity or the biosphere as a whole. They do not cause damage, or problems – they are innocent until proven guilty so should be protected.

Activity

Consider the following extract and answer the questions.

Kakadu National Park in Australia's Northern Territory, contains rugged woodlands, swamps and waterways supporting a rich variety of life; it contains species found nowhere else, including some, such as the Hooded Parrot and the Pig-nosed Turtle, which are endangered. Kakadu affords aesthetic enjoyment and recreational and research opportunities. Many think it is a place of immense beauty and ecological significance. It is of spiritual significance to the Jawoyn aboriginals. Kakadu is also rich in gold, platinum, palladium and uranium, which some think should be mined. If this happens then, environmentalists claim, aesthetic, recreational and research opportunities will be reduced, the beauty of Kakadu will be lessened, species will disappear, ecological richness will decrease, the naturalness of the place will be compromised and the spiritual values of the Jawoyn discounted. Mining already goes on in the Kakadu area and there is pressure to allow more. Should more mining be allowed? Should any mining at all be allowed? How exactly might we reach answers to these ethical questions?

Elliott, 1991, pp284–293

■ Should the mining in this example be allowed?

■ Should any mining at all be allowed?

■ How might we go about answering these ethical questions?

■ Do human beings have a greater claim to the planet's resources than any other life-form?

■ Should humans be forced to accept a simpler lifestyle, to protect and preserve the environment?

■ Developing countries

Developing countries present a challenge to the application of environmental thinking. The poorest of countries are desperately in need of reliable power sources and other resources to improve their education and health provision and reduce poverty levels, lengthen life-expectancy, reduce child mortality and so forth. However, when they industrialise following the Western model with power stations that consume non-renewable resources and emit high levels of pollution they damage the environment. Some developing countries have rapidly growing economies because they trade very successfully with the rich West and help to satisfy the high consumer demands with low-cost production. The low standard of living in developing countries means they can produce goods very cheaply to attract the business from rich countries. This is precisely what developing countries need to develop, but the speed of development encourages environmentally damaging development. Should developing countries forgo the fruits that have made the rich world rich? Even at the expense of their people? Can the rich world hold the developing world to task when they are only growing to meet developed-world consumption needs? Are rich Western shoppers interested only in goods made in environmentally sustainable ways, or do they wanted the cheapest goods?

It is developing countries which will be most at risk from climate change and so there is considerable self-interest in pursuing a more sustainable route to development. The risks are particularly acute for poorer, developing countries which will be disproportionately exposed to those risks and are less able to respond to them. Less developed countries seeking to gain similar benefits from industrialisation now face demands to limit their development in response to climate change. The development they seek to gain from industrialisation will leave them better protected from the changes in the environment but at the same time will cause increased changes in the environment. However, they also have immediate threats from disease, poverty, low life-expectancy, high child mortality and, in some cases, the political instability which follows from the more precarious situation in which they find themselves.

■ Religious and philosophical perspectives

💡 A deep ecology

Many of the concerns about the environment are about damage and destruction which will negatively affect human life and society. Environmental ethics can be focused on the interests and goods of humanity. However, there is also a wider movement for a broader concern about the environment to include the whole biosphere and **geosphere**. **Deep ecology** recognises value in all life-forms, and perhaps even the geological and biological systems and diversity of planet earth, and rejects **anthropocentric** ethics. Shallow ecology sees humans as separate from their environment. It sees them as the only source of value. Deep ecology looks at the whole field – the interrelational, interconnected moral sphere. American environmentalist Aldo Leopold (1887–1948) led this attempt, calling in his posthumously published *A Sand County Almanac* (1949) for a new ethic to deal with man's relationship to the land and to the animals and plants that thrive upon it. He sought to enlarge the boundaries of the moral community to include soils, waters, plants and animals, or collectively the land (Leopold, 1949). It is not enough for Leopold to see the environment in terms of its contribution to human life. This tendency is illustrated well by the American poet William Cullen Bryant (1794–1878):

> ... The hills
> Rock-ribbed and ancient as the sun. – the vales
> Stretching in pensive quietness between –
> The venerable woods – rivers that move
> In majesty, and the complaining brooks
> That make the meadows green; and, poured round all
> Old oceans grey and melancholy waste, –
> Are but the solemn decorations all
> Of the great tomb of man ...

Bryant, 1817

The non-human is also intrinsically valuable. The Norwegian philosopher Arne Naess (b. 1912) argued that deep ecology sought to 'preserve the integrity of the biosphere for its own sake', not for any possible human benefits. Leopold says: 'A thing is right when it tends to preserve the integrity, stability and beauty of the biotic community. It is wrong when it tends otherwise.' In a paper published in 1984, Arne Naess and George Sessions proposed that:

1 The well being of human and non-human life on Earth have value in themselves. These values are independent of the usefulness of the non-human world for human purposes.

2 Richness and diversity of life-forms contribute to the realization of these values and are also values in themselves.

3 Humans have no right to reduce this richness and diversity except to satisfy vital needs.

Naess and Sessions, 1984

Arguably, this ethic can be extended to include natural objects or systems, and in *Deep Ecology* (1985), Bill Devall and George Sessions argue that, 'all organisms and entities in the ecosphere, as parts of the interrelated whole, are equal in intrinsic worth.' Peter Vardy and Paul Grosch (1994) note that James Lovelock's **Gaia hypothesis** sees the ecosystem as a whole as an entity in its own right, which must be considered in any moral deliberation (see Lovelock, 1979, p279); while Paul Taylor (quoted in Vardy and Grosch, 1994) argues that there should be respect for every life, as every living thing is 'pursuing its own good in its own unique way'.

Deep ecology is also critical of what the American philosopher Warwick Fox describes as mechanistic materialism, the industrialisation of the world, and the political and economic force which drives that industrialisation, namely capitalism. Deep ecology challenges accepted norms and asks the question why do things have to be this way? This is a particularly powerful point when it is considered that it is precisely the industrialisation of the last century which has brought on the climate change which threatens to destabilise millions of people's lives. At the same time it is that industrialisation which has powered the economic expansion which has produced the civilisation that enables the reader of this book to be studying ethics.

The attempt to extend intrinsic value to all of the elements of the earth is problematic. Singer maintains that while all life-forms can have value as part of the diverse interrelated 'geophysiological' structure of the planet, it is only justifiable to give intrinsic value to sentient life-forms, as plants and other organisms cannot truly be said to desire to flourish or have experiences. Lovelock's use of the Greek goddess Gaia to describe the world may be appealing, but it seems to confer on the earth a consciousness that is not there (Singer, 1993, p282). There is a danger that by using metaphorical or romantic language we will confer sentiency on things that do not possess it.

However, this criticism of deep ecology makes a mistake, argues Naess, because it misrepresents that way of thinking. It suggests that these ecologists do not think humans have extraordinary traits or any overriding obligations to their own kind, both of which are not the case (Naess, 2003).

☑ Jewish perspectives

David Vogel in his 1999 article 'How Green is Judaism? Exploring Jewish environmental ethics' (based on a paper published in *Business Ethics Quarterly*) reviews Jewish perspectives on this issue. Ancient and medieval texts placed restrictions on the human use of the natural environment (p3). Nevertheless he notes:

> ### Key terms
>
> **Gaia hypothesis:** Gaia was the Greek 'mother earth' goddess. The Gaia hypothesis is that the earth as a whole is a single organism made up of living and non-living parts. The system is incredibly complex and interactive, and works as a whole to regulate life on earth as a whole.

> Judaism does not regard the preservation or protection of nature as the most important societal value; it holds that humans are not just a part of nature but have privileged and distinctive moral claims; it believes that nature can threaten humans as well as the obverse; it argues that nature should be used and enjoyed as well as protected. In short, the Jewish tradition is complex: it contains both 'green' and 'non-green' elements.

Vogel, 1999, p3

Nature exists both for its own sake, independent of any human needs, and for the benefit of humans and the two must be kept in balance. Vogel notes that medieval Jewish commentators wrote in terms that seem similar to ideas of sustainable development and conservation of the environment. Acts which bring about the extinction of animals are not permitted because of the future needs for which those species might provide.

Genesis 1:26 seems to justify the exploitation of the environment in the interests of humanity suggesting man has dominion over the natural world. However, a classic **midrash** interpretation of that text emphasises the responsibility that came with such dominion:

> When God created Adam he led him past all the trees in the Garden of Eden and told him, 'See how beautiful and excellent are all My works. Beware lest you spoil and ruin My world. For if you spoil it there is nobody to repair it after you.'

Stahl, 1993

> ### Key terms
>
> **Midrash:** in Judaism, explains biblical text from the ethical and devotional point of view.
>
> **Kosher:** prepared in accordance with Jewish dietary laws.

There are biblical restrictions on what foods can and cannot be eaten, whether humans can eat plants or animals, which trees can and cannot be cut down in times of war (Gen 1:30, Deuteronomy 20:19–20) suggesting a much more measured approach to the use of the environment that does not allow for a plundering attitude. God's creation of animals which are of no direct benefit to humankind implies they have value of their own (Job). Equally the idea of the day of rest limiting human activity expresses a value that activity should not be unrestrained. One contemporary scholar writes: 'The essence of the prohibition against melacha (productive work) on Shabbat is to teach that the productive manipulation of the environment is not an absolute right' (Berman, 1992) and this is complemented by rules about the treatment of animals (Deuteronomy 22:10, 25:4 and Leviticus 22:28, Exodus 23:4). In addition the laws of **kosher** slaughtering seek to minimise the pain suffered by animals.

Human life takes precedence over animals as illustrated by the binding of Isaac (Genesis 22) and he sacrificed an animal instead of a human being. On the other hand, humanity is not the whole purpose as God says to Job, 'Where were you when I laid the earth's foundation?' (Job 38:4, 6–7) and Maimonides, in his *Guide for the Perplexed*, wrote:

> It should not be believed that all the beings exist for the sake of the existence of humanity. On the contrary, all the other beings too have been intended for their own sakes, and not for the sake of something else.

Vogel argues that the Jewish tradition is both respectful of nature and also critical of it. Nature can be presented as a malevolent force which can bring great death and destruction. The story of Noah is one that suggests the importance of species protection as the continuation of every species had to be ensured by Noah, yet involves the slaughter of countless millions. There is an ambiguity in the relationship between human and the non-human natural world, and Judaism as a source for environmental ethics. Vogel concludes that while Judaism can be a source for environmental ethics, there are certain non-green values within it:

> First, while Judaism clearly regards the preservation and protection of nature as an important value, it is certainly not the most important value …
>
> Second, the notion that humans are not just a part of nature, but have distinctive – and privileged – moral claims is an integral part of Jewish thought. Thus preserving and maintaining human life is more important than protecting or preserving nature …
>
> Third, while it is certainly true that a strain of self-denial runs through the observances of many Jewish holidays – including the Shabbath – it is equally true that Judaism regards nature as something to be used. Recall that the Promised Land is described as one of 'milk and honey,' and thus a place where nature is to be used to benefit humans …
>
> Finally, Judaism does not view nature as inherently benevolent. While recognizing the beauty and majesty of the natural world, it also perceives that nature can also be terrifying and threatening.

Vogel, 1999, pp20–23

Nevertheless there are a number of limitations on the use of natural resources which provide guidance for ethical conduct at a time when there is concern about the environments. There are prohibitions about wastage, both of fuel in warning about wasting oil in a lamp by not properly adjusting the air flow, and also in the destruction of anything useful. As everything belongs to God, the wanton destruction of things is the destruction of things which do not belong to you and is to be avoided, and indeed resources must be used productively and not wastefully (Vogel, 1999, pp18–20).

☑ Christian perspectives

Christian views on the environment have been accused of placing an emphasis on human domination of the world. The account of creation in Genesis says, 'let them [humans] have dominion over the fish of the sea, and over the fowl of the air, and over the cattle, and over all the earth, and over every creeping thing that creepeth upon the earth' (Genesis 1:26b). This anthropocentric emphasis on the idea that the world is for human use is also seen in the writings of the ancient Greek philosopher Aristotle: 'Since nature makes nothing purposeless or in vain, it is undeniably true that she has made all animals for the sake of man.' Similarly, St Thomas Aquinas maintains that 'all animals are naturally subject to man'. Peter Singer is critical of this Christian tradition and argues that the Hebrew and Greek traditions place humans at the moral centre while the environment is regarded as morally insignificant. Genesis makes mankind dominant over the world and encourages him to multiply over it and subdue it. Singer notes that Aquinas did not recognise sin against the environment, and that the main Western view has been that the natural world exists for the benefit of humans: in this view, nature has no intrinsic value and its destruction cannot be sinful.

It can be argued that the Christian tradition presents a more positive environmental ethics (see Anderson, 1986). Christian ethics is necessarily theocentric (God-centred) as God is the underlying reason for moral behaviour and this includes environmental ethics. It is also anthropocentric in that the Christian/agape love of the neighbour is the fundamental principle for human relations. Moreover the condition of the environment can affect the quality and ease of human life. It is also arguably geo/biocentric, in that creation is God-made and good, and therefore must be preserved because it is a good in itself. Anderson notes that 'The recognition that nonhuman creatures have intrinsic value is present in the Christian tradition (Basil the Great, Chrysostom, Augustine, Francis)' (Anderson, 1986, p197). Roger Crook argues that these latter obligations have authority because of God. Christians see their relationships with one another in terms of their relationship with God. The value that the environment has comes from its relationship with God – that which God created (Crook, 2002, p267).

The Christian view understands the environment in terms of God's sacred creation. The idea of stewardship is present in the Bible, which emphasises that humans are responsible to God for their use of God's world. Humans are part of that creation: Crook argues that human activity has worth as part of God's creative process, and so technology and science are not bad. God works in and through nature, and nature is important to God (see Psalm 19). He goes on to suggest that as human beings manipulate nature more than any other life-form, they have a special responsibility to care for it. The irreparable damage being done to the planet and the natural order comes about because of human selfishness in taking a short-term view: 'Man is so intrinsically related to nature that when he sins against God, nature suffers; and when he obeys God, nature rejoices' (Barnette, 1972, p37). Pope John Paul II has written:

> Man thinks that he can make arbitrary use of the earth, subjecting it without restraint to his will, as though the earth did not have its own requisites and a prior, God-given purpose ... Instead of carrying out his role as a co-operator with God in the work of creation, man sets himself up in place of God and thus ends up in provoking a rebellion on the part of nature, which is more tyrannized than governed by him.

Pope John Paul II, Centesimus Annus, 1991, Section 37

In a paper entitled 'The call of creation: God's invitation and the human response: the natural environment and Catholic social teaching', the Catholic Church argues that:

> A way of life that disregards and damages God's creation, forces the poor into greater poverty, and threatens the right of future generations to a healthy environment and to their fair share of the earth's wealth and resources, is contrary to the vision of the Gospel.

Catholic Bishops' Conference of England and Wales, July 2002

Christians are duty bound to observe several principles, which imply a religious moral responsibility to care for the environment out of love for God, love for each other and love for God's creative work:

1 *Creation has value in itself and reveals God.* Genesis 1–2 records that God created everything and his creation is good and loved for its own sake. Creation has a distinct relationship with God – it glorifies and worships God (see Psalms 96:12, Isaiah 55:12). The environment is special not because humans need it but because it has value in itself

as the work of God and to an extent reveals God. St Thomas Aquinas argued that the diversity of the life on earth reveals the richness of God's nature and therefore Christians are bound not to degrade or damage it.

2 *Human beings are dependent but responsible*. Human beings are co-creators with God as they use and transform the natural world. Human acts should reflect God's own love for creation and should show care for creation as human life depends on creation.

3 *Creation reveals human sin*. Sin has distorted the human relationship with the natural world damaging the balance of nature. This idea is in the Old Testament: 'The earth dries up and withers, the world languishes and withers; the heavens languish together with the earth. The earth lies polluted under its inhabitants; for they have transgressed laws, violated the statutes, broken the everlasting covenant' (Isaiah 24:4–5). 'Therefore the land mourns, and all who live in it languish; together with the wild animals and the birds of the air, even the fish of the sea are perishing' (Hosea 4:2–3). Our immoral treatment of the environment damages our relationships with God, with each other and between humanity and the earth.

4 *Creation participates in human redemption*. A Christian's relationship with God is affected by how he or she uses the gifts of creation. Loving God includes giving thanks and praise for these gifts, honouring and respecting them for their own sake and because they are destined by God to be fairly shared for all people. Care and respect must replace exploitative greed.

5 *Creation in the world to come*. Part of being a Christian is to work to bring about the Kingdom of God. Humans are called to renew the face of the earth until there is peace and harmony, life and health for all. In the words of Revelation, 'the curse of destruction will be abolished' (Revelation 22:1–3), and the bounty of the world shared among all peoples.

For Pope John Paul II there must be a change of attitude towards material possessions:

> It is not wrong to want to live better. What is wrong is a style of life which is presumed to be better when it is directed towards having rather than being and which wants to have more, not in order to be more but in order to spend life in enjoyment as an end in itself.

Pope John Paul II, Centesimus Annus, 1991, Section 37

Humans must observe environmental justice, which means taking account of the impact of their lifestyles on others and the world. The desire for affluence and greater wealth can dominate. Advertising encourages the idea that we have a right to use the luxury goods of creation entirely as we wish. All people should remember the emphasis placed by the world religions on simplicity.

Muslim perspectives

Izzi Deen explores some principles of the Muslim approaches to environmental ethics. First, the conservation of the environment is based on the principle that the natural world was created by God and that all elements of the world exist with distinct purposes in balance. Humanity is not the only reason God made the world. Second, all aspects of this creation exist in continuous praise of God:

Activities

1 Explain how a Christian environmental ethic could be anthropocentric, geo/biocentric and ultimately theocentric.

2 In your view, do the biblical sources support an environmental ethic?

3 Should a Christian's love of God necessarily extend to care for creation?

> The seven heavens and the earth and all that is therein praise Him, and there is not such a thing but hymneth his praise; but ye understand not their praise. Lo! He is ever Clement, Forgiving.

Sura 17:44

Third the natural laws are God's laws and, fourth, there are other communities, beyond the human communities which live in the world. Izzi Deen notes Surah 6:38: 'There is not an animal in the earth, nor a flying creature flying on two wings, but they are peoples like unto you.' Fifth, all human relationships are based on justice and equity. Human relationships with the environment are based on these principles. He goes on to say that humans must not only 'enjoy, use and benefit from their surroundings. They are expected to preserve, protect and promote their fellow creatures'. The earth is mentioned hundreds of times in the Qur'an. It is described as being subservient to humans and it is described as a receptacle. These on their own would seem to point to a less eco-friendly ethic but there is more than this. Earth is seen as a source of purity, blessedness and, indeed, a place for the worship of God.

Deen argues that, 'A theory of the sustainable utilization of the ecosystem may be deduced from Islam's assertion that life is maintained with due balance in everything'. Humans are maintainers of the environment and not owners and must sustain it and conserve it. Since the time of the Prophet there is also the idea of *himil*, a protected zone for the benefit of the people which cannot be built on or developed. A further concept for supporting conservation is *harim*, a space, frequently a spring or water channel, river of woodland, which must be preserved and protected.

There are, then, approaches within Islam which support environmental ethics and not simply anthropocentric ideas of environmental ethics, as there is in Judaism, a sense in which the purpose of creation is not simply about humanity.

Hindu perspectives

O. P. Dwivedi (1996) argues that the principle of the sanctity of life is ingrained in the Hindu religion. He writes that human beings do not have dominion or sovereignty over all creatures, only God has this:

> ... humanity cannot act as a viceroy of God over the planet, nor assign degrees of relative worth to other species.

Dwivedi, 1996, p148

Dwivedi continues:

> ... all lives, human and nonhuman, are of equal value and all have the same right to existence. According to the Atharvaveda, the Earth is not for human beings alone, but for other creatures as well.

Dwivedi, 1996, p149

This means that human beings do not have a special privilege or position of authority over other living things and, what is more, they have special duties to animals and birds. Indeed human beings may experience rebirth as any animal or bird and so they deserve respect. In the Gita, Lord Krishna says: 'God, Kesava, is pleased with a person who does not harm or destroy other non-speaking creatures or animals' (Visnupurana 3.8.15). Beyond animals and birds, trees and flora are also respected. Dwivedi also notes plants as having divine powers including healing properties with a hymn in Rig veda devoted to their praise (Rg. 10.97). Water is also sacred,

'The waters in the sky, the waters of rivers, and water in the well whose source is the ocean, may all these sacred waters protect me' (Rg. 7.49.2), and so many rivers are considered sacred such as the Ganges. The killing of creatures, the pollution of wells or ponds are prohibited. Hinduism teaches against materialism and worldly goods. Dwivedi concludes:

> In Hindu culture, a human being is authorized to use natural resources, but has no divine power of control and dominion over nature and its elements. Hence, from the perspective of Hindu culture, abuse and exploitation of nature for selfish gain is unjust and sacreligious. Against the continuation of such exploitation, the only viable strategy appears to be satyagraha for conservation.

Dwivedi, 1996, p151

There is in Hinduism a significant basis for an environmental ethic which is not anthropocentric.

Buddhist approaches

Damien Keown argues that Buddhism is thought to be far more closely integrated with the natural world than some other religious traditions, especially Christianity. He writes:

> Buddhism … is perceived as pursuing a path of harmonious integration with nature and as fostering identification and mutual respect within the natural world. Since, according to Buddhist teachings, human beings can be reborn as animals, and vice versa, the Buddhist world view suggests a much closer kinship between species whereby different forms of life are interrelated in a profound way.

Keown, 1996, p39

However, he also argues that human beings remain the primary focus of Buddhism, which seeks to bring human beings from suffering to liberation, and so is much closer in focus to Christianity than might be thought at first glance. Buddhism with the basic principle of non-violence (ahimsa) requires the abstention from harming living beings, something which can be seen to happen when the industrial use of natural resources spreads and grows unabated. The destruction of habitats brings animals to extinction. The Sutta Nipata says:

> Let him neither kill, nor cause to be killed any living being, nor let him approve of others killing, after having refrained from hurting all creatures, both those that are strong and those that tremble in the world.

v.393 in Keown, 1996, p41

The Buddhist concern for human beings means the over-consumption of resources is unacceptable. Resources must be used responsibly. The ever-increasing demands of the burgeoning population mean that the eating of luxury goods such as meat is unethical.

Keown suggests that respect for plant life and trees is not on a par with humans and there is not much evidence to support the conservation of wilderness, beyond the observation that it is beautiful. They are borderline in terms of being a sentient life-form (Harvey, 2000, p174). However, wilderness as a place to which one can withdraw, to meditate, is important for Buddhist hermits, and Buddha spent many important phases of his life in the forest, including his enlightenment. Theravada monks who specialise in meditation are known as forest monks (Harvey, 2000, p174). If there is no forest or wilderness then these spaces would not be there to withdraw to (Keown, 1996, p44).

There are possibilities of tensions between the aims of conservation and Buddhist principles, for instance killing animals to maintain or protect a habitat being encroached by foreign predators. Harvey argues that in premodern time, conservation of species and habitat was not something given much attention as the environment had not been over-exploited, but this has changed as Buddhist countries have been influenced by Western values and become industrialised (Harvey, 2000, p178). This conflicts with the Buddhist ideal of co-operation with nature, rather than domination or submission to it, and has led to the growth of an active conservation movement based upon the Dalai Lama's idea of universal responsibility. In his 1989 Nobel Peace Prize lecture the Dalai Lama said that the Tibetan plateau would become a 'Zone of Non-violence' which

> … would be transformed into the world's largest natural park or biosphere. Strict laws would be enforced to protect wildlife and plan life; the exploitation of natural resources would be carefully regulated so as not to damage relevant ecosystems; and a policy of sustainable development would be adopted in populated areas.

*Quoted in **Harvey**, 2000, p170*

For Buddhism humans are not stewards of non-human nature, but neighbours of less sentient beings. The concern for the destruction or damage to the environment is motivated by a concern for sentient life, including, and most importantly, human life. It is human-centred but it does extend a duty to conserve human and non-human life, and by extension, the habitats which preserve that life.

Sikh approaches

Vladimir Tomek, in his survey 'Environmental concerns: Sikh responses', notes that the Sikh Gurus saw that human beings had some responsibility towards the natural world and urged people to study and respect it. Guru Nanak (1469–1539) said: 'The earth is your mother. Respect for "mother earth" is the only solution to these problems [meaning destruction of forests leading to soil erosion]' (Sidhu). Sikhs are expected to cultivate an awareness and respect for the dignity of all life.

Tomek claims that an important idea in Sikh thinking is that human beings live in harmony with creation. There is a sacred relationship between humans and all creation, and knowledge and understanding of this is called eco-sophism, the wisdom of the universe. However, the current threats facing the environment reflect human attempts to dominate all creation, to exploit, to dominate and to enslave, and represent a loss of that wisdom. Human surroundings reflect their inner state and the desperate situation in the world. The values underpinning human activity are what is fundamentally wrong, not simply the actions. The idea of equality, important in Sikhism's rejection of the caste system, suggests a balance which includes an ecological equilibrium, and that balance is no longer maintained. In 1999 the next 300-year cycle that Sikhism follows was named 'The Cycle of Creation', which has already led to an increase in environmental practices by Sikh temples. Sikhs, then, have a responsibility to listen to the wisdom of the universe, and restore the balance that has been lost. The pursuit of this must also be through prayer and the spirit of humility before God's will.

Conclusions

Different themes can be found within the different religious traditions examined here but there are also common themes. Nevertheless, religion in general terms has received some criticism that it has not adequately addressed environmental concerns, and that it to some extent is lagging behind the environmentalists.

In a recent Channel 4 documentary, 'God is Green' (see www.channel4.com/culture/microsites/C/can_you_believe_it/debates/green.html) Mark Dowd argued that religion should have a greater role in preventing imminent disaster and so far can be seen to be lacking. He observes fundamentalist Christians who seem to look with hope towards the end of time, Muslims who rarely espouse green ideas, and a slow-moving Catholic Church. He also notes the huge industrial expansion in India contrasting the ideas espoused within Hinduism. In other words religions and religious leaders seem not to be taking responsibility for educating, encouraging and setting an example for ordinary people to save the planet. There seems to be much more interest in other ethical issues, such as sexual ethical issues and medical ethical issues. Strangely the interest in environmental ethics seems to not be quite so important.

Scott I. Paradise has suggested that certain common religious beliefs need to be revised, and below are his revisions:

1 'Only man and the things he treasures have any value' must be replaced by 'All things have value.'

2 'The universe exists for man's exclusive and unconditional use' must be replaced by 'Man has been given responsibility for the earth.'

3 'In production and consumption, man finds his major fulfillment' must be replaced by 'In producing and consuming, man finds only a small part of his humanity.'

4 'Production and consumption must increase endlessly' must be replaced by 'Improvement in the quality of life takes precedence over increasing the quantity of material production.'

5 'The earth's resources are unlimited' must be replaced by 'Material resources are limited and are to be used carefully and cherished.'

6 'A major purpose of government is to make it easy for individuals and corporations to exploit the environment for the amassing of wealth and power' must be replaced by 'A major purpose of government is to regulate the exercise of property rights and to supervise a planning process that will prevent the impairment of the quality of the environment.'

Paradise, 1971

Some of these values echo existing theologies within existing approaches to environmental ethics and Paradise's proposals certainly clarify a possible position of agreement between the world's principal religions. However, the question will remain about the priority which religious leaders and believers will give to such an approach which, in richer countries and developing countries, will have a profound effect on lifestyle.

Activities

1 Compare and contrast the contributions made by a religious tradition and deep ecology to the environmental debate.

2 Are criticisms of religious approaches to the environment justified or not? Why/why not?

Activity

Environmental ethics is both about behaviours and about attitudes. Compare two or more religious and philosophical views of environmental ethics. What sorts of attitudes do they encourage and what sort of behaviours do they encourage? What differences or similarities emerge from your comparison?

Only an issue for the rich?

It is quite apparent that a concern for the well-being of the environment is in the interest of every sentient being on the planet, and if non-sentient beings can be said to have interests, it is in the interest of all life-forms. There is only one earth and until and unless we find other planets that can sustain life, there is only one chance at survival for the biosphere.

Of course the poor will suffer first and most from the deterioration caused by global warming and rising sea levels. Rich people and rich countries will be able to better fend off the shortages of food and water, the spread of disease and political instability that are likely to result from climate change. However, mass immigration from impoverished areas into the rich world will bring the problem to everyone.

Moral responsibility falls on all, but especially those with power and wealth for the system which drives climate change is industrialisation and development, and that, in turn, is based on capitalism. Environmental ethics are linked to issues of materialism and business ethics. Here religion has a potential to make a difference for it concerns other values than material ones, and reaches deeply into people's behaviour and attitudes. Religion has the capacity to change lifestyles. It remains to be seen whether this capacity is used.

Protecting the environment for the good of humankind?

Some ethical approaches to the environment are strictly concerned with human beings. They are said to be anthropocentric. Religions tend to give human beings a higher status than other creatures. For instance, Western religious traditions tend to see human beings as having the image and likeness of God. Other aspects of nature do not reflect the divine image in this way.

There are also those who, for philosophical reasons, do not give moral significance to animals or other living beings because they do not have the capacities of free will, rational thought, and moral deliberation, that mark human beings out.

Both these approaches tend to lead towards an idea that ultimately it is the human good that should be protected and environmental ethics should keep that as the focus. Of course there are many wonderful aspects of the environment which bring aesthetic and other pleasures to human beings, but in this analysis it is human beings who matter.

Against this view are a number of opinions. First it can be argued that this perspective encourages the kind of selfish thinking that has led to the exploitation and, ultimately, the endangering of the environment. In short it is not in human interests to simply be concerned about human interest because it encourages self-destructive behaviour.

In addition to this argument there is the case that other creatures are sentient and should be considered and valued. A further argument holds that we live in an interconnected biosphere and geosphere. In other words we cannot simply separate ourselves from the world which sustains us when we try to decide what is morally valuable. We have to consider the complicated interrelationships which we have with other living creatures and the natural habitat.

Should we be forced to be environmentally responsible?

Is the environment a moral issue which goes beyond persuasion and good conduct? Should it carry the weight of law behind it? While many think adultery is wrong, in most Western countries it is not illegal. However this is not the case for assault. Is concern for the environment important enough to move from the kind of moral in which we place adultery, to the kind of category in which we place assault? Should the force of law be used to change behaviours? Should people be forced to be environmentally friendly?

In thinking about this question there are a number of different factors to consider. First, who is it that is doing the forcing? Presumably what is meant here is the state or international community. In effect then we are thinking about the point at which the community overrules the freedom an individual has. This is quite an extreme measure in moral terms. Once we compel people to act they are no longer freely acting moral agents. Nevertheless there are good reasons to compel people to act on occasion. The law restricts drivers from driving at any speed they like and punishes those who ignore speed limits in the interests of the wider community (in this case protecting other road users and pedestrians). So if the danger is serious enough to the community, then certain freedoms are withdrawn from individuals by the public authorities in the interests of the community. This should not be done lightly but is justified. The question then is whether the concerns about the environment fall into this category, and if they are as serious as the science suggests, perhaps they do.

There is a softer way in which public authorities can influence individual moral behaviour: the way in which governments tax and regulate individuals and businesses, and encourage or discourage certain kinds of behaviour. Heavily taxing goods made from unsustainable resources, power from non-renewable sources while reducing tax and encouraging environmentally friendly options, is a way of exerting influence. Governments can also regulate against certain products and activities if they consider them too environmentally unfriendly, driving them out of the market.

However, these top-down methods of influence and control do reduce the sense of individual responsibility that people have for their own moral conduct. Environmentalists want individuals to change as well as governments. They want people to realise that they need to learn to live sustainably. There must be a recognition that individuals have a responsibility for the consequences of their actions, or else they might not strive to be moral.

Extracts from key texts

Peter Singer, Practical Ethics, *1993*
From p266

'And God said, Let us make man in our image, after our likeness: and let them have dominion over the fish of the sea, and over the fowl of the air, and over the Earth, and over every creeping thing that creepeth upon the Earth. So God created man in his own image, in the image of God created he him; male and female created he them. And God blessed them, and God said upon them, Be fruitful, and multiply, and replenish the Earth, and subdue it; and have dominion over the fish of the sea and over the fowl of the air, and over every living thing that moveth upon the Earth.'

Today Christians debate the meaning of this grant of 'dominion'; and those concerned about the environment claim that it should be regarded not as a license to do as we will with other living things, but rather as a directive to look after them, on God's behalf, and be answerable to God for the way in which we treat them. There is, however, little justification in the text itself for such an interpretation; and given the example God set when he drowned almost every animal on Earth in order to punish human beings for their wickedness, it is no wonder that people should think the flooding of a single river valley is nothing worth worrying about. After the flood there is a repetition of the grant of dominion in more ominous language: 'And the fear of you and the dread of you shall be upon every beast of the Earth, and upon every fowl of the air, upon all that moveth upon the Earth, and upon all the fishes of the sea; into your hands are they delivered.' The implication is clear: to act in a way that causes fear and dread to everything that moves on the Earth is not improper; it is, in fact, in accordance with a God-given decree. The most influential early Christian thinkers had no doubts about how man's dominion was to be understood. 'Doth God care for oxen?' asked Paul, in the course of a discussion of an Old Testament command to rest one's ox on the Sabbath, but it was only a rhetorical question – he took it for granted that the answer must be negative, and the command was to be explained in terms of some benefit to humans.

Aldo Leopold, 'The land ethic' (in LaFollette, 1997)

From pp634–643

When god-like Odysseus returned from the wars in Troy, he hanged all on one rope a dozen slave girls of his household whom he suspected of misbehaviour during his absence. This hanging involved no question of propriety. The girls were property. The disposal of property was then, as now, a matter of expediency, not right and wrong.

Concepts of right and wrong were not lacking from Odysseus' Greece: witness the fidelity of his wife through the long years before at last his blackprowed galleys clove the wine-dark seas from home. The ethical structure of that time covered wives, but had not yet extended to human chattels. During the three thousand years which have since elapsed, ethical criteria have been extended to many fields of conduct, with corresponding shrinkages in those judged by expediency only.

This extension of ethics, so far studied only by philosophers, is actually a process in ecological evolution. Its sequences may be described in ecological as well as in philosophical terms. An ethic, ecologically, is a limitation on freedom of action in the struggle for existence. An ethic, philosophically, is a differentiation of social from anti social conduct …

… The first ethic dealt with the relation between individuals; the Mosaic Decalogue is an example. Later accretions dealt with the relation between individual and society. The Golden Rule tries to integrate the individual into society; democracy to integrate social organisation to the individual.

There is as yet no ethic dealing with man's relation to land and to the animals and plants which grow upon it. Land, like Odysseus' slave girls, is still property. The land relation is still strictly economic, entailing privileges but not obligations.

The extension of ethics to this third element in human environment is, if I read the evidence correctly, an evolutionary possibility and an ecological necessity. It is the third step in a sequence. The first two have already been taken. Individual thinkers since the days of Ezekiel and Isaiah have asserted that the despoliation of land is not only inexpedient but wrong. Society, however, has not yet affirmed their belief. I regard the present conservation movement as the embryo of such an affirmation …

All ethics so far rest upon a simple premise: that the individual is a member of a community of interdependent parts. His instincts prompt him to compete for his place in the community, but his ethics prompt him also to cooperate. The land ethic simply enlarges the boundaries of the community to include soils, waters, plants, and animals, or collectively: the land.

This sounds simple: do we not already sing our love for and obligation to the land of the free and the home of the brave? Yes, but just what and whom do we love? Certainly not the soil, which we are sending helter-skelter downriver. Certainly not the waters, which we assume have no function except to turn turbines, float barges, and carry off sewage. Certainly not the plants, of which we exterminate whole communities without batting an eye. Certainly not the animals, of which we have already extirpated many of the largest and most beautiful species. A land ethic of course cannot prevent the alteration, management, and use of these 'resources,' but it does affirm their right to continued existence, and, at least in spots, their continued existence in a natural state.

Chapter summary

- Environmental ethics is concerned with our attitudes towards and impact on the biological and geological dimensions of the planet.

Threats to the environment: pollution and global warming

- Climate change presents very serious global risks and demands an urgent global response.

- It is very likely that the increase in temperatures in the 20th century is due to the increase in greenhouse gases.

- Systems that nurture and sustain life, providing clean air, water and soil, are breaking down through pollution and abuse.

- The world's finite natural resources are being depleted at an unsustainable rate.

- Environmental damage will disproportionately affect the poor.

- Industrialisation and technological and scientific development has led to the destruction of wildernesses.

- Technological advancement and scientific investigation are threatening humanity's long-term survival.

Conservation, preservation and protection

- Holmes Rolston III argues that we should not be exclusively concerned with human poverty, but should also be concerned with other aspects of civilisation as well as the value of the natural world.

- Animals have rights because they have some intrinsic value.
- We should avoid the mistreatment of animals and seek to improve their quality of life.
- Animals also have inherent value and all beings who have inherent value have it equally.
- Singer argues that equality should be applied for animals as well as humans.
- Fox argued that animals are not members of the moral community and that we have no moral obligation towards them – moral capability arises from faculties that animals don't have.
- However, not all human beings display these moral capabilities (babies, etc.) and yet we give them moral status and regard them as deserving of special protection.
- Arguably wildernesses contain untapped, undiscovered valuable natural resources or scientific treasures, they are a kind of life-support system for the world, they provide a retreat for human beings from the built environment, they should be preserved for the diversity of life-forms within, they should be protected simply because of what they are, rather than what they might offer humanity or the biosphere as a whole.

Developing countries

- Poorer countries need to develop to improve the lot of their people but industrialising in the way rich countries did increases pollution and greenhouse gases.
- Rich countries are encouraging unsustainable economic development of developing countries as they can produce goods more cheaply to satisfy wealthy consumers.
- Rich countries have got rich through unsustainable development.
- Failure to develop leaves poorer countries poor.
- Poorer countries are more exposed to the dangers of climate change.

Religious and philosophical perspectives

A deep ecology

- Deep ecology recognises value in all life and others aspects of the natural world as part of an interconnected whole and so the whole bio/geosphere has moral significance.
- Deep ecology preserves the biosphere for its own sake, not just for the benefit of humanity.
- James Lovelock's Gaia hypothesis sees the ecosystem as a whole as an entity in its own right, which must be considered in any moral deliberation.
- Some argue the Gaia hypothesis gives the biosphere a consciousness which is not there – it is romantic language.
- Deep ecology is also critical of mechanistic materialism, industrialisation and capitalism.

Jewish perspectives

- Humanity has a special place in nature above other aspects of the natural world, though nature should be protected.
- Nature exists for humanity and for its own sake.

- Genesis seems both to encourage exploitation and also restrict which animals may be eaten – the Sabbath laws imply restraint in human activity and there are restrictions about the use of natural resources.
- Nature can be seen as dangerous (e.g. the flood).

Christian perspectives

- Built on Jewish perspectives.
- Aquinas maintained that 'all animals are naturally subject to man' and did not recognise the possibility of sin against the environment.
- However, Christian ethics is necessarily God-centred, rather than human-centred.
- Concern for your neighbour should include concern for your neighbour's environment.
- Non-human creatures have intrinsic value in the Christian tradition, e.g. St Francis.
- The environment has value because it was created by God.
- Poor treatment of the environment reflects human sin.
- Humans are called to renew the face of the earth until there is peace and harmony, life and health for all.

Muslim perspectives

- The natural world was created by God and all elements of the world exist with distinct purposes in balance.
- Creation exists in continuous praise of God, and humanity has duties as stewards of creation.
- Natural laws are God's laws and there are other communities, beyond the human communities, which live in the world.
- Human relationships with the environment should be based on justice and equity.
- Humans are maintainers of the environment and not owners, and must sustain it and conserve it.

Hindu perspectives

- The principle of the sanctity of life is ingrained in the Hindu religion.
- Human beings do not have dominion or sovereignty over all creatures, only God has this.
- Human and non-human lives are of equal value and all have the same right to existence – the earth is for other creatures as well as humans.
- Beyond animals and birds, trees and flora are also respected – plants have divine powers including healing properties.
- A human being is authorised to use natural resources, but has no divine power of control and dominion over nature and its elements.

Buddhist perspectives

- Buddhism is thought to be a path of harmonious integration with nature which fosters identification and mutual respect within the natural world.
- However, human beings remain the primary focus of Buddhism which is to bring human beings from suffering to liberation.

- The basic principle of non-violence (ahimsa) requires the abstention from harming living beings, which includes the industrial use of natural resources.

- The Buddhist concern for human beings means the over-consumption of resources is unacceptable.

- Respect for plant life and trees is not on a par with humans and there is not much evidence to support the conservation of wilderness, beyond the observation that it is beautiful.

- In Buddhism humans are not stewards of non-human nature, but neighbours to less sentient beings.

- The concern for the destruction or damage to the environment is motivated by a concern for sentient life including, and most importantly, human life.

Sikh perspectives

- The Sikh Gurus saw that human beings had some responsibility towards the natural world and urged people to study and respect it – Guru Nanak said: 'The earth is your mother. Respect mother earth.'

- Important in Sikh thinking is that human beings live in harmony with creation.

- There is a sacred relationship between humans and all creation, and knowledge and understanding of this is called eco-sophism, the wisdom of the universe.

- The idea of equality, important in Sikhism's rejection of the caste system, suggests a balance between humanity and nature.

Conclusions

- Different themes can be found within the different religious traditions examined here but there are also common themes.

- Religion has received some criticism that it has not adequately addressed environmental concerns.

- Scott I. Paradise has suggested that certain common religious beliefs need to be revised to give value to all things, to turn away from the emphasis on consumption and production as leading to fulfilment, and to care for limited resources.

- All living creatures have an interest in sustaining the environment.

- The poor stand to lose more at first, though the rich will also lose in the end.

- Those with wealth and power have a special responsibility in how they use it and for what ends.

- However, saving the planet requires individuals to change the way they live their lives.

- Some argue that human interests should be the motive for environmental concern rather than other life-forms, though the environment might have instrumental value, in that it can make human life better.

- Anthropocentric thinking might encourage selfishness, and also encourage a false view that human life is separate from the eco-system around it – such a view is responsible in part for the problems the world faces now.

- Life on earth is interconnected and so it is difficult to identify single parts of life only as having moral value or significance.

- The state should only intervene to force people to act in a certain way if the community is seriously threatened by environmental disaster, as individual freedoms will be lost.

- The state can also intervene in a softer way, e.g. taxes, to influence behaviour.

- There is also a moral concern that individuals have a sense of responsibility for their actions.

Further reading

Very readable explorations can be found in:

Singer, P., *Practical Ethics*, Cambridge University Press, 1993, pp264–288
Vardy, P., *The Puzzle of Ethics*, Fount, 1992, pp213–226

Not forgetting my favourite anthology:

Singer, P., *Ethics*, in the Oxford Readers series, Oxford University Press, 1994

In this chapter you have:

- explored the main ethical areas of debate related to environmental ethics: the threats to the environment, the issues of conservation, pollution and preservation and the role of developing countries

- considered religious and non-religious approaches to problems within the environment

- considered the strengths and weaknesses of the different approaches.

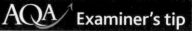

AQA Examiner's tip

As this textbook illustrates, there is often a marked difference between religious rhetoric about the environment and what actually gets done. Given that environmental destruction is probably the greatest current threat to human survival, why do you think that action by the world's religious authorities is generally so limited?

What is ethics?

(a) Explain the differences between deontological and teleological theories of ethics.

(b) 'It cannot be right to base an ethical theory on the consequences of our actions.' How far do you agree with this statement?

Absolutism and relativism

Practice essays

This subject does not appear on the specification as such, although two papers include examples of absolutist and relativist theories: Kant and natural law in paper B2 are absolutist, utilitarianism in paper B1 is relativist. Situation ethics in B1 is based on an absolute principle (the law of love), but that principle is interpreted relatively. Questions on these subjects therefore involve consideration of the absolutist/relativist debate in ethics.

(a) Using examples from the ethical theories you have studied, explain the differences between absolutist and relativist theories of ethics.

(b) Consider the view that absolutism must be wrong, otherwise there would be no disagreement in ethics.

Utilitarianism

(a) Examine the differences between act and rule utilitarianism.

(b) How far is it true that the pursuit of happiness is not a worthwhile goal in ethics?

Situation ethics

(a) Examine any four of the six fundamental principles on which Fletcher bases his theory of situation ethics.

(b) 'Love is not a good basis for making ethical decisions.' How far do you agree?

Religious perspectives on the nature and value of human life

(a) Consider the importance of free will in the debate about the value of human life.

(b) 'We have no free will: our fate is already decided for us.' How would you respond to such a statement?

Kant

(a) Examine the concept of the *summum bonum* in Kant's theory of ethics.

(b) Assess the view that the concept of the *summum bonum* is the weakest point in Kant's theory of ethics.

Natural moral law

(a) Explain how Aquinas made use of Aristotle's ethics in developing his own theory of natural law.

(b) How far do you agree that there is such a thing as natural good?

Abortion

(a) Explain the importance of the different definitions of the start of human life in the debate about abortion.

(b) 'The right to life begins at birth.' Assess this view.

Euthanasia

(a) With reference to religious teaching, explain arguments for and against euthanasia.

(b) Assess the claim that humans have a right to death.

Religion and the created world

(a) With reference to the religion you have studied, what does it mean to say that God 'sustains' the world?

(b) 'God sustains the world, so humans have a moral responsibility to look after it.' To what extent is this true?

Environmental ethics

(a) 'Environmental conservation is not just important – it is *vital* in the 21st century.' Explain the reasoning behind this statement.

(b) How far do you agree that all humans share equally the responsibility of caring for the environment?

Glossary

A

Abh: the human being as the slave or loving servant of God.

Abortion: the deliberate termination (ending) of a pregnancy, usually before the foetus is twenty-four weeks old.

Absolutism: in ethics, the view that moral rules have a complete and universal authority that derives either from God, or from the internal authority/consistency of the rule.

Active euthanasia: carrying out some action to help someone to die.

Act utilitarianism: a version of utilitarianism according to which the rightness or wrongness of individual acts are calculated by the amount of happiness resulting from these acts.

Agape love: in Christian terms, the unconditional love that they must show their neighbours.

Analytic: analytic statements are true by definition, e.g. a bicycle has two wheels. Here the predicate says something necessary about the subject. Since mathematical statements are also said to be true by the terms used, $1+1 = 2$ is often said to be analytic a priori.

Animal welfare: ethical concern for the care of domestic, farming or wild animals.

Anthropocentric: the idea that, for humans, humans must be the central concern, and that humanity must judge all things accordingly.

Antinomian ethics: the view that there are no moral principles or rules at all.

A posteriori: sentences/propositions/ judgements are a posteriori (literally 'after') when their truth depends on how our experience/ observation turns out.

A priori: sentences/propositions/ judgements are a priori (literally 'before') when their truth is not dependent on sense experience. Many philosophers hold that maths is a priori, because no sense experience is needed to know that $1+1 = 2$, but some dispute this.

Atman: individual immortal soul, or true self.

Autonomous: free to make decisions.

Autonomous moral agents: the idea that humans are beings capable of free moral decision-making.

Ayatollah: high-ranking religious leader among Shiite Muslims, especially in Iran.

B

Behaviourist: in psychology, behaviourism can be described as the theory that human and animal behaviour can be explained in terms of conditioning, without appeal to thoughts or feelings, and that psychological disorders are best treated by altering behaviour patterns.

Bhagavad-Gita: the sacred 'Song of God', composed c.200 BC; a holy text revered by followers of Hinduism.

Brahman or Paramatman: the universal absolute being or supreme soul.

Brahmin: a higher caste, holy, man; not the same as Brahman, or supreme soul.

Buddha: the title given to the founder of Buddhism, Siddartha Gautama (c.563–c.483 BC), but also in the sense of full Buddha, a person who has achieved enlightenment.

C

Caste: a hereditary social class among Hindus; stratified according to ritual purity.

Casuistry: casuistry is the practice of applying moral principles to particular cases, or types of case. It can be contrasted with situational approaches to ethics, which consider each moral situation as it arises.

Categorical imperative: categorical imperatives are laws whose forces are absolute and undeniable, e.g. 'Do not murder', 'Honour your parents', etc. Their force is discernible by contrasting them with the weak command in hypothetical imperatives.

Christological: Christology is a field of study within Christian theology which is concerned with the nature of Jesus the Christ. In particular, how the divine and human are related in his person.

Conscience: used in a special sense in situation ethics. Fletcher rejects the idea that conscience is (1) intuition, (2) a channel for divine guidance, (3) the internalised values of the individual's culture, or (4) the part of reason that makes value judgements, because all of these treat conscience as a thing, which Fletcher believes is a mistake. Rather, for him, conscience is a verb rather than a noun – it is something you do when you make decisions, as he puts it, 'creatively'.

Consciousness: a state of being awake, aware of, or sensitive to one's surroundings.

Consequentialist/consequential thinking: thinking, in this case, about the rightness or wrongness of an action, that takes only the consequences of an action into consideration. Contrasted with deontological thinking.

Cosmology: reflection on and account of the world or universe.

Covenant: an agreement which brings about a relationship of God and his people.

Cultural relativism: the form of relativism which maintains that what is good or bad, right or wrong, for a person varies in relation to the culture in which the person lives.

D

Dalai Lama: the spiritual head of Tibetan Buddhism.

Deep ecology: an ethical theory which recognises value in all life-forms, and perhaps even the geological and biological systems and diversity of planet earth, and rejects anthropocentric ethics.

Definism: or ethical naturalism is the theory that ethical facts are known in the same way as mathematical or scientific facts.

Deontological/deontological ethics: in contrast to consequential thinking – this is only concerned with the moral law, or duty, that makes a particular action right or wrong regardless of the consequences.

Descriptive ethics: looks at how different people and societies have answered moral questions.

Dharma: has different shades of meaning, but can be taken in this context as the 'right way of living' or 'proper conduct'.

Dominion: this refers to the view that the scriptures give humans power over animals and the environment, as opposed to theories of stewardship.

Double effect: this is a doctrine devised to deal with moral conflicts in natural law theory. It says that it is always wrong to do a bad act intentionally in order to bring about good consequences, but it is sometimes permissible to do a good act while at the same time knowing that it will bring about bad consequences. In rough terms, this is sometimes translated as, 'Provided your intention is to follow the rule, you can "benefit" from any unintended consequences.'

Duty: the central plank of Kant's ethics. Duty is based on moral obligation as shown by the categorical imperative, and it must not be confused with desire.

E

Earth yoga: spiritual practice which values the physical natural world, enhances health and senses, and encourages a concern about the destruction of the natural world.

Ectopic pregnancy: a pregnancy in which the foetus develops outside the uterus.

Embryo: an unborn human baby (especially in the first eight weeks), after implantation but before the development of organs.

Emotivism: A. J. Ayer's theory, which argues that moral choices are based on emotional reactions to what we see. If we dislike the sight of blood, for example, then our emotional reaction to it will make us predisposed to outlaw murder.

Ensoulment: the process in Christian belief, by which a body is endowed with a soul.

Episcopal Church: the name given to the Anglican (Church of England) Church in Scotland and the US.

Ethical theory: covers religious and philosophical systems or methods for making moral decisions or analysing moral statements.

Ethics: the principles by which people live.

Euthanasia: inducing a painless death, by agreement and with compassion, to ease suffering. From the Greek meaning 'Good Death'.

Excommunication: the act of banishing a member of a Church from the communion of believers and the privileges of the Church; cutting a person off from a religious society.

Exterior act/interior act: an interior act is an act of the will, which contrasts with an exterior act, which is what you do. In Aquinas's natural law system, both are important. The motive and purpose of an act is just as important as the exterior act, because its ultimate end is God.

Extrinsic: not part of the essential nature of someone or something; coming or operating from outside.

F

Fall of man: when Adam and Eve ate of the fruit of the tree of knowledge of good and evil in the Garden of Eden, God punished them by driving them out of the Garden of Eden and into the world where they would be subject to sickness and pain and eventual death.

Fatalism: the view that everything that happens is predetermined and that we have no control over it.

Fertilised ovum: a female reproductive cell which has been fertilised by a male reproductive cell (sperm).

Foetus: an unborn human baby after eight weeks.

Free will: having the ability to choose or determine one's own actions.

G

Gaia hypothesis: Gaia was the Greek 'mother earth' goddess. The Gaia hypothesis is that the earth as a whole is a single organism made up of living and non-living parts. The system is incredibly complex and interactive, and works as a whole to regulate life on earth as a whole.

Geosphere: the soils, sediments, and rock layers of the earth's crust, both continental and beneath the ocean floors.

Good: in a moral sense, refers to actions, consequences, situations, people, characters, choices and lifestyles.

Greater jihad: unlike the outward-looking lesser jihad, greater jihad concerns the inner struggle for sanctity.

Guru: a spiritual leader or teacher.

H

Hadith: the sayings of the Prophet Muhammad, as recounted by his contemporaries. The Hadith is a major source of Islamic law.

Hedonic calculus: created by Bentham, this is a utilitarian system whereby the effects of an action can be measured as to the amount of pleasure it may bring.

Hedonism: the belief that pleasure is the chief 'good'.

Hippocratic oath: an oath stating the duties and proper conduct of doctors.

Holistic: characterised by the belief that the parts of something are intimately interconnected and explicable only by reference to the whole.

Hukam: the Divine Will by which all forms were created.

Hypothetical imperative: statements that take the form: 'If x, then y' are hypothetical, e.g. If you want to be happy, then you should take regular exercise. Statements such as this are hypothetical in that they describe instrumental good – good as a means to an end. An imperative is a command, so a hypothetical imperative is a weak command. Kant used hypothetical imperatives to illustrate the power of categorical imperatives, such as 'Do not murder', which he argues has a force that cannot be denied.

I

Incarnation: the Christian doctrine of the union of God and man in the person of Jesus Christ.

Intrinsically good: intrinsic good is 'built-in' good, e.g. one does not have to ask why health is good. Intrinsic good for Kant is in the good will – duty for duty's sake.

Intuitionism: or non-naturalism disagrees with ethical naturalism, stating that moral properties cannot be reduced to entirely non-ethical properties; they are not like mathematical facts.

Involuntary euthanasia: helping a person to die when they are unable to request this for themselves.

J

Jainism: founded in India in the 6th century BC as a reaction against orthodox Brahmanism. The religion teaches salvation by perfection through successive lives, and non-injury to living creatures.

Jihad: literally, translated from the Arabic, 'striving in the way of God', though this striving can take a number of forms, from the internal to the external.

Justice: the principles underpinning law and their relationship to those laws.

Just war: a war that is deemed to be morally or theologically justifiable by established conditions.

K

Kantian ethics: the ethical theory defined by Immanuel Kant, consisting of the primacy of duty, good will and the categorical imperative.

Karma: in Hinduism and Buddhism, the sum of a person's actions in this and previous states of existence, viewed as deciding their fate in future existences.

Khalifa: the idea that the human being is vice-regent of God on earth and must act in God's interests.

Kingdom of ends: Kant's term for the ethical community as a whole. One version of the categorical imperative is that humans should act always as if they were not just individuals but law-abiding members of a kingdom of moral ends.

Kosher: prepared in accordance with Jewish dietary laws.

L

Legalistic ethics: an ethical system that contains rules for every situation and/or the association of doing good with simply following those rules.

Lesser jihad: can be taken to mean an actual fight against infidels, or non-Muslims, contrasted with greater jihad. Characterised sometimes as a 'holy war'.

Liberty: freedom.

Life is sacred: has a special, holy value, beyond a material, exchangeable price.

Liturgy: a liturgy comprises a prescribed ceremony, according to the traditions of a particular group or event.

Living will: a document that specifies an individual's wishes regarding care and treatment if he or she becomes incapacitated, such as limiting life-support that would only prolong death.

M

Means: in any action, we distinguish between the end result to be achieved, and the way in which it is achieved – the means.

Metaethics/philosophical ethics: explores the meaning and function of moral language.

Midrash: in Judaism, explains biblical text from the ethical and devotional point of view.

Moral agents: in ethics, the person who acts in accordance with some ethical belief or teaching is referred to as a moral agent, in the sense that what is said or done is through his/her agency.

Morality: concerned with which actions are right and wrong, rather than the character of the person.

Moral relativism: the idea that moral or ethical propositions do not reflect objective, universal truths, instead making claims relative to social, cultural, historical or personal circumstances.

Mufti: a Muslim legal expert who is empowered to give rulings on religious matters.

N

Naturalistic fallacy: G. E. Moore's claim that the concept of 'good' is indefinable and therefore not valid in philosophical discussion.

Natural law: the name of Aquinas's ethical system, derived partly from Aristotle, in which the good is defined by acts which are within our common human nature. Good actions are those which help us become fully human, whereas bad actions are those which hinder us from being fully human.

Natural moral law: the name of Aquinas's ethical system, derived partly from Aristotle, in which the good is defined by acts which are within our common human nature. Good actions are those which help us become fully human, whereas bad actions are those which hinder us from being fully human.

Nirvana: a transcendent state in which there is neither suffering, desire, nor sense of self, and the subject is released from the effects of karma. It represents the final goal of Buddhism.

Normative ethics: decides how people ought to act, how moral choices should be made and how the rules apply.

O

'Ought' implies 'can': the argument that an act must be possible before it can be required.

P

Palliative care: the care of patients with a terminal illness, not with the intent of trying to cure them, but to relieve their symptoms.

Passive euthanasia: not carrying out actions which would prolong life.

Pastorally: pastoral care is typically guidance, in the way of counselling, given by a religious figure.

Personalism: the ethic that demands that human beings are not treated as 'means' but are subject.

Personhood: the ethical quality or human condition which denotes a morally significant or valuable individual being.

Pneumatology: brand of Christian theology concerned with the Holy Ghost and other spiritual concerns.

Positivism: the situational principle that Christians freely choose to believe that God is love and then act in a way reasonable with this faith statement.

Practical (or applied) ethics: focuses on debates about specific dilemmas, such as abortion or euthanasia.

Practical reason: the consideration of basic human goods when deciding how to live.

Pragmatism: any theory of ethics must be practical and work towards the end that is love.

Predestination: the belief that one's actions and eventual fate are already determined before one is born.

Preference utilitarianism: a utilitarian theory interested in the best consequences for those involved rather than what creates the most pleasure and least pain.

Prescriptivism: the moral theory of R. M. Hare, that moral statements have a prescriptive quality about them (meaning that we want them to apply to others) and in that sense are universalisable (which Hare imports from Kant).

Primary precepts: in natural law ethics, primary precepts are the 'first' level of rules which apply to all human beings by virtue of their common human nature, e.g. the primary precept of sexual behaviour is that all acts of sex should lead directly to the possibility of procreation, from which a number of interesting secondary precepts are then derived.

Primitive streak: the faint streak which is the earliest trace of the embryo in the fertilised ovum of a higher vertebrate, often regarded as day 14.

Proportionalism: a modification of natural law ethics which seeks to take account of the consequences of actions. It suggests that moral rules may sometimes be broken if there is a proportionate reason. Where this happens, the act remains objectively wrong but is morally right: e.g. contraception is an objective wrong which can be morally right in order to prevent the damaging effects of over-population.

Q

Qualitative: concerned with the value and nature.

Quantitative: concerned with the amount.

R

Relativism: in moral terms, moral relativism is the view that there are no moral absolutes, so that our moral judgements relate to upbringing, milieu, psychology, society, and so on. Philosophers have sought to justify relativism culturally, metaethically and normatively. Cultural relativism simply notes that moral values vary between societies, and so assume that this reflects the fact that moral values are relative. Metaethical relativism argues that the discussion about the meaning of moral language cannot reach an agreed conclusion between the competing theories of naturalism, non-naturalism and non-cognitivism; so in the absence of such an agreement, it seems safest to conclude that this is because values are indeed relative and not factual. Normative relativism is the view that right and wrong are defined by the situation.

Right reason: uncorrupted reason which serves its own ends rather than the ends of special interests.

Rule utilitarianism: a version of utilitarianism in which general rules are assessed for the happiness-making properties rather than individual decisions. Often associated with John Stuart Mill. Actions are therefore 'right' or 'wrong' depending on whether they conform to a happiness-making rule, not because of their individual effects.

S

Samsara: wandering on.

Secondary precepts: these are the rules which Aquinas derived from the primary precepts which are at the centre of his natural law theory. The set of secondary precepts most commonly referred to is that containing the rules for sexual conduct, which have caused much controversy.

Self-determination: the process by which a person controls and directs their life.

Self-willed death: the decision to accept death in the hope of enlightenment.

Situation ethics: the moral theory proposed by Joseph Fletcher which requires the application of love to every unique situation.

Slippery slope: the idea that once one seemingly insignificant ethical restriction is lifted, much more serious ones are likely to follow; the thin edge of the wedge.

Stewardship: the religious doctrine that humans are responsible to God for animals and for the rest of the environment/created world, since the mode of the creation of humans singles them out as the species that rules the earth on God's behalf. Stewardship in theory should lead to the preservation of both the human and the non-human world, although in practice the diversity of interpretation of what appears to be a simple idea leads also to environmental destruction.

Summum bonum: in Kant's ethics, Kant assumed that the force of the moral 'ought' implied that we 'can' achieve our moral goals and complete our duty perfectly. Perfect duty ought to be rewarded by perfect happiness. This is the *summum bonum* – the highest good. Since it is hardly possible to achieve this during one's lifetime, Kant surmised that there must be life after death in which to achieve it, which in turn presupposes the existence of God as the only being capable of providing immortality, and of judging that the *summum bonum* has been achieved. Kant did say that these assumptions and their basis in God were collectively a 'postulate of practical reason', i.e. they are probabilities, not facts.

Sunni: one of the two main branches of Islam, commonly described as orthodox, and the most widely followed. The other main branch is Shia, with approximately 10 per cent of Muslims, though Shiites represent a majority in Iran.

Synthetic: knowledge is said to be synthetic if it is based on observation/measurement/testing. Synthetic statements can be true or false. Statements like, 'Scooby is a dog' are synthetic, and since they are known after experience, they are a posteriori, so 'Scooby is a dog' is synthetic a posteriori (and given that Scooby can talk, it is probably synthetic a posteriori false).

T

Teleological ethics/teleological thinking: a description applied to utilitarianism. It stresses that an action is right or wrong depending on its purpose/intended outcome.

U

Universalisability: a central focus of Kant's ethical theory; a form of the categorical imperative, which states that reason is correct in holding a moral law to be true if it can be universalised, i.e. if the one who proposes to act on it is satisfied that it should apply to all humans – to everyone in the universe.

Upanishads: philosophical teachings that form the later part of the Vedas.

Utilitarianism: a philosophical system concerned with consequences rather than motives and in which the happiness of the greatest number should be the result.

Utility principle: the rightness or wrongness of an action is determined by its 'utility' or usefulness.

V

Vedic religion: the ancient religion of the Aryan peoples who entered NW India from Persia (*c*.2000– 1200 BC). It was the precursor of Hinduism, and its beliefs and practices are contained in the Vedas.

Viability: in the context of abortion, the point at which the developing foetus/child becomes capable of living outside the womb. A viable ovum/embryo is one that has the potential to develop into an adult organism.

Vinaya: the monastic discipline, or the scriptural collection of its rules and commentaries.

Voluntary euthanasia: helping a person who wishes to die to do so.

W

Women's rights: freedoms and liberties guaranteed to women in law.

Bibliography and websites

Abortion Rights, the national pro-choice campaign. More information on this organisation can be found here: www.abortionrights.org.uk

Abu-Sway, M., 'Towards an Islamic Jurisprudence of the Environment'. A paper based on a lecture given at the Belfast Mosque in February 1998. See http://www.iol.ie/~afifi/Articles/environment.htm

Anderson, 'Environmental ethics', in Childress, J. F. and Macquarrie, J. (ed.), *A New Dictionary of Christian Ethics*, SCM, 1986

Aquinas, St T., *Summa Theologica*, trans. The Fathers of the English Dominican Province, Benziger Bros, 1947

Aristotle, 'Eudemian Ethics', in Barnes, J. (ed.), *The Complete Works of Aristotle vol. 2*, Princeton University Press, 1984

Aristotle, *The Nicomachean ethics*, trans. with an introduction by W. D. Ross, Oxford University Press, 1980

Austin, J., *The Providence of Jurisprudence Determined*, John Murray, 1832

Ayer, A. J., *Truth, Language and Logic*, Victor Gollancz, 1936

Barclay, W., *Ethics in a Permissive Society*, Collins, 1980

Barnette, H., *The Church and the Ecological Crises*, Eerdsmans, 1972

Bauman, Z., *Postmodern Ethics*, Blackwell, 1993

Bentham, J., *A Fragment on Government*, Montague, F. C. (ed.), Greenwood Press, 1980

Bentham, J., *Principles of Morals and Legislation*, Prometheus, 1988

Berman, S., 'Jewish environmental values: the dynamic tension between nature and human needs', in *Human Values and the Environment*, Conference Proceedings, Institute for Environmental Studies, University of Wisconsin-Madison, 1992

Berry, T., 'A new story', in *Teilhard Studies*, New York, Winter, 1978

Biatch, J., Beth El Hebrew Congregation, Alexandria, VA, Union of Reform Judaism. For more information about Reform Judaism and abortion, visit http://urj.org and select the 'FAQ – by subject'

Bowker, J. (ed.), *The Oxford Dictionary of World Religions*, Oxford University Press, 1997

Bradley, F. H., *Ethical Studies*, 2nd edn, Oxford University Press, 1927

Brockopp, J. E., *Islamic Ethics of Life: abortion, war and euthanasia*, University of South Carolina Press, 2003

Bryant, W. C., 'Thanatopsis', in the *North American Review*, September, 1817

Butler, S., *The Way of All Flesh*, Kessinger Publishing, 1916

Cahn, S. M. and Markie, P., *Ethics: history, theory, and contemporary issues*, Oxford University Press, 1998

Cairns, D., *The Image of God in Man*, Collins, 1973

Chapple, C. K., 1998, 'Hinduism, Jainism, and ecology', *Earth Ethics*, 10, no.1. See www.environment.harvard.edu/religion, click on the image to access the site, then select 'Hinduism'

Childress, J. F. and Macquarrie, J., *New Dictionary of Christian Ethics*, SCM, 1986

Church of England (2004), Bishops oppose 'misguided and unnecessary' euthanasia bill. See www.cofe.anglican.org, select the 'media centre' link, then pick from the 2004 archive

Cicero, *De Re Publica (On the Republic), De Legibus (On the Laws)*, Trans. Clinton Walker Keyes, Loeb Classical Library No. 213, Cambridge, 1928

Cohan, C., 'The case for use of animals in biomedical research', in (eds) Cahn, S. M. and Markie, P., *Ethics: history, theory and contemporary issues*, Oxford University Press, 1998, pp829–837

Cole, W. O., *Understanding Sikhism*, Dunedin Academic Press, 2004

Coward, H., 'World religions and reproductive technologies', *Social Values and Attitudes Surrounding New Reproductive Technologies*, Ottawa: Royal Commission of New Reproductive Technologies, Research Studies, vol. 2, 1993, pp454–456

Coward, H. and Sidhu, T., 'Review, bioethics for clinicians: 19. Hinduism and Sikhism', *Canadian Medical Association Journal*, 163 (9), 2000, pp1167–1170

Coward, H. G., Lipner, J. J. and Young K. K., *Hindu Ethics: purity, abortion, and euthanasia*, State University of New York Press, 1989

Crook, R. H., *Introduction to Christian Ethics*, Prentice Hall, 2002

Deen, I. and Mawil, Y., 'Islamic environmental ethics, law and society', in Gottlieb, R. S., *This Sacred Earth: religion, nature, environment*, Routledge, 1996, pp152–164

Denny, F. M., 'Islam and ecology: a bestowed trust inviting balanced stewardship', *Earth Ethics*, 10, no.1, 1998. See www.environment.harvard.edu/religion, click on the image to access the site, then select 'Islam'

Department of Health, Abortion statistics, England and Wales: 2006. See www.dh.gov.uk/en, click on the 'Publications' link, then the 'Publications' sub-head

Devall, B. and Sessions, G., *Deep Ecology*, Smith, Salt Lake City, 1985

Dhand, A., 'The Dharma of ethics, the ethics of Dharma: quizzing the ideals of Hinduism', *Journal of Religious Ethics*, 2002, pp347–372

Dwivedi, O. P., 'Satyagraha for conservation: awakening the spirit of hinduism', in Gottlieb, R. S., *This Sacred Earth: religion, nature, environment*, Routledge, 1996, pp147–151

Dyck, A., 'Beneficent euthanasia and benemortasia alternative views of mercy', in Kohl, M. (ed.), *Beneficent Euthanasia*, Prometheus Books, 1975

Elliott, R., 'Environmental ethics', in Singer, P. (ed.), *A Companion to Ethics*, Blackwell, pp284–293

Fields, R., 'The time is now', *Yoga Journal*, 138, February, 1998

Fink, D. B., 'Judaism and ecology: a theology of creation', *Earth Ethics*, 10, no.1, 1998. See www.environment. harvard.edu/religion, click on the image to access the site, then select 'Judaism'

Finnis, J., *Natural Law and Natural Rights*, Clarendon Press, 1980

Fletcher, J., *Moral Responsibility: situation ethics at work*, Westminster Press, 1967

Fletcher, J., *Situation Ethics: the new morality*, Westminster Press, 1963

Fletcher, J., 'The patient's right to die', in Downing, A. B. (ed.), *Euthanasia and the Right to Death: the case for voluntary euthanasia*, Peter Owen, 1969

Fletcher, J., 'The "right" to live and the "right" to die', in (ed.) Kohl, M., *Beneficent Euthanasia*, Prometheus Books, 1975, p119

Fox, M. A., *The Case for Animal Experimentation*, University of California Press, 1986

Frame, J. M., *Medical Ethics: principles, persons and problems*, P&R, 1988

Gallagher, J., *Is the Human Embryo a Person?*, Human Life Research Institute Report, 4, 1985

Glover, J., *Causing Death and Saving Lives*, Penguin, 1977

Goldberg, R. T., 'The "right" to die: the case for and against voluntary passive euthanasia', *Disability, Handicap & Society*, 2, (1), 1987

Goldsmith, O., 'The Traveller', in *English Poetry II: From Collins to Fitzgerald*, (1909–14), Vol. XLI, The Harvard Classics, P.F. Collier & Son, 2001

Goodman, L. E., *Judaism, Human Rights, and Human Values*, Oxford University Press, 1998

Gruen, L., 'Animals', in Singer, P. (ed.), *A Companion to Ethics*, Blackwell, 1991, pp343–353

Gula, R. M., 'Conscience', in Hoose, B., *Christian Ethics: an introduction*, Cassell, 1998, pp110–122

Hare, R. M., *Freedom and Reason*, Clarendon Press, 1963

Hare, R. M., *The Language of Morals*, Oxford University Press, 1952

Harvey, P., *An Introduction to Buddhism: teachings, history and practices*, Cambridge University Press, 1990

Harvey, P., *An Introduction to Buddhist Ethics*, Cambridge University Press, 2000

Hazlitt, W., the quotation in Chapter 3 is widely attributed to Hazlitt, for instance by Hadden, P., *The Quotable Artist*, Allworth Communications, 2002

Hedayat, K. M., Shooshtarizadeh, P. and Raza, M., 'Therapeutic abortion in Islam: contemporary views of Muslim Shiite scholars and effect of recent Iranian legislation', *Journal of Medical Ethics*, 32, 2006, pp652–657

Herodotus, *Histories*, trans. G. Rawlinson, Wordsworth Classics, 1996

Hessel, D. T., 'Christianity and ecology: wholeness, respect, justice, sustainability', Harvard University Center for the Environment, 1998. *Earth Ethics*, 10, no.1. See www.environment.harvard.edu/religion, click on the image to access the site, then select 'Christianity'

Hewer, C., *Understanding Islam*, SCM, 2006

Hoffman, J. and Rosenkrantz, G., 'Omnipotence' in Quinn, P. L. and Taliaferro, C. A. (eds), *Companion to Philosophy of Religion*, Blackwell, 1997, pp229–235

Honderich, T., *Oxford Companion to Philosophy*, Oxford University Press, 1995

Hooker, B., 'Rule utilitarianism and euthaniasia', in LaFollette, H. (ed.), *Ethics in Practice: An Anthology*, Blackwell, 1997, pp42–52

Hoose, B., *Christian Ethics: an introduction*, Cassell, 1998

Hoose, B., *Proportionalism: the American debate and its European roots*, Georgetown University Press, 1987

Hughes, J. J. and Keown, D., 'Buddhism and medical ethics: a bibliographic introduction', *The Journal of Buddhist Ethics*, Vol. 2, 1995

Hull, J. M., 'A spirituality of disability: the Christian heritage as both problem and potential,' *Studies in Christian Ethics*, 16 (2), 2003, pp21–35

Intergovernmental Panel on Climate change, *Synthesis Report of the IPCC Fourth Assessment Report*, 16 November 2000. See www.ipcc.ch for a link to the report

Islamic Organization of Medical Sciences, Kuwait, 1981, p65

Jakobovits, I., *Jewish Medical Ethics*, Bloch Publishing, 1959

Jakobovits, I., quoted by the BBC on the 'Religion and Ethics: Judaism' page: www.bbc.co.uk. Click on 'Religions', then 'Judaism', then 'Ethics'

Jarvis Thompson, J., 'A defence of abortion', *Philosophy and Public Affairs*, 1, (1) (Autumn), 1971, pp47–66

Kamali, M. H., *The Dignity of Man: an Islamic perspective*, Islamic Texts Society, 2002

Kant, I., *Critique of Practical Reason*, trans. L. W. Beck, Bobbs-Merrill, 1977

Kant, I., *Groundwork of the Metaphysics of Morals*, trans. H. J. Paton, Routledge, 1948

Kant, I., *The Metaphysics of Morals*, Cambridge University Press, 1996

Kelly, K. T., *New Directions in Moral Theology*, Chapman, 1992

Keown, D., 'Attitudes to euthanasia in the Vinaya and Commentary'. See www.urbandharma.org, and type '/udharma/euthanasia.html' after the web address to read the full article

Keown, D., *Buddhism and Bioethics*, Macmillan, 1995

Keown, D., *Buddhist Ethics, a very short introduction*, Oxford University Press, 1996

Krawietz, B., 'Brain death and Islamic traditions: shifting borders of life?', in Brockopp, J. (ed.), *Islamic Issues of Life: abortion, war and euthanasia*, South Carolina Press, 2003, pp194–213

Kuhse, H., 'Euthanasia', in Singer, P. (ed.), *A Companion to Ethics*, Blackwell, 1991, pp294–302

LaFleur, W. A., 'Contestation and confrontation: the morality of abortion in Japan', *Philosophy East and West*, 40, 1990, pp529–542

LaFleur, W. A., *Liquid Life: abortion and Buddhism in Japan*, Princeton University Press, 1995

LaFleur, W. A., 'The Cult of Jizo: abortion practices in Japan and what they can teach the West', *Tricycle*, Summer, 1992, pp41–44

LaFollette, H. (ed.), *Ethics in Practice: an anthology*, Blackwell, 1997

Lane, D. A., 'The doctrine of the incarnation: human and cosmic considerations', in Hayes, M. and Gearon, L. (eds), *Contemporary Catholic Theology: a reader*, Continuum, 2000, pp209–233

Law, S., *The War for Children's Minds*, Routledge, 2006

Lehmann, P., *Ethics in a Christian context*, Harper and Row, 1963

Leopold, A., *A Sand County Almanac*, Oxford University Press, 1949

Lesco, P., 'A Buddhist view of abortion', *Journal of Religion and Health*, 25 (I), 1987, pp51–57

Ling, T., 'Buddhist factors in population growth and control: a survey based on Thailand and Ceylon', *Population Studies*, 23 (I), 1969, pp53–60

Lipner, J. J., 'The classical Hindu view on abortion and the Moral Status of the Unborn', in Coward, H. G.,

Lipner, J. J. and Young, K. K. (eds), *Hindu Ethics: purity, abortion, and euthanasia*, State University of New York Press, 1989, pp41–69

Lovelock, J., *Gaia: a new look at life on Earth*, Oxford University Press, 1979

McGrath, A. E., *Christian Theology: an introduction*, Blackwell, 2006, pp381–382

MacIntyre, A., *A Short History of Ethics*, Routledge, 1966

Mackie, J. L., *Ethics, Inventing Right and Wrong*, Penguin, 1977

Maimonides, *Guide for the Perplexed*, trans. M. Friedlander, Courier Dover, 1956

Marquis, D., 'An argument that abortion is wrong', in LaFollette, H. (ed.), *Ethics in Practice: an anthology*, Blackwell, 1997, pp83–93

Mavrodes, G., 'Omniscience', in Quinn, P. L. and Taliaferro, C., *A Companion to Philosophy of Religion*, Blackwell, 2000

McLaren, A., 'Ethical and social considerations of stem cell research', *Nature*, November, 414, 2001

Mill, J. S., *On Liberty*, Penguin, 1982

Mill, J. S., *Utilitarianism*, Hackett, 1979

Moore, G. E., *Principia Ethica*, Cambridge University Press, 1993

More, T., *Utopia*, Penguin, 2004

Morton, A., *Philosophy in Practice*, Blackwell, 1996

Naess, A., 'Pluralism of tenable worldviews', in Stadier, F. (ed.), *The Vienna Circle and Logical Empiricism: reevaluation and future perspectives*, Kluwer, 2003

Naess, A. and Sessions, G., 'Basic principles of deep ecology', in *Ecophilosophy*, 6, 1984

Nelson, M. P., 'An amalgamation of wilderness preservation arguments', in Light, A. and Rolston III, H. (eds), *Environmental Ethics: an anthology*, Blackwell, 2003, pp413–437

Nielsen, K., *God and the Grounding of Morality*, University of Ottawa Press, 1991

North, C., *Noctes Ambrosianae*, Hamilton, Adams & Co., 1888

Paradise, S. I., 'Rehabilitation for cosmic outlaws', in Stone, G. C. (ed.), *A New Ethic for a New Earth*, Friendship Press, 1971, pp133–142

Pence, G. E., *Flesh of my Flesh, the Ethics of Human Cloning*, Rowman & Littlefield, 1997

Pence, G. E., 'Why physicians should help the dying', lead essay in LaFollette, H. (ed.), *Practical Ethics*, Blackwell, 1997

Pitaka, V. (Th.), *The Book of Discipline*, Vol. IV, trans. I. B., Horner, PTS, 1966

Plato, *The Republic*, 2nd edn, trans. D. Lee, Penguin, 1979

Pojman, L. P., *Ethics: Discovering Right and Wrong*, Wadsworth, 1988

Pope John Paul II, *Centesimus Annus: encyclical letter of Pope John Paul II on the Hundredth Anniversary of Rerum Novarum*, 1991. Available in full at www.vatican.va. Follow links to the 'Vatican Publishing House', then 'The Holy Father', then 'John Paul II', and finally 'Encyclicals'

Pope John Paul II, *The Gospel of Life: encyclical letter on abortion, euthanasia, and the death penalty in today's world*, Random House, 1995

Prichard, H. A., 'Does moral philosophy rest on mistake?', in *Mind*; reprinted in *Moral Obligation: essay and lectures*, Clarendon Press, 1949.

Protagoras only survives in fragments such as in Plato's Protagoras, in Cooper, J. M. (ed.), *Plato, Complete Works*, Hackett Publishing, 1997

Rachels, J., 'Active and Passive Euthanasia', in Velasquez, M. and Rostankowski, C., *Ethics: Theory and Practice*, Prentice Hall, 1985

Ramadan, T., *Western Muslims and the Future of Islam*, Oxford University Press, 2003

Ramaswami Aiyar, C. P., *The Gazetteer of India, Volume 1: Country and People*, Publications Division, Government of India, 1965

Regan, T., *Animal Rights, Human Wrongs: an introduction to moral philosophy*, Rowman and Littlefield, 2003

Regan, T., 'The case for animal rights', in Singer, P. (ed.), *In Defence of Animals*, Blackwell, 1985

Religion and Ethics News Weekly, Cover Story: Sex Selection in India, 1 June, 2001. See http://www.pbs. org/wnet/religionandethics/index_flash.html, and choose the relevant edition

Robinson, J. A. T., *Honest to God*, SCM Press, 1963

Rolston III, H. and Light, A., *Environmental Ethics: an anthology*, Blackwell, 2003

Roman Catholic Church, *Catechism of the Roman Catholic Church*, Geoffrey Chapman, 1992

Roman Catholic Church, *Declaration on Euthanasia* – Available in full at www.vatican.va. Follow links to the 'Vatican Publishing House', then select the 'Roman Curia' link, 'Congregations', 'Doctrine of the Faith', 'Documents', and finally 'Doctrinal Documents', to find the text in full

Roman Catholic Church, Pastoral Constitution – *Gaudium et spes*, http://www.vatican.va/archive/ hist_councils/ii_vatican_council/documents/vat-ii_cons_ 19651207_gaudium-et-spes_en.html

Roman Catholic Church, *The call of creation: God's invitation and the human response: the natural environment and Catholic social teaching*, Catholic Bishop's Conference of England and Wales, July, 2002

Rosen, D. 'Religions and environment: a Jewish perspective'. See www.rabbidavidrosen.net. Click on 'Articles', then 'Judaism'

Sarma, D. S., *Essence of Hinduism*, Bharatiya Vidya Bhavan, 1971

Selling, J., 'The human person', in Hoose, B. (ed.), *Christian Ethics: an introduction*, Cassell, 1998, pp95–109

Sherwin, B. L., *Jewish Ethics for the Twenty-First Century*, Syracuse University Press, 2001

Sidhu, G. S., 'Sikh religion and science'. See www.sikhs. wellington.net.nz

Sidgwick, H., *The Methods of Ethics*, Macmillan, London, 1962

Sikhism101.com, 'What is the Sikh attitude towards abortion?' For more information, visit www.sikhism101. com, select 'Sikh Faith FAQ', then 'Sikhism and Modern Issues'

Singer, P., *Animal Liberation*, Pimlico, 1995

Singer, P., *Ethics*, in the Oxford Readers series, Oxford University Press, 1994

Singer, P., *In Defence of Animals*, Blackwell, 1985

Singer, P., *Practical Ethics*, Cambridge University Press, 1993

Singh, N., *Faith and Environment – A Sikh Perspective*, 2002. See www.sikhreview.org: select 'Archive', then

'January 2002', and click on the 'Ecology' link in the side-bar

Skinner, B. F., *Beyond Freedom and Dignity*, Knopf, 1971

Smith, D., 'Abortion: a moral controversy', *Dialogue: a Journal for Religious Studies and Philosophy*, 8, April, 1997, pp9–14

Smith, D., 'Hinduism', in Woodhead, L. *et al*. (eds), *Religions in the Modern World*, Routledge, 2002, pp15–40

Soulen, R. and Woodhead, L., *God and Human Dignity*, Eerdmans, 2006

Stahl, A., 'Educating for change in attitudes toward nature and environment among oriental Jews in Israel', *Environment and Behavior*, January, 1993, pp3–21

Staniforth, M., (trans.) *Early Christian Writings: the Apostle Fathers*, Penguin, 1968

Stevenson, C. L., *Ethics and Language*, Yale University, 1945

Sumner, W. G., *Folkways*, Ginn, 1906

Taniguchi, S., 'Biomedical ethics from a Buddhist perspective', *The Pacific World: Journal of the Institute of Buddhist Studies*, New Series, no. 3, 1987, pp75–83

Temple, W., *Mens Creatix: an essay*, Macmillan, 1923

Tillich, P., *Systematic Theology*, vol. 1, University of Chicago Press, 1951

Tomek, V., 'Environmental concerns: Sikh responses', 2006. See www.religioustolerance.org/tomek17.htm

Vardy, P. and Grosch, P., *The Puzzle of Ethics*, Fount, 1994

Veatchi, R. M., *A Theory of Medical Ethics*, New York, 1981, pp33–43

Vickers, B., *Francis Bacon*, Oxford University Press, 1996

Vogel, D., 'How green is Judaism? An exploration of Jewish environmental ethics, *Business Ethics Quarterly*, April 2001; revised version, *Judaism*, Winter 2001; online version http://faculty.haas.berkeley.edu/vogel/ judaism.pdf

Warren, M. A., 'Abortion', in Singer, P. (ed.), *A Companion to Ethics*, Blackwell, 1991, pp303–314

Warren, M. A., 'On the legal and moral status of abortion', in LaFollette, H. (ed.), *Ethics in Practice: an anthology*, Blackwell, 1997, pp79–90

White, L., 'The historical roots of our ecological crisis', *Science* 155, 1967, pp 1203–1207. See www.aeoe. org, click on 'Resources', then 'Spiritual EE', select the 'Resources for Spiritual Environmental Education' link and finally the PDF link 'The historical roots of our ecological crisis'

Williams, B., 'A critique of utilitarianism', in Smart, J. J. C., and Williams, B., *Utilitarianism: for and against*, Cambridge University Press, 1973, pp75–150

Yun, H., *Being Good: Buddhist ethics for everyday life*, trans. T. Graham, Weatherhill, 1998

Zagzebski, L., 'Foreknowledge and human freedom', in Quinn, P. and Taliaferro, C. (eds.), *A Companion to Philosophy of Religion*, Blackwell, 1997, pp291–312

Index